Table of Contents

character

staying sane

academics

building a bridge
between home & school

character

Good character is more to be praised than outstanding talent.
Most talents are to some extent a gift.
Good character, by contrast, is not given to us.
We have to build it piece by piece by thought, choice, courage and determination.

– JOHN LUTHER

(H)eather

Good people don't just happen. Raising our children to develop positive character traits is one of the most important jobs we have as parents. Parenting takes time, work and commitment. Regardless of our busy schedules, we must make teaching and nurturing our children a priority through quality family time. We can use teachable moments, such as discipline, to be specific in defining what it means to be an honorable person and why it's important to make good choices. We also need to focus on praising our children for positive actions, as they will invariably repeat the behavior that gets our attention.

Our lives are a model, hopefully of good character, with the intention of instilling genuine qualities in our children. Even when we are unaware of it, our words and actions influence them. We create the environment for our children to grow and develop virtues like courage, kindness, honesty, respect and compassion. They will use these virtues as a guide to making ethical decisions in life.

(M)elissa

When I think of character, numerous words and images pop into my head: my parents, my two brothers, and the words strength, honesty and trustworthiness. What does not pop into my mind is any image of a famous athlete, movie star or politician. I look to those close to me for examples of character, and I want my children to always think of my husband and me when they picture role models in their lives that represent character. It is through our actions, our deeds and our words that we can capture our children's attention and teach them what it means to be character-driven individuals.

(J)ennifer

My greatest hope for my children is that they will know that they are deeply, fiercely, unconditionally loved, and that they will have the courage and ability to love others with passion and integrity. This hope is at the forefront of my mind and heart as my husband and I make choices about disciplining our children and shaping their character. Our approach is long-term in focus. Even when my children were infants, I wanted my responses to them to be consistent with those I imagined giving them as teenagers—a balance of "You are strong, capable, and you have what it takes to make it in the world" and "I am your mommy, and I will always be here for you." Love is powerful, sacrificial and transformative. To love our children is to accept them as they are and to bring out the best in them. Love isn't passive admiration; it requires action. Love means allowing your child to feel the painful consequences of her actions; knowing that to rescue her would be momentarily gratifying but ultimately detrimental. Love is planning ahead, making tough choices and constantly striving to be a better parent. Loving your child is a marriage of acceptance and hope. Who you are right now is enough. Let's journey together to see who you will become. True discipline finds its source in love.

(P)atina

Character is who you are. It determines your response, regardless of the circumstances. I tell my children that it isn't just what you do in front of others, but what you do when no one is looking that counts. Our character isn't something we're born with; it is built. Discipline (to teach) and building your child's character are tied closely together. Character is the sweet fruit of your labor. As a mother of young adults, I have had the good fortune to see my years of hard work pay off. And I'm struck by two powerful emotions: sadness and pride. Sadness because I know they'll be leaving my home soon to build their own lives, and pride because of the choices they have made. They aren't perfect and I know they'll make mistakes. But it has been truly satisfying to see the boundaries I put in place for them as children develop into a code of ethics they have embraced for themselves.

Today's Lesson:
Developing Children's Gifts and Love of Learning

Use what talents you possess; the woods would be very silent
if no birds sang there except those that sang best.

– HENRY VAN DYKE

Chalk Talk

The words "gifted" and "talented" can be a bit confusing. In our world of "America's Got Talent," we tend to think of a talent as a performance to entertain others. When you hear the phrase "gifted and talented," you may think of special school programs designed to meet the needs of students who tested well. Just hearing the word "gifted" may make you think of brainiacs, kids who are extremely intelligent or have high IQs. Stop right there. Don't get caught up in labels for our children. Most of us are typical people, and there is beauty in that. In this lesson, when I speak of children's "gifts or talents," I am referring to their strengths, things they are good at doing. In order to see our children's gifts, we must be willing to be flexible with our own personal wishes and expectations for our kids. Let your child take the lead as you discover her gifts, and together you can discover a lifetime of passion and adventure.

We all want our children to be successful members of society. We want them to be happy, healthy and live fulfilling lives. But what does this mean? How do we get our kids to that place in life? We help them discover and develop their natural talents.

It's exciting to think of what your children will be when they grow up. It's exciting for all parents. But it's just a dream. Because in reality, we don't get to choose the path our child follows. It is her decision to make, and we are here to give her the tools and support to choose wisely. If we all had our first childhood choice, the world would be full of ninjas and ballerinas. Be supportive of each attempt your child makes to figure out who she is and what she wants to do, knowing that some will stick and some won't. Of course, it's hard to do when you see your child going down a path you don't approve of or don't see as a good fit. Maybe you thought your daughter would be a fabulous surgeon, and instead she is an incredibly gifted drummer. Let her grow into what she is good at doing. Teach her to cultivate a love of herself from the inside out. The key to contentment comes from within. So it's up to us, as parents, to remember that in the end, we want our children to be happy and fulfilled. And that's what counts.

Teacher's Conference

Teachers begin the year with a classroom full of diverse and eager learners. Most of the time, the teacher doesn't know the students. It takes time to get used to one another and feel secure. Some children are very outgoing, displaying interests or talents right away, while others are more reserved. Not everyone has visible talents; some are hidden, waiting to be discovered and nurtured. The teacher provides opportunities for all students to try new things in a safe, non-intimidating environment. She encourages new ways of thinking and exploring, while promoting acceptance and understanding of others. In the classroom, there's a lot of talk about being alike and different. Learning these concepts allows children to embrace their differences and accept others and other ways of thinking. After all, wouldn't the world be a boring place if we were all the same?

Teachers spend a lot of time reaching all learners through their varying ability levels or learning styles, recognizing that children learn in different ways and at different paces. Howard Gardner's Theory of Multiple Intelligences has greatly influenced the education world, encouraging educators to reach out to all learners with diverse lessons. There are nine multiple intelligences, and while we all possess each type of intelligence, we tend to show dominance in one or two. These intelligences are:

- Linguistic intelligence ("word smart") Does your child have a gift with words? Could he talk you into painting the house neon green or write a poem to make you weep? Think writers, librarians and lawyers.

- Logical-mathematical intelligence ("number/reasoning smart") Does your child have a gift for solving problems through numbers, sorting or patterns? Accountants, scientists or computer programmers use this intelligence.

- Spatial intelligence ("picture smart") People with this gift often visualize their goal before obtaining it. It focuses on pictures, patterns or images. Can your child take the map from your lost spouse and direct you to the destination? He may be a future artist, engineer or inventor.

- Bodily-kinesthetic intelligence ("body smart") This intelligence focuses on bodily movements and handling objects. Does your child take off on his bike easily? Or do you have a young child that can string beads a mile long? Athletes, dancers, mechanics, jewelers and surgeons possess this talent.

- Musical intelligence ("music smart") Those with this gift have an ear for rhythm, pitch, melody and tone. Just listen and notice who has a gift for music. Musicians, composers and DJs show musical intelligence.

8

- Interpersonal intelligence ("people smart") Is your child a social butterfly, always aware of feelings and connecting with those around him? This talent is an essential one for teachers or nurses to have.

- Intrapersonal intelligence ("self smart") Is your child in tune with himself, or does he prefer playing alone? Entrepreneurs, theologians and psychologists display a strong sense of self.

- Naturalist intelligence ("nature smart") Has your bathroom turned into a science laboratory for your child to dissect bugs? Can she tell you every fact about dinosaurs or the name of every tree in the forest? If your child displays a deep interest in the natural world, she may have a gift in this area. Zoologists, meteorologists and landscape architects are examples of those who use this intelligence.

- Philosophical-ethical ("world smart") If your child is interested in other cultures and conscious of moral and ethical issues, he may be gifted in this intelligence. A judge, diplomat or missionary is an example of someone strong in this intelligence.

Teachers use their knowledge of these intelligences as tools to meet the needs of all students and teach them in the way they learn best. By doing this, teachers also create a positive environment in which children enjoy learning. As parents, the use of multiple intelligences may help you see your child in a new light as you discover her hidden talents. Use this information to recognize, celebrate and support your child's strengths at home.

One year when I was teaching Kindergarten, I had a student with no prior exposure to math skills or literacy skills, such as letter recognition—nor did she know how to write her name. I quickly realized that she had a gift for music and dance. She was amazing! She could remember any song, belting it out as she grooved to her beat. We learned through fun skill songs throughout the day. She picked up new skills so quickly and even learned to write her fourteen-letter name with lightning speed. She just needed exposure to the skills through her musical learning style.

Another example of using multiple intelligences in my classroom was in teaching addition and subtraction. Some students just "got it" right away. They showed the gift of mathematical intelligence. Others needed to see it. Some quickly learned the concept by building with blocks, drawing, singing songs or solving problems with Cheerios. They also enjoyed solving problems by acting them out or listening to addition or subtraction concept books. Some students enjoyed moving right along, solving problems with a number line, while others needed to see several different solutions and explanations of the concepts before they truly understood. In the end, they all learned the concept in their own way and at their own pace.

Homework

- Set high expectations for your child, and encourage him to take pride in his strengths. We want our children to reach for the stars and believe that anything is possible. We also want them to know that we're right behind them every step of the way. Your child may look to you for encouragement through positive words, or she may just need you to be a good listener. Find books that focus on positive role models who display similar interests and strengths as your child.

- Write a list of gifts your child has and ways in which you could give specific praise, support and encouragement. Having it on paper will remind you of the importance of building up your child's self confidence. For an older child, write a letter to him. Who doesn't love reading and hearing good things about themselves? This will be a special present your child will hold dear and continue to revisit.

- Give your child opportunities to explore new activities and develop interests without the fear of failure. He must feel secure about diving into unfamiliar territory. Expose your child to the nine intelligences so he has an opportunity to discover interests that you may not have originally thought were a natural fit. Encourage independence by letting your child make decisions. Remember, your dream for your child may not be the same one that your child has in mind. In the end, he will decide which path he wants to follow.

- Model a strength of your own. Let your child see you doing something you love. Show him what it looks like to take pride in something. Talk about your spouse's strengths (or those of other family members) to illustrate different types of talents. Maybe you are a wonderful baker. Let your child see you in action as you take your goods to a neighbor. The smile on your neighbor's face is a result of your talent. What a great lesson for your child; seeing you use your talent to make others happy! Model life-long learning as well. It is never too late to develop new talents and discover hidden ones. We'll never get the opportunity to nurture new talents if we don't try.

- At the beginning of the school year, write your child's teacher a short letter introducing your child. Let her know of special interests and things your child is good at doing. Be specific and brief. Teachers are incredibly busy preparing for the new school year. This isn't the time to tell her how smart and bright your child is and how she'll need to be challenged. Instead, it's the time to give her specific examples of your child's interests and personality. It is extremely helpful for the teacher to hear, "Suzy can be shy and quiet at first, but she loves to read. She will really open up to you if you ask her about the books she read this summer." Or "Sam loves to draw. He can really express himself through art. Would you consider allowing him to include illustrations with his journal entries or science reports?" Don't just tell your child's teacher that your child has gifts, tell her what those gifts are.

- Become active in your child's school. Find out what programs are offered. Partner with the school and even community organizations to encourage growth and development in your child's talents. Talk to your child's teacher about enrichment activities you could do at home.

Words of Wisdom

Think of your child's gifts as you would a packet of seeds. Water them, tend them and watch them grow into beautiful individual blossoms.

Continuing Education

From an early age, there is constant pressure to label children as "gifted" or "talented" in a language, sport, musical instrument, etc. Let your child take the lead in wanting to pursue countless hours of practice or lessons in an area. Pushing your child to achieve your dream will lead to frustration and disappointment. Encouraging your child to follow his dreams by providing opportunities will lead to life-long learning, success and fulfillment. Let your child find his bright spot.

HIGH FIVE to **Julie Ellerbrock**, director of children's ministries at St. Luke's Methodist Church in Houston, TX and mother of two.

(High Fives throughout *Answer Keys* recognize individuals who shared their expertise with us on a particular lesson.)

Sources

Gardner, Howard. *Frames of Mind: The Theory of Multiple Intelligences*. New York: Basic, 1983.

Gardner, Howard. *Multiple Intelligences: The Theory in Practice*. New York: Basic, 1993.

Gardner, Howard. *Intelligence Reframed: Multiple Intelligences for the 21st Century*. New York: Basic, 2000

Armstrong, Thomas. "Multiple Intelligences," Dr. Thomas Armstrong Website http://www.thomasarmstrong.com, ©1998-2000

Fitzgerald D. Ed., Ronald. http://www.successinteaching.com

Today's Lesson:
Choices

It is our choices...that show what we truly are,
far more than our abilities.

– J. K. ROWLING, FROM HARRY POTTER AND THE CHAMBER OF SECRETS

Chalk Talk

Choices are the essence of life. Mundane or mind-blowing, we are faced with thousands of them everyday. Paper or plastic? Decaf or regular? Work out or sleep in? Tell or keep a secret? Keep trying or give up? Our choices propel us forward through life. They make us who we are. Every choice, no matter how small, contains elements of control and responsibility. Teaching your child how to make wise decisions is one of the most critical aspects of parenting, and starting when your children are young can make all the difference.

When I was pregnant with my daughter, I envisioned myself as one of those carefree moms who let her daughter wear dress-up clothes to church and pajamas to preschool. I guess this daydream stemmed from being dressed to match my younger siblings on special occasions like Easter, Christmas, birthdays and trips to the grocery store. Okay, maybe it wasn't that bad. But as the oldest of four, I vividly recall wearing a shocking yellow Easter dress that exactly matched my sister's dress (she's five years younger than I am), my little brother's overalls (seven years younger) and my baby brother's romper (ten years younger). Ouch. So I guess I wanted to make up for this torturous humiliation (sorry, Mom) by giving my daughter limitless freedom in the wardrobe department. Well, like most pre-natal daydreams, achieving this state of blissful creativity wasn't so easy when faced with the limits of a four-year-old's decision-making abilities. I guess I always pictured my daughter's outfits as cute Punky Brewster-ish ensembles. I did not foresee that she would want to wear a stained skirt two sizes too small with a not-so-white tank top, black Halloween knee socks poking out of pink sandals and a sparkly headband around her forehead. Eventually we came up with a compromise: I get to choose her outfits for parties and church, and Katie can choose whatever she wants to wear on "free dress days." We pick out school clothes together.

As much as we know it's the right thing to do, it is often very difficult to allow our young children to make their own decisions. We want to catch the brimming cup of water before it spills over onto the floor. We want to avoid the hassle of pulling off sweaty woolen tights in July when it was obviously way too hot to wear them. It is easier, quicker and less messy just to do it ourselves. As parents, the temptation to think for our children is almost irresistible. My challenge to all parents, including myself, is to fight this temptation tooth and nail.

Teacher's Conference

In the classroom, I often encountered students who had very little practice thinking for themselves. If they had a question or got "stuck," they fell into a habit of helplessness. Through no fault of their own, they had come to believe that the last place they should look for the solution to a problem was in their own brains. They would immediately look at the ceiling, at me or at their friends for help, when most of the time the answer was well within their reach. We must allow our children to use and trust their own minds and hearts so that when the time comes, they'll be able to make wise and thoughtful decisions. Trust takes time to develop. It is essential that as parents, we teach our children to make wise choices as early as possible. By allowing young children to make age-appropriate choices, we are giving them the opportunity to practice valuable life skills. Decisions that greatly impact a toddler's life are incredibly low-risk: Do you want to wear the red shirt or the blue shirt? Do you want peas or carrots? How much better to practice making choices when the stakes are low.

As a middle-school teacher, I dreaded the inevitable clamor every year for a class pet. I knew that I would end up taking care of it. One year I gave in, and—since I don't do rodents—chose hermit crabs. My students were excited at first, but the novelty eventually wore off and the weekly "class zookeeper" kept forgetting to feed the crabs. Without warning, I sent the hermit crabs to live in my friend's classroom. After recovering from their initial outrage, my students initiated a movement to "bring back the crabs!" They independently established a reminder system, which included strategically placed sticky notes and messages on the chalkboard. When the crabs returned, they ended up being very well loved. I was thankful for my students' previous irresponsibility. Having to face the consequences of their actions taught them more than I could have with lectures and nagging.

answerkeys

Put to the Test

Although most choices a toddler can make are low-risk, they are not risk-free; the consequences of a young child's mistakes usually involve increased mess or inconvenience, rather than anything life-altering. When my daughter, Katie, was first learning to clear her dishes from the table after each meal, she tried to make things more interesting by carrying a half-full bowl of cereal and milk on her head. By the time I saw her, all I could say was "Oh!" before it all came tumbling down on her. It was a sad moment, but since then I have not needed to say a word to her about being careful. Being covered in sticky milk was more powerful than any number of warnings. It took awhile to rinse her off, change clothes, and clean up but overall it saved me countless moments of nagging. She will be careful whether I'm watching her or not, because she knows exactly what happens when she is careless. This is what we have to keep in mind as we parent our young children: Someday we won't be right there, and our children need to know how to think for themselves. Let your children make mistakes! And more importantly, let them feel the consequences of their actions.

Homework

Assignment #1:

Give your toddler or preschooler small choices. *Would you like to brush your teeth or your hair first? Do you want one or two scoops of peas? Would you rather hold my hand in the parking lot or should I carry you?*

Try providing choices when things are going well. Present a choice that doesn't really make a big difference to you, but would be fun for your child. *Do you want to put your shirt on first or your shorts? Do you want me to wash your toes first or your tummy? Do you want the pink cup or the red cup?*

Assignment #2:

Offer choices as tantrum-tamers. Try offering your young child choices when things are not going so well, or when you can see a potential crisis on the horizon. Examples: When trying to get your child to leave the park, ask "Would you rather run or walk to the gate?" Or a recent favorite at our house: "Would you rather buzz like a bee or hiss like a snake?" — your child won't be able to keep this up for very long, and either of these two noises seem preferable to shrieking elephant sounds coming from the back seat of the car. Giving your child practice with decision making is not only incredibly valuable for the future; it can also save your sanity right now.

Character

Mom Tip

Always give choices that are safe, possible and equally appealing. Offering your child marshmallows or cauliflower is not the same as offering cauliflower or broccoli. Don't ask your child if she would rather stay outside or come in, unless you are happy with either choice. Children have an uncanny ability to pick your least favorite option.

Always make sure you can follow through when giving your child options. If she picks a third, unacceptable option or refuses to choose within a few seconds or so, you must choose for her. Stick with your original options: Make the choice and move on. Resist the temptation to lecture or scold your child.

Adapted from *Parenting with Love and Logic* by Foster Cline, M.D. and Jim Fay.

Sources

Cline, Foster W. and Jim Fay. *Parenting with Love And Logic* (Updated and Expanded Edition). Colorado Springs: NavPress, 2006.

Fay, Charles and Jim Fay. *Love and Logic Magic for Early Childhood: Practical Parenting from Birth to Six Years*. 1st ed. Golden, CO: Love & Logic Press, 2000.

Today's Lesson:
Making Good Decisions

In a moment of decision, the best thing you can do is the right thing to do. The worst thing you can do is nothing.

- THEODORE ROOSEVELT

Chalk Talk

As your child gets older, she will spend less and less time with you. No longer can you present her with two safe, approved options and have her choose. The foundation you have laid by teaching her about making good choices moves into a more independent phase: making good decisions.

Making good decisions is a learned skill. It is probably one of the most important skills our children will ever need. We all know a smart girl whose parents sheltered her and made all of her decisions while she was growing up. When she got a taste of freedom in college, she chose not to go to class, but partied all night. Or then there's the great, church-going family whose son went from school detention to rehab to jail. What happened?

While we never know what goes on behind the scenes in any family but our own, we do know that some people make a pattern of making bad choices, even when the stakes are high. Just as we taught our young children to make a good choice when we had control of the choices, there are ways for us to help them become good decision-makers as they get older.

Teacher's Conference

Classroom teachers are aware that their students' decision making skills will be at various levels of development throughout the year. As a fifth grade teacher, one of my responsibilities was to prepare the students for up-coming middle school. In middle school, students have complex curricula; therefore cooperation, time management and responsibility for learning are essential to mastering the material. I found some of the common roadblocks to success were students staying up too late playing video games, not turning in assignments, being disruptive in class and being disrespectful to the other students. Most of these poor classroom decisions were minor and easy to fix with a little time and attention. But some required support from home.

By the end of the first couple of weeks, if the student continued to have difficulty making good decisions in class, I would start with a phone conference with the parents. Most often, the parents were thankful that I had brought this to their attention so early in the year. Next, they were eager to discuss how we could work together to solve the problems. We would discuss strategies, tools, consequences and rewards that could be used both at home and at school to improve decision making. If additional interventions were needed, the parents and I would draw up a contract with the student that would chart his daily progress. It would be signed and returned weekly. With the help of supportive parents, most children improved their decision making skills with patience, practice and maturity.

If you want your child to make good decisions based on your family values, you and your spouse are the best teachers. Don't assume that a nanny, daycare center, school or even church or synagogue can do this important work for you. Helping your child to internalize values and the ability to use them "on the go" are your responsibility, no matter how many obstacles seem to be put into your path by the media, friends or fashion. You can't control every influence in his life, but you can help him to build a method of responding to choices that is based on what is important to your family. The hard work you do in this area pays off when you have a child who is a happy, contributing member of society.

The prime time for teaching decision making skills is from about age two to twelve. At these ages, your child is eager for your input. This is the time to act out different scenarios and talk about possible outcomes. Remind your children that their decisions affect others. Tell them that we need to be mindful of other people's feelings and that our choices tell people who we are.

Homework

Assignment #1
Come up with a "safe" word. Your older children will need help handling peer pressure and getting out of bad situations. Not having a clear and easy plan to get out of a bad situation can cause teens to panic. Using a "safe word" has given my teens, John Henry and Murphy, an out from an unsafe or sticky situation without the fear of embarrassment or ridicule from friends. For example, Murphy's safe word is "jacket." When she has found herself in an unsafe situation where risky activities are taking place, she will call me. She will simply say something about "leaving her jacket in the car," and then I know to get her immediately. No questions asked.

Assignment #2
Create a list of acceptable choices. Sit with your spouse and think about pitfalls and problem areas that you have with your children. Brainstorm and write down possible choices to use in advance or in response to a difficult situation with your child.

answerkeys

Assignment #3

Make a special effort to get to know your child's friends. Include them in some of your fun family activities. Many times friends can influence the decisions your child makes. Try not to make snap judgments based on appearance before getting to know them.

Mom Tip

As the mother of older children, I see how choices evolve over time. Since John Henry is a senior and will be leaving home soon, he and I have a standing lunch date on Fridays. It is free discussion time, and might include topics like school, activities, dates, college or family. There are also opportunities to discuss his decision making regarding subjects like making new friends, tobacco, drugs, alcohol use and safety concerns.

Words of Wisdom

Once your child becomes a teenager, opportunities to provide coaching become fewer and less effective. But that doesn't mean that there are no opportunities to help strengthen her decision making process. At that point, rather than trying to tell her specifically what to do, it is better to listen and not be judgmental. The more you listen, the more she will talk. If you freak out, or overreact, she will usually shut down completely. If you can learn to hold your tongue until she feels heard, you provide a safe environment. Often you will be asked for your opinion or you can find a way to insert it without stopping the communication. Ultimately, you want to be the one that your child turns to when she has a big decision or needs help. Preserving the relationship and the dialogue at this stage is critical. Be clear with your child that you respect her decision making abilities, and continue to be just as clear with her that as she grows your expectations and boundaries for her will evolve, but your family's values will not.

Keys to Good Decision Making:

Model wise decision making in your home. The best way to teach your child to make good choices is to make good choices. Let your child see you apologizing to your spouse when you lose your temper. Be honest. Even "white lies" set a poor example for your child. When you parent with a purpose all your acts of integrity and compassion will make a big impression on your children—not because you told them what to do, but because you showed them.

Practice. Allow your child to practice making choices at an early age. Giving your child plenty of practice at a young age helps him to develop the problem-solving skills necessary to make wise decisions and the confidence to do so independently. Putting a great deal of energy and intent into your parenting in the early stages will lead to tremendous benefits in the future. Waiting until adolescence to teach your child about wise decision making makes the job more challenging. When your children are young, they are captivated by what you say; they imitate your every move. When they become teenagers, the frequency of teachable moments plummets, while the cost of poor decisions rises dramatically. If you have not focused on making choices when your child was younger, remember to use your own good listening skills before you try to influence his decision making.

Natural Consequences. Allow your child to experience the natural consequences of her actions. Feeling the painful consequences of our actions is often the only thing that leads us to choose more wisely in the future; the same is true for our children. Showing your child that you care about her when she's in pain is very different from rescuing her from the outcome of her mistakes. We learn more from our failures than we do from our successes, so don't be afraid for your child to be in a little uncomfortable. Discomfort usually promotes thoughtfulness and caution.

Self-confidence. Children need to be confident in order to be successful. Build your child's confidence. Allow him to make lots of decisions and mistakes while he is still living in your house with your support. He needs practice to build his skills. Tell your child that you believe in him and demonstrate your sincerity by trusting him to make his own decisions. If your child believes that you have confidence in him, then he will be more likely to make wise choices and to seek your advice when needed. As he validates your trust with good decisions, let him know, and reward him with more opportunities to make decisions.

Discuss impulsive decision making. Being impulsive sounds very romantic, but it is usually not the stuff from which good decisions are made. Because our brains are not fully developed until our mid-twenties, skills like evaluating possible outcomes are difficult. Teach your child that the bigger the decision the more thought it requires. Sometimes more opinions are needed. If your child believes that you have confidence in him, then he will be more likely to seek your advice. Help him to identify other trusted adults he can turn to in a variety of situations.

Put to the Test: One Teenager's Story

I often tell young mothers that I have found all the hard work I have done as a parent to be like a savings account at the bank: The more you put in, the greater reward you will reap when they are teenagers. I assure you that once your child reaches those years, sometimes you will feel you are burning through that account rather quickly. But, I am happy to say that as a mother of two teenagers, I am now seeing the fruit of my labor, and it is sweet. I do not worry myself sick every time they walk out the door. I do not check their rooms and cars for drugs and alcohol. I am not forced to be an amateur private detective in my own house. I do still worry and know they will make mistakes, but the lines of communication are open. More importantly, perhaps, I live with a sense of peace, and truly enjoy and continue to learn from my teenagers.

I feel comfortable trusting my teens because they have proven to me they can make good choices when it really counts. My children have always made friends easily. This was a great comfort to me when we moved across town, and changed churches and schools. I was so excited when Murphy's new classmates began asking her to go to the movies on the weekends. The theater was very nice and close to our house. As I dropped the girls off into a sea of middle schoolers, I thought to myself, "What a great safe activity." Dropped off in a safe place and picked up by me, what could be better?

After several weeks, I noticed Murphy stopped asking to go to the movies, although I knew that she had been invited. Instead, she was having girls over or doing other things. One Friday night as we drove past the theater, I asked her why she was not going to the movies anymore. There were so many kids from her school there, and it looked like fun. After a minute she said, "Mom, some older girls are bringing vodka in hair spray bottles and getting drunk in the back of the theater. Some kids are smoking in the bathroom and doing a lot of stuff with boys. I just decided I didn't want to hang out there anymore." I was shocked! My brain was screaming, "Are you kidding me? These kids are fifteen years old!" I took a moment and then calmly said, "How could this be, these kids can't drive?" Murphy said, "They get an older brother or sister to bring them home or take them to a friend's house." Their parents never knew a thing. I asked her what she thought about it, and she said, "I think it's sad."

I told Murphy I was proud of her because she had demonstrated good judgment. I gave myself a time out to think about what more needed to be said and how I could best encourage my daughter. You want your child to come to you when she has a problem or needs help. You should be their soft place to land. Remember, you will only know as much about your child as she is willing to share with you. You won't be able to help, encourage or guide your child unless she comes to you. If you are getting most of your information about your child though the school or other parents, you may be getting it too late to help.

Later the next day, I told Murphy again how proud I was of her. She had proven to me that she could make decisions for herself, and I didn't always need to be there. I told her I knew that she would make mistakes; everyone does. Good kids sometimes make bad choices; no one is perfect. We will all suffer consequences, and that is how we learn. (I am in my forties and still learning from my consequences.) No one gets through his or her teen years without some mistakes. As a parent, I just don't want my children's big mistakes to be about sex, drugs, alcohol or personal safety. All bad decisions are not created equally. As your child becomes older, some consequences are much greater than others. The bottom line is to make sure your children understand that you love them no matter what and that they will always have your full support.

Sources

"Using Adolescent Brain Research to Inform Policy: A Guide for Juvenile Advocates." National Juvenile Justice Network. (September 2008), http://www.njjn.org/media/resources/public/resource_847.pdf

Today's Lesson:
Approaching Bullying

You will never reach higher ground if you are
always pushing others down.

– JEFFREY BENJAMIN

Chalk Talk

It's raining. I'm eating my lunch alone in the library…again. I entered my freshman year of high school with high hopes and dreams of football games, friends, dances and playing sports. By April of that year, however, my dreams had been dashed, and I had run for cover to the only place I wouldn't be mortified to be alone.

It is extremely difficult for me to recount my miserable experience of becoming the "odd girl out," but I am writing about it now because I want to offer something to parents whose child has been or is being bullied or excluded. Your child is not the only one. More importantly, she can survive and thrive after an experience with bullying.

My own story started when a group of girls I thought were my friends turned on me and left me with no one to talk to. That time of my life was lonely, frightening and confusing. I couldn't figure out why my friendship wasn't good enough for them anymore. And while I wasn't the victim of public ridicule, being ostracized was a very demeaning experience. I even considered transferring to another school to escape the constant reminders of what a "loser" I had become.

Fortunately, my story had a happy ending. I didn't leave my high school. After much thought, I decided that running away would not solve the problem. I made a choice to forge new friendships, hang tough and become a better person. I remember chanting, "I will win," as I got ready for school each morning. It was tough. Some days were excruciating because I knew I might eat alone again. But I did it. And in time, I made new friends and stopped needing to prop myself up with, "I will win."

The point is that I didn't allow the actions of a few mean girls drive me away. By the second semester of my junior year, I was voted Sadie Hawkins dance princess and won a school-wide election to student government; senior year I was crowned Homecoming Queen. I believe my classmates awarded me that honor because after my experience, I made it my policy to be nice to everyone.

But before I polish and buff my halo, I have to admit that I have been on the bullying end of situations, too. I remember joining with a friend to taunt a second-grade classmate because she had gotten lice. I can still see the look of embarrassment on her face. I should have been embarrassed because of how I made her feel. In middle school, I was part of a clique who excluded a classmate not deemed to be cool enough. One year later, I discovered for myself exactly how she felt.

I think I was able to successfully survive my bullying experience because my parents helped lay a strong foundation for my value system. While I stumbled a little along the way, their guidance and example gave me the strength to overcome obstacles in my own life and learn to treat everyone with respect and dignity. Additionally, I played on my high school tennis and soccer teams. Being part of a team helped me through that time. I was also very active in a volunteer organization, the Assistance League; helping others forced me take the focus off of my own troubles. Lastly, I had my faith, and I knew that if I stayed true to that faith, I could make it through anything.

Childhood can be tough road to ride. Parents need to know that what they say to their children and how they treat other people matters, because their kids are watching and listening. We should give them all the tools we can to deal with bullying and to help them avoid becoming bullies themselves.

Teacher's Conference

When parents think of school safety, they may imagine fire drills and disaster preparedness lessons. But with school violence in the news and on many parents' minds, more and more schools are creating bullying policies and adopting programs to combat the issue. Research reveals that students report the majority of bullying takes place on school grounds, most often in the classroom, on the playground, in the cafeteria, in bathrooms and in the halls.

Schools should take multiple steps to combat bullying and educate teachers, parents and students about the short- and long-term affects that bullying can have on both the victim and the perpetrator. Strong schools have programs that include the following elements: a clear school policy, faculty training, a curriculum that teachers can use in the classroom, a support system for students and an open line of communication with parents. Perhaps most important is the idea that all adults and children in the school community should foster a culture of caring. When everyone involved has no tolerance for bullying, bullies have no choice but to stop their negative behavior.

These steps are positive ones that will help ensure a safe school campus. However, as your child's primary educator, you are still the first line of defense in keeping your child from being bullied or from becoming one.

Homework

First and foremost, parents need to understand some of the dynamics involved in bullying and the affects that bullying can have on both the victim and the perpetrator.

Types of Bullying:

Physical/Direct: hitting, punching, scratching, kicking, spitting or other physical attacks.

Emotional/Indirect: spreading rumors or stories about someone; systematically excluding a student from activities; tormenting a student by making fun of a handicap or related issue; using sexist or racist slurs; name-calling and the like.

Cyber: using the Internet or cell phones to inflict emotional harm on another child by posting negative images, sending threats, leaving nasty voice mails, creating negative websites or posting negative information on a social networking site.

Male bullying tends to be physical or involve intimidation and coercion (handing over lunch money), while female bullying tends to be indirect in nature. Girls are more likely to exclude one another, spread rumors and use cyber-bullying as a tool for harassment. That doesn't mean that girls never get physical, or that boys never use the Internet to bully. These patterns simply expose how gender can affect the type of bullying that takes place in a given situation.

Roles Children can Play in the Bullying Process

Current research reveals different roles children play in the bullying cycle:

Ringleader: the person who leads or dictates the act of bullying through intimidation and influence.

Assistant: the person who participates in the bullying so as to avoid being a target of the ringleader.

Reinforcer: the kid who shows positive encouragement toward the main bully.

Bystander: the student who witnesses the act of bullying but is afraid to say anything, and appears to condone the act because of his silence. It is very easy for children to fall into this category.

Defender: the student who stands up against a bully or group of bullies.

A common myth is that bullies are anti-social and outcasts among classmates. This could not be further from the truth. Recent research indicates that many of today's bullies are typical kids who do not exhibit the stereotypical bully profile. Many students engage in group bullying that allows them to feel they are not really responsible for their behavior. It can be extremely difficult for children to walk away when the popular kids are the bullies.

answerkeys

Signs of Bullying
- Torn, dirty or wet clothing; damaged books or backpack, and the child cannot give a good explanation of what happened to cause the damage
- Bruises, injuries that cannot be explained, cuts, scratches
- Loss of interest in school and a drop in academic performance
- Loss of friends
- Afraid or unwilling to go to school in the morning
- Complains of physical ailments
- Has nightmares or cannot sleep at all
- Sadness, depression
- Anxiety
- Quiet, overly sensitive, passive
- Low self-esteem and a loss of self-confidence

Effects of Bullying on the Victim
- Depression
- Thoughts of suicide
- Low self-esteem
- Loss of desire to attend school or outside activities
- Feelings of anxiety
- Becoming shy or withdrawn
- Physical ailment (stomach ache, headaches)

Effects of Bullying on the Perpetrator
- May lead to additional negative behavior, such as drug use, truancy or vandalism
- If a bully is antisocial, that behavior may extend into adulthood
- More likely to perform poorly in school
- One in four boys that bully will end up with a criminal record by age thirty
- Failure to develop empathy and compassion for other people

With so much information, parents need concrete strategies they can implement to help their child deal with various bullying scenarios.

Homework

Before bullying occurs:
- Keep a clear head. Talk to your child about the difference between casual back-and-forth teasing and bullying.
  - Although they are often used interchangeably, there is a difference between bullying and teasing. Teasing is a non-threatening back and forth that takes place between children on the same emotional and physical level. Bullying, on the other hand, is when one or more children engage in systematic and organized behavior that is threatening, hurtful, physically harmful or spreads negative information via the Internet.

- Research conducted over the past fifteen years has found that teasing can be a positive force in relationships. School-age children can use happy, fun teasing as an important part of play, and it can actually enhance their ability to express positive feelings toward one another. Parents and children can enjoy teasing each other, too. Teasing is even present in the animal world! Juvenile monkeys pull the tails of other monkeys to engage them in play.

- Teasing should be fun and mutual. Make sure your child knows when enough is enough.

- Play the game, "What does a bully look like?" Have your child draw a picture of what he thinks a bully looks like. Talk about the personality characteristics of someone who bullies and what your child should look out for at school.

   Example: A child may draw a picture of a cute little girl. Next to the girl, she may draw another picture of a snake to illustrate that a bully engages in sneaky and mean behavior, just like a snake.

- Set up standards of behavior, and create a family approach to bullying. For example:
   - We do not bully.
   - We always help others.
   - We will include students who are left out.
   - If we know someone is being bullied, we will seek help from a trusted adult.
   - We will create a game plan for dealing with a bully.

- Practice "walking away" with your child. Practice makes perfect, and your child will feel more empowered to do something positive if he has practiced with you at home.

- Find out about the school's bullying policy. See if there is anything you can do to assist with the program or enlist the participation of other parents.

- Partner with the school to create a culture and community of caring, a community that does not tolerate harassment of abuse of any kind.

If your child tells you he is being bullied:
- Stay calm and gather facts before acting.

- Talk with and listen to your child.

   - Get the whole story; find out the circumstances of the bullying and what exactly happened.

   - Help your child decide which friends he can count on, and promote the value of protecting positive relationships. Encourage your child to participate in activities that include these friends. Invite them over and create a safe, fun environment for your child to enjoy friends who support him.

   - Give him a healthy outlet for his frustrations by allowing him to vent, get angry, cry, even scream. This can help relieve stress (see lesson on *Anger Management*, page 36).

25

- Make an action plan together.

- Give him unconditional love.

- If the bullying is taking place at school, find a trusted school official whose help you can enlist and discuss the situation. Consider contacting the bully's parents if you feel it will improve the situation. If school rules have been violated, trust the school to handle it.

- Work with the principal to ensure that the school is implementing its bullying policy effectively.

- Find like-minded parents to talk to the school if other students are being bullied, too.

If your child is the bully:
No parent wants to hear that her child is a bully. You should first give yourself credit for acknowledging that your child is engaging in negative behavior and realize that you cannot blame yourself for his actions. Even so, you should take a critical look at what takes place in your home on a daily basis and immediately address your child's desire to bully others.

- Make it clear that bullying is never allowed. If you have a negative reaction to your child's efforts to bully, your child is more likely to stop than if you ignore the behavior or try to let the school handle the situation on its own.

- Set up strict consequences for negative/bullying behavior. Set up a contract with the teacher, a coach or with the school principal. Enforce all consequences, and acknowledge positive behavioral strides.

- Spend quality time with your child every day. There is a reason your child has chosen to bully other kids. Get to the root of the issue through conversation, physical contact and unconditional love.

- Teach your child empathy and compassion through service projects and other outside activities (see lesson on Promoting Service Projects & Volunteerism, page 45). Research shows that children who bully often lack empathy toward their victims. For example, if your child teases a child with a disability, involve him with the Special Olympics so that he can begin to see others in a new light.

- Encourage your child to participate in sports or some after-school program where she can vent frustration in a constructive manner, forge meaningful friendships and build genuine self-esteem.

- Enlist of the support of your family and the school. Bullies are people too, and if we want to break the cycle, we need to help them change their attitude and their behavior through consequences and positive reinforcement.

Systemic bullying is a larger issue than any one person can solve. It takes a cooperative effort on the part of students, teachers, parents and administrators.

If your child is witness or bystander to bullying:

- Follow the strategies for when your child is being bullied. Many children are bystanders because they are afraid of being bullied themselves.

    ◉ Talk about how being bullied makes your child feel. Have him transfer those feelings to the child who was being bullied.

    ◉ Talk to your child about the courage it takes to stand up to your "friends" when they are mistreating another student. Encourage him to take steps to help address the issue (tell a teacher, stand up for his friend, get other kids to rally around the child being bullied, etc.). Again, practicing with your child will better prepare him for the real thing.

Cafeteria Line

Additional coping tips for kids

- Avoid the bully and use the buddy system when walking the halls or using the restroom.
- Resist the urge to become angry and react in a way that will encourage the bully. Yelling or crying may encourage the bully to continue, and physically reacting may get you in trouble.
- Tell an adult.
- Talk about it with your parents or a trusted friend.
- Remove possible incentives.
- Use confident body language. It sends a message that you will not be a victim.
- Engage in activities that make you feel good (sports, music or a service project).

Teacher Toolbox Tips

Teach you child how to stop a cyber bully.

- **Don't respond.** Sinking to her level perpetuates the problem. Try to block all communication from her.

- **Don't retaliate.** It exacerbates the problem and empowers the bully.

- **Save the evidence.** Make copies of all negative correspondence. Alert the authorities if the behavior continues or if you feel you are in danger.

- **Be polite.** Avoid the urge to be mean or start an argument with a bully. Try to be courteous until the situation is resolved.

- **Don't be a bully.** Never pick on someone else, even if you have been bullied. Engaging in negative behavior makes you no different than the bully.

- **Be a friend, not a bystander.** Refuse to forward or comment on negative pictures or information. Stand up for friends and classmates. A bully is only as powerful as you allow her to become. Take away her power by using your voice for good.

answerkeys

HIGH FIVE to **Sue Arnold**, third grade teacher at Holy Family School in South Pasadena, CA. and mother of three

HIGH FIVE to **Maryanne Leupold** of Tustin Hills, CA, editor and mother of three, including me

HIGH FIVE to **Andrea Richmond Schmidt**, 5th grade teacher in Ashburn, VA

Sources

http://www.safenetwork.org

http://www.kidshealth.org

http://www.bulliestobuddies.com)

http://www.mentalhealth.samhsa.gov

http://www.parentsconnect.com

http://www.kidsareworthit.com

http://www.drphil.com (his son has an entire bullying program)

http://www.ama-assn.org -The Educational Forum on Adolescent Health: Youth Bullying, American Medical Association (2002)

Keltner, Dachler, "In Defense of Teasing," *New York Times*, December 5, 2008, online edition. http://www.nytimes.com/2008/12/07/magazine/07teasing-t.html?scp=1&sq=In%20Defense%20of%20Teasing&st=cse

Bishop Mills, Carol, "The Ups and Downs of Teasing," *Communication Currents*, April 2009. This article was translated from the scholarly article: Mills, C.B. & Carwile, A.M. (2009). http://www.communicationcurrents.com/index.asp?bid=15&issuepage=153

Bishop Mills, Carol, "The Good, the Bad and the Borderline: Separating Teasing from Bullying," *Communication Education* 58, 276-301 (April 2009).

Character

Today's Lesson:
Discipline versus Punishment

Discipline must come through liberty…We do not consider an individual disciplined only when he has been rendered as artificially silent as a mute and as immovable as a paralytic. He is an individual annihilated, not disciplined.

– MARIA MONTESSORI

Chalk Talk

If there ever was a "hot button" parenting issue, discipline is it. Everyone has their own stories from childhood: scary, humiliating, even humorous at times. Parents have to decide if they will follow the example of their parents, or choose a new way. I believe that discipline is such an emotionally charged issue because it taps into our deepest vulnerabilities: our most potent childhood memories, our passionate love for our children, and our hopes and fears about who we are as parents. Most often, we are making parenting decisions on the fly: "If you don't stop feeding your vitamins to the tadpoles I will…" What? Never give you vitamins again? Make you eat the nasty, algae-covered vitamin? Pour all the tadpoles down the drain? Empty threats are ineffective, and really do no more than make us look foolish. Yet all of us have done it at some point. Making decisions about your "parenting philosophy" in the midst of chaos never seems to go well. While a certain amount of flexibility and improvisation are necessary parenting talents, nothing will improve your ability to discipline your children like being proactive and planning ahead.

I hope that reading this lesson will inspire some passionate and thoughtful conversations about discipline between you and your spouse, your parents and your friends. Before any intelligent conversation can begin, however, there needs to be clarification about three significant words: discipline, punishment, and consequences. The word discipline comes from the same root as the word disciple, which means the follower of a teacher. To discipline means to train or to teach. Punishment is any pain, suffering, or loss inflicted upon a person because of wrongdoing. Many people use discipline and punishment interchangeably, but I think they're significantly different. Discipline is a much broader term that incorporates all the things you do as a parent to teach your child about what's right and wrong and what is appropriate. Punishment is always reactive, usually negative, and at times harmful. Consequences are the results or outcome of an earlier action. As parents, we often fall into the trap of shielding our children from the real consequences of their own actions in an effort to protect them. Instead, we spend hours trying to invent consequences of our own to take their place. Productive and healthy discipline allows children to learn from their mistakes rather than making them suffer for them. In fact, when we impose suffering on a child it actually shifts the focus from the child's mistake and its consequences to the "mean parent" who is making his life miserable. Punishment requires the parent to be responsible for controlling a child's behavior, rather than the child controlling his own actions. Instead, we should look for the natural consequences that arise from our children's actions and take advantage of them.

Teacher's Conference

All of this is great in theory and on paper, but what does it really mean for me? How does that help me when my kids are throwing tantrums, talking back, biting the cat, and making "soup" in the toilet? The essence of effective discipline comes down to being prepared. As a teacher, I spent a great deal of time and energy troubleshooting. Which parts of my day were the most difficult? Well, the first five minutes of math class were always a nightmare. But instead of blaming the kids, I searched for things I could change in advance to help the situation. Math was right after lunch, and my students always had a tough time transitioning from socializing to studying. I tried starting class with a group problem-solving activity at the beginning of each math class, instead of jumping into the new lesson right away. I also recognized that this was one of the times I really had to be "on my game" and not sitting behind my desk. I found that putting creative energy into tweaking my routine and keeping my expectations reasonable saved me time and emotional energy. Preventing discipline problems is much easier and more pleasant than resolving them once they have erupted.

No matter how good a strategist you are, it is impossible to prevent every discipline problem. You simply can't anticipate every crisis. Problems will arise, no matter how much you plan and prepare, so be sure you know how you will handle unexpected problems. It will make all the difference. When I was a first-year teacher, I had an unusually creative class. My students constantly amazed me with their ability to not just break the rules, but to come up with behavior that I could not possibly have created a rule to prevent. For example, just before we were headed out the door to take class pictures, I asked if anyone needed to go to the restroom or check themselves in the mirror. One student said "I'll be right back!" and so we waited and waited. Finally he emerged from the restroom dripping wet, having submerged his head in the sink. He thought it would look cool if his hair was wet and spiky "with drips that looked like sweat" in his school picture.

Well, I never ever thought I would have to say, "Please don't bathe in the sink immediately before school pictures, or ever for that matter." I gave him some paper towels and off we went. I told him that I would have to think of what to do and how to tell his mother, and since I was going to have to spend so much of my time thinking about his hair that he would need to help me out by picking up trash and cleaning up the classroom. After he had cleaned for awhile he tentatively came up to my desk and said, "I have an idea. I could write my mom a note to tell her what I did and say sorry." So that's what he did. I may not have been able to anticipate that particular crisis, but I knew that I needed to respond calmly and give myself some time to think. Having a plan at home is essential. Know what you will do ahead of time and follow through, even if it is difficult—especially if it is difficult. A calm, consistent response is key.

Homework

Most of my happiness in both marriage and in motherhood has hinged upon being conscious of my expectations and managing them wisely. Often I have faced great disappointment and frustration when an expectation that I hadn't consciously realized, much less verbalized, went unmet. My children have enough trouble following the expectations I set before them clearly and repeatedly. It's unreasonable to expect them (or my husband) to be mind readers.

Assignment #1
Consider and clarify your expectations for yourself, your spouse and your children. Many of us have "unwritten rules" to which we hold ourselves and others. Sometimes we aren't even aware of them until these expectations go unfulfilled. Take some time to write a short list of your unwritten and unspoken "rules," and evaluate them to see if they are really feasible. Often we carry over rules and expectations from our childhood that may not fit our own families.

Here are some examples of expectations (some healthy, some not) to which you might relate:
- Expectations for self:
  - Always be busy. Only lazy people take breaks or naps.
  - Spending money is fun. Saving is boring and frustrating.
  - Never raise your voice.

- Expectations for your spouse:
  - Whoever cooks dinner should not have to do the dishes.
  - When there is a problem, talking about it immediately is essential.
  - Vacations are for adventuring and trying new things, rather than resting and relaxing.

- Expectations for your children:
  - Every child should play a sport.
  - Children should always clean their plate at every meal.
  - A consistent bedtime should always be strictly enforced.

answerkeys

Assignment #2

Evaluate your expectations. Putting your expectations down on paper can help you determine if they are appropriate and useful, or outdated and ineffective. The way your mother and father shared household responsibilities may not be the best fit for your marriage, given your different gifts, needs and lifestyle. Just because your mother kept her house spotless doesn't mean that you have to freak out if your kids track mud all over the living room floor. Your spouse may have a completely different perspective than you do. These differences can be liberating and enlightening if discussed openly and in advance. The key is to consider whether your expectations are a good fit for your family at this time, given your circumstances and your children's ages and level of maturity. Be prepared to reevaluate and adapt your expectations as needed.

Question for the Teacher

How do I know if my expectations for my child are age-appropriate?
Answer: If you are having consistent struggles over certain behavioral issues, it may mean that your expectations are too high. However, if your child shows regression in a certain area that she had previously "mastered," then your expectations are probably appropriate. Her development will seldom be linear, and setbacks are to be expected. Respond to your child with love and support when she struggles, but continue to keep your expectations intact. Dr. T. Berry Brazelton explains this typical, non-linear pattern of child development in his book, *Touchpoints, Birth to Three: Your Child's Emotional and Behavioral Development*:

"Emotional, behavioral, motor, and language development all occur at their own pace but also affect each other. A child's advances in any one of these areas are preceded by temporary backslides, or regressions, in the same area, or another. The cost of each new achievement can temporarily disrupt the child's progress—and the whole family's stability. Yet each of these disruptions also offers parents a chance to reflect, consider a change in direction, and grow along with the child...When seen as natural and predictable, these periods of regressive behavior are opportunities to understand the child more deeply and to support his or her growth, rather to become locked in a struggle."

Character

Assignment #3

Communicate your expectations to your spouse and then to your children. Having reasonable expectations is a critical part of being an effective parent. Communicating those expectations is equally important. If you're aware of your expectations and are able to communicate them to your family, then you will be able to eliminate a great deal of confusion and frustration. Don't let this be a one-sided conversation. Encourage your spouse to clarify his or her own expectations. Try to come to a consensus, especially on your expectations for your children. It is absolutely essential that you present a united front to your kids, even if you have differences in opinion on certain issues. Support your spouse in front of your child. Work out your differences about discipline in private.

Assignment #4

With your spouse, create a discipline plan that flows out of your expectations for your family. Your expectations may be broad and somewhat vague, i.e. "I expect our children to be respectful." The next step is to think about how to live out these expectations in a practical, day-to-day sense. With your spouse, list your top three (or five or ten) current discipline problems, and make a plan for dealing with each of them. This doesn't have to be anything more than bullet points or a few words. A few examples: When Maggie squirts me in face with the rubber ducky, then bath time is over. When Conner throws a tantrum, I will lead him to his room to let him finish it without an audience. If Julia uses more than her allotted cell phone minutes, we will take away her phone until she pays us back for the extra charges.

Assignment #5

Practice (out loud, if you want) what you will say to your child when she misbehaves. Have some short, calm "go-to" sentences that will send a clear message to your child and give you a moment to gather yourself. Redirection is often easier for your child to receive than correction.

- "Oh, no you threw sand. It's time to leave the playground, and go home."
- "Hmm…you still haven't put on your shoes. I'll let you carry them to the car instead."
- 'Would you like me to wash your hands with soap, or would you like to wash mine with lots of bubbles?" (Either way, your child's hands get clean. Thanks to my dad for this one!)
- "I'll be happy to listen to you when you use a polite voice."

Example #1 If your child refuses to clean up his toys, even when you offer to help, quickly and calmly collect all the toys on the floor in a bag and tell him he may have them back tomorrow (or later if need be). Proactive and preventive steps to take: Limit the number of toys your child has out in his room. Box some up and trade them out to keep things interesting. Make sure your child's toy storage is kid-friendly. Large baskets or bins that are low to the ground help make cleaning up a reasonable request.

33

answerkeys

Example #2 If your child breaks something valuable, she needs to help clean it up and pay to replace it. If she only has a handful of pennies, she can give you some of her toys to sell or earn money by doing extra chores. Proactive and preventive steps to take: Take another crack at "baby proofing" your house. As your child grows, you may need to adjust and edit your décor. If your child is especially active, you may want to schedule more time for outside play.

Mom Tips

- Focus on being calm, even bored by your child's misbehavior. This lack of emotion will often surprise your child and will eliminate screaming matches. We have all seen that impish glint in a child's eye when he knows he's got you at your wit's end. There is no fun or excitement in boring someone. Save your emotional energy for dangerous situations and enthusiastic responses to right choices.

- Keep moving. This strategy works especially well for toddlers and young children. Even if your child is putting up a fight, if you move on to the next thing, your child will not want to be left behind. When my daughter is taking an inordinate amount of time to get out the door, I simply walk out the front door and get in the car. She invariably grabs her things and runs outside. It takes much less energy to walk back and shut the front door than it does to convince her to hurry up. When my son fights bedtime or naptime, I sit in the rocking chair and start reading aloud. He settles down in my lap to hear the story within seconds.

- When on vacation, traveling or out of your normal routine, strive to strike a balance between being flexible and retaining a helpful level of structure. On our last plane trip, I fed my kids an airline "snack" of salami, crackers and mysterious cheese spread coupled with cookies, apple juice and fruit snacks and called it dinner. As soon as we were off the plane, my adherence to normal nutritional goals was back in place. Sometimes you just do what you have to, but if you repeatedly let your rules and expectations fall apart —your kids will fall apart, too.

- When we constantly repeat ourselves, not only do we sound like a broken record, but our words lose their effectiveness because our children simply tune us out. We should strive to be thoughtful when choosing our words, and wise about when and how often we use them. Limit your use of the word "no." Saving it for dangerous situations and serious infractions helps the word retain its power. As a parent, I have found that you can say "yes" to almost any request. For example, if your child asks to go to the park at eight o'clock at night you can cheerfully respond, "I would love to take you to the park tomorrow afternoon, but now it's time for bed."

Adapted from *Parenting with Love and Logic* by Foster Cline, M.D. and Jim Fay.

Words of Wisdom

- If you can't come up with a reasonable response to your child's misbehavior on the spot, then wait. Tell her not to worry and that you will be sure to get back to her about what the consequences of her action will be.

- Handle your child's misbehavior quietly and privately as often as you can. No one likes to feel cornered or embarrassed, and she will likely do anything to save face. Public humiliation is not an appropriate consequence.

- Celebrate right choices with emotion and fanfare. React to poor choices with an efficient, matter-of-fact tone and no emotion. Act bored.

- Be consistent. Always.

- Never do anything to injure or humiliate your child in an attempt to reprimand him. A violent response is one of weakness and desperation. It takes strength and creativity to discipline a child with love.

- Sarcasm is never an effective discipline tool. You are basically saying with your tone of voice: "I am smart, and you are stupid." Your child will mostly likely be confused and embarrassed by sarcastic remarks. It is better to say nothing at all then to let a biting comment or negative remark escape your lips.

- Apologize to your children when you make a mistake. More than once, I have completely lost my cool and screamed at my children. The only thing that I could possibly do to regain my children's trust was to kneel down and look them in the eyes and say "I'm sorry. I was wrong. Will you forgive me?" It is humbling and uncomfortable to ask for forgiveness—without tacking on any extras like "I was so angry because you took forever to get in the car!!!" A simple, sincere apology can go along way toward building your relationship with your child.

- Keep your love and hopes for your children in the forefront of your mind when making decisions about discipline.

35

Sources

Brazelton, T. Berry, and Joshua Sparrow. *Touchpoints 3 to 6*. New York and Washington D.C.: Da Capo Press, 2002.

Cline, Foster W. and Jim Fay. *Parenting with Love and Logic* (Updated and Expanded Edition). Colorado Springs: NavPress, 2006.

Fay, Charles and Jim Fay. *Love and Logic Magic for Early Childhood: Practical Parenting from Birth to Six Years*. 1st ed. Golden,CO: Love & Logic Press, 2000.

Today's Lesson:
Anger Management

Anyone can become angry. That is easy. But to be angry with
the right person, to the right degree, at the right time,
for the right purpose and in the right way...that is not easy.

– ARISTOTLE

Chalk Talk

Your face gets hot, your jaw clenches, your heart begins racing, your breathing speeds up. Are you having a heart attack? Doubtful. Sounds like you're getting angry. Don't worry. Anger is a natural emotion. It can't be avoided. At some point, everyone gets angry, and that's okay. What's not okay is to take your anger out on other people or their stuff. And that's why we have to teach our kids how to appropriately manage their anger and stay in control of their emotions.

Pop Quiz

You are driving along when suddenly, a woman cuts you off. You have to slam on your brakes, spilling your coffee. Your reaction would be:

    a. to stick your middle finger out the window while laying on the horn
    b. to shout out your favorite four-letter word while laying on the horn
    c. to wish she would die as you race to cut her off
    d. to take a deep breath and count to 10

Character

If you answered a, b or c, would you consider yourself a "hothead" or the type of person that flies off the handle in the blink of an eye? Maybe it's time to think about better ways to vent your anger, as you are a role model for your children.

Mom Tip

I am sure we have all found ourselves in a situation where someone's anger has spiraled out of control. It is important to talk to our children about these types of situations and what to do if they find themselves at the wrong place, at the wrong time. Talk about how an angry person may look (red face, clenched fists, flared nostrils, etc.). Is he threatening others, verbally attacking someone, or becoming physical? We cannot predict how someone will react to their anger so it is best to walk away immediately. Tell your child that even if he is just watching a heated situation, he can accidentally wind up in the middle and get hurt. Stress the importance of not becoming involved, getting out of danger and seeking help if needed.

Teacher's Conference

Throughout my teaching career, I have been exposed to many angry people, varying angry reactions and unpredictable situations. Some of the kids I have worked with weren't angry at anyone in particular, they were just angry. Some didn't know how to release this built-up anger, so they would take it out on whomever or whatever was around; others repressed their anger and built a wall around themselves. They may have been angry because: they didn't sleep well; they heard gunshots in the night; their mother's boyfriend gave her a black eye; or they had been evicted yet again. These are all good reasons to be angry; it was my job to help them vent and manage their anger in a safe, effective way. Of course, these situations were more on the extreme side. I also had students become angry during everyday situations, such as: "Emily said red was her favorite color, but it is my favorite color," or "John held the door, but I am the door holder," or "My mom made me eat cereal this morning, but I wanted yogurt." There are countless reasons why we get angry. What's important is how we manage our anger. As parents, we can give our kids outlets for promoting positive, productive anger management.

What we can't do is give our kids inappropriate advice for social situations, such as school. There are rules in school and in life that we must follow, or face consequences. More times than I'd care to count, I would have a student become physically aggressive with a classmate. The reasons would vary, but often the student

answerkeys

would tell me that their mom told them to hit the offender. After years of teaching inner-city kids, I finally figured out that hitting and punching were street survival skills for many of my students. They had to know how to stand up for themselves and members of their family. Whenever possible, I would speak to the child's mother, and she would confirm her advice to use physical aggression if someone was bothering her child. I would explain that at school, advice like that didn't apply because school wasn't just a place for learning, it was also a place where kids should feel safe.

Homework

Assignment #1

Take a few minutes to think about your own reactions to anger. Do you cry, scream, throw things, shut down or just tend to hold it in until you think you might explode? Now think of your children or spouse. Each person's reaction to anger may look different. Does your child's response to anger need to be drawn out or reigned in? One child may have an explosive response, while another child withdraws. Whatever your child's response to anger may be, be sure to acknowledge that her feelings are real and valid—and address them. It isn't easy for everyone to express themselves and discuss their feelings.

Assignment #2

As the parent, it is your job to get to the root of the problem when your child is angry. There is a reason your child feels angry. If she becomes angry and has an outburst, you must remain calm.

- Don't fuel the fire. Give your child time and space to cool off and calm down.
- Be consistent.
- Provide tools and outlets for your child to channel anger, keeping in mind her personality.
- Talk about how she handled her anger, and praise her for positive, appropriate behavior.

It takes time and patience to help children deal with feelings of anger.

Teacher Toolbox Tips

How to avoid power struggles with children: *

- Stick to rituals and routines.
- Sings songs that aid in transitions.
- Warn them ahead of time about transitions.
- Slow your pace to that of a young child.
- Remember that young children do not share, take turns, sit still for long or wait for things.
- Avoid too many changes in a child's life.
- Use games to make things happen (e.g. cleaning up toys).
- Don't tackle too much in one day.
- Give children a choice between two options.
- Know your child and read her cues.
- Let your child know exactly what will happen in advance.
- Distract and redirect.
- Warn your child about a behavior.
- Remind your child about rules.
- Talk about feelings.
- Use humor.
- Decide which battles are worth fighting and which are not.

* **March 2003 Family Information Services, Minneapolis, MN ISSN 1042-0878**

Assignment #3

Think about the television shows, movies, video games and music you allow in your home. Are they violent or negatively influencing your child? Some kids, especially young children, may have difficulty distinguishing between what is real and what is make-believe. Take an active role in keeping up with what your child sees or listens to. Promote bravery and confidence, not violence.

Cafeteria Line

Tools to help younger children deal with anger:

- Color red on a piece of paper.
- Draw a picture.
- Write about feelings.
- Use a squeeze ball.
- Squeeze clay and let it ooze through your fingers.
- Tear paper into small pieces.
- Practice deep breathing.
- Count or count backwards.
- Jump up and down as high as you can.
- Punch a pillow.
- Talk to someone about your feelings.
- Turn up the radio and belt out a favorite song (use headphones if available).
- Get moving: run, take a bike ride, etc.
- Take a mental vacation. In your mind, picture a peaceful place, a tree house way up in the sky, or floating in a raft on the water.

Additional tools to help older kids manage anger:

- Write in a journal.
- Meditation
- Don't react, just walk away.
- When you are calm, decide on a "sign" that you can give a parent to let them know you are angry and need some time. Examples: set out a red note card; tie a bandana on the doorknob, etc.
- Tune into how your body feels when angry. When your face becomes flushed, or your heart begins to race, it may be time to step away from a person or situation before becoming really angry.
- Learn your own "triggers" and take steps to avoid them.
- Play out reactions in your head when you feel calm. You are more likely to remain calm if you visualize that state of mind when you're not angry.
- Talk it out. Cut off a potential argument before it gets out of hand by using reason to get to the heart of why an issue or situation makes you angry.
- Vent to someone you trust.
- Repeat a calming word or phrase to yourself, or close your eyes picture yourself somewhere more peaceful.

Mom Tips

Create an "angry box" with items such as clay, paper, crayons and stress balls. You and your child will be prepared instead of hunting for tools in the heat of the moment. Sports and art are great anger management tools. Art lets students release their emotions in a more positive way, and sports help them let off steam.

39

answerkeys

Ways to remain in control when your child makes you angry:

- Give yourself a time out.
- Shut yourself up in a room.
- Do not talk to your children until you feel calm.
- Count to ten.
- Write your angry thoughts on paper to get them out of your system.
- Blow off steam with intense exercise.

If you or a loved one is experiencing out-of-control anger or displaying destructive behaviors, practical advice isn't enough. A professional can investigate and help address deeper, emotional struggles. When there is a persistent pattern of behavior occurring over a six- to twelve-month period, in which the rights of others are violated, you need to seek professional help. If, for example, you can cite three or more of the following behaviors, it's time to get help: bullying; threatening and intimidating others; initiating fights; using a weapon that could hurt someone; being physically cruel to people or animals; actively defying or refusing to comply with adults' requests or rules; deliberately annoying people; blaming others for mistakes or misbehaviors; often annoyed, angry, resentful, spiteful or vindictive; often losing temper or arguing with adults. These are red flag behaviors, and while they may be reflective of a stressful season in a child's life, they are indicative of more serious problems that need a professional's attention.

Words of Wisdom

Listen to your child. Really listen to your child and find out how she is feeling. Help her think through options to save face with others, build self-esteem and find ways out of difficult situations. Don't tell her how she should feel. Give her ways to deal with her own feelings, and let her know you are always there for her.

HIGH FIVE to Beth Stanley, Licensed Professional Counselor and mother of four.

Today's Lesson:
The Proper and Effective Use of Time Out

Never be afraid to sit awhile and think.

– LORRAINE HANSBERRY

Chalk Talk

When disciplining your child, the most important part is the "buy-in." You and your spouse must be on the same page with discipline. Both of you should understand and be committed to why you will use time out. And you should know the desired outcome for you child. I choose to use time out because I want to teach my children about making good choices. I love them, and want them to be happy and successful with others. I want to teach them patience and respect for others.

Time out can also teach them how to collect themselves. The goal is to teach skills that allow them to stop, gather their thoughts, and then make good choices. It's a big part of emotional intelligence. As adults, we would look pretty silly if we threw ourselves on the floor every time we didn't get our way. The sooner we learn how to solve problems, the easier our life with others will be.

Teacher's Conference

Discipline is a skill required for effective teaching. As classroom teachers, we don't have only one or two children that we're trying to engage in the daily lessons; we have a class of twenty-five kids. Getting twenty-five kindergartners down the hall to the cafeteria in an orderly manner takes skill, not luck. Handling an angry, disruptive high-schooler who's twice your size takes confidence and skill, not panic buttons or pepper spray. Good teachers know not to get into an emotional struggle with a frustrated child at any age or size. It's a lose-lose situation. Staying calm is easier said than done. It's a skill that takes lots of practice, especially when your son takes a bite out of his little sister. I promise that your children will give you plenty of opportunities to practice and perfect that skill.

answerkeys

Using time out effectively. You must be consistent. Being consistent builds trust between you and your child. Children want to know that your words mean something, and they need to know to expect consistent consequences when they make poor choices. This will mean everything to you when your children are teenagers.

Toddlers are smart. Even if you let only one major offense out of twenty slide, they will remember. It is their job to wear you down. If you are working on correcting a particular behavior, one slide can sabotage you and your child.

Another important key to success is that you and your spouse act as one unit. Children will shop for the answer that they want. They need to understand early on that both parents will give the same answer.

Using time out appropriately. Time out should be used when a child is not making good choices or not following directions. In my opinion, time out should not be used on a child younger than eighteen months old. Most situations at that age can be handled by redirecting. If your ten-month-old keeps digging in your plant, give a firm "no" and move the plant. Give him something fun to play with and later talk about why the plant needs to stay in the dirt and why houseplants are not good to eat.

A Practical Example

You have discussed with your child many times how she must hold your hand until you get inside the park gates. You have talked about how important it is to keep her safe and how much fun you are going to have at the park. Your child has also told you how the two of you are going to get from the car to the inside of the park. You have checked for understanding and gotten both " Yes, Mom" and eye contact. All of this has to happen before you open a single door.

Not two minutes out of the car, your child takes off through the parking lot without you. You immediately pick her up and tell her that you are going home. Remind her why: She must hold your hand until you're inside the gate. Put her straight in the car seat kicking, screaming and all. She will probably kick and scream the entire way home. Kicking and screaming are no big deal; all that matters is that she is safe and you keep your word. If you are a busy mom on the go, the car seat can be your best friend. It can save your child in a fiery crash and, when necessary, be a safe place to hold your child until you can get to your time out space at home.

I roll down the windows and turn on my favorite music. This is not a time to get upset and engage in a battle. Try not to scream over an upset child—it's really not a teachable moment. Use the ride home as a time to quietly gather your thoughts. When you get home, take her out of the car seat and straight to time out. Now, her thinking time starts. If she's still having a fit, that's okay, as long as she's sitting in her time out space. After time out is finished, you should squat down and look her in the eyes. Ask her why she's in time out and not at the park. Go over again about safety, following directions and how much you love her. Have her tell you how you both get out of the car and why you do it this way. You can also tell her that you understand how disappointed she is and that you also love the park and all of the fun equipment. Next, it is important to talk about how you know that she will make a better choice next time, and that you're looking forward to trying again next week. Now drop it, be positive and go on with your day.

Changing your child's location and putting her in the car seat works well in grocery stores, friends' houses, or anywhere you need to stop a behavior and make a big impression. Never be embarrassed about leaving quickly with your child. Other parents appreciate it when you take control of a bad situation. Just give a polite "good-bye" and "I will call you later."

Words of Wisdom

In my opinion, discipline is not about punishment, it's about training your child to use appropriate behavior and self-control, and to make good choices. Like all mothers, you want your child to be well liked, have friends and be a good friend. Children aren't born with these skills — you, the parent, must model, teach and practice.

Besides car talk, the most effective thing I have done to teach appropriate behavior is to act it out. Roleplay and make it fun! You pretend to be the waiter and let them be the guest at the restaurant. Then switch. Children love to pretend.

Do not expect your toddler to be naturally gracious and well-mannered at a birthday party. The truth is you don't have to teach your two-year-old to say "no" or "mine," but you do have to teach them to say "please" and "thank you". As humans, we're just hard wired to be egocentric. We want to take all the presents, blow out all the candles, and get the first slice of cake.

This is why all good teachers know not to give a spelling test until their students have written the words at least three times, learned the definitions and used them in a sentence. It's the same way with your child. In other words, do not expect success in a particular behavior that you have not modeled, taught and practiced.

One more thing to keep in mind: Sometimes adults need a time out. When you find yourself saying, "I will ground you until you are thirty," or "I will never take you back to another birthday party for the rest of your life," stop and walk away. Or tell your child you will talk to him about the consequences of his behavior after dinner when you are less upset. Don't you remember as a child worrying about a punishment that you

answerkeys

knew you were going to get? Sometimes the anticipation was worse than the punishment. You want to avoid making any threats that you are not fully prepared to back up. Empty threats will undermine your authority.

Homework

Guide to follow:
- Give a warning, and check for understanding.
- Take your child and sit him in a designated time out place.
- Put him in a safe corner without a chair (so he doesn't hurt himself).
- Don't get upset. In fact, don't talk to him at all while he's in time out.
- Set the timer (One minute per year of age).
- Put him back in the corner as many times as it takes, I don't care if it is sixty-two times, you must win. The next time it will be forty-eight and by about the fifth time, it will be once. Do not talk, just put him back. Then, start the timer.
- Go about your business while he is in time out.
- After he has completed the minutes:
  - Get down at eye level and, in a pleasant tone, ask him why he is in time out.
  - Ask why he did not make a good choice.
  - Listen to his response.
  - Briefly explain the behavior you expect to see.
  - Be positive. Talk about how he will make a better choice next time.
  - Move on and make the rest of the day better for you and your child.

POP Quiz

- **Only one _____ in a room.**
  - a. Barrel of monkeys
  - b. Double stroller
  - c. Hysterical person
- **No one ever _____ from not getting their way.**
  - a. Died
  - b. Melted
  - c. Swallowed their tongue.

- **What is the purpose of time out?**
  - a. For you and your child to become partners in building character.
  - b. To teach your child good decision-making skills
  - c. To give your child a chance to stop and gather himself emotionally.
  - d. All of the above

Key: c, a, d

Mom Tip

- No groceries are worth compromising your authority.
- Never negotiate with terrorists or toddlers. (Hopefully you have better judgment than a two year old.)
- Do not expect a behavior that you have not taught, role played and practiced. (Teaching a behavior should be fun.)
- Do not ever get out of the car until you have discussed your expectations for your child's behavior and checked for understanding.
- Be positive!
- Meet with your spouse about how your family will handle discipline.
- Discuss appropriate consequences and rewards.
- Learn what your child's currency is and know that it may change every week.
- Make the decision to always be aware and ready to point out when your child is loving, kind to others and making good choices.

Cheat Sheet

Currency: A standard of value for your child. For example, John Henry is seventeen, and his currency is his cell phone; Whitley is five, and her currency is going to the park before dinner.

Car Talk: The discussion of expectations before you get out of the car. In the car, your children are a captive audience. It's a perfect time to role-play different situations and check for understanding.

Buy-In: This is when you and your spouse have made a decision. You know why you will do it this way and are hopeful about the long-term outcome for your family.

Emotional Intelligence: This refers to the ability to perceive, control and evaluate emotions.

Today's Lesson:
Promoting Service Projects & Volunteerism

Each one should use whatever gift he has received to serve others,
faithfully administering God's grace in its various forms.

– 1 PETER 4:10

Chalk Talk

Looking back, I remember anxiously awaiting the arrival of my first child, John Henry. When he was about six weeks old, I recall saying to my husband, "I have never served anyone or anything this much in my entire life." I was exhausted. As parents, we gladly meet the needs of our children. We want their tummies full and their diapers dry. We attend to their every whimper, thankful to be blessed with this tiny miracle. Although at three o'clock in the morning, sleeping through the night seems like the real miracle.

Soon our little ones learn that they are the center of our universe. They see how the slightest cry is met with open arms and full attention. Infancy is quickly followed by the second year, better known as the "me," "mine" and "no" stage. This is normal. At this age, the only perspective our little egomaniac is capable of understanding is her own. By the age of two, she could care less if little Johnny wants a turn or Emma didn't get a cookie. As long as she has a turn and she gets a cookie, that's all that matters.

We gladly serve our children, but when can they learn to serve others? The exciting news is that around the age of three or four, children start wanting to do things for themselves. It is through this process of learning and growing that you will find fertile ground to plant the seeds of compassion for others.

As your child becomes more independent, you can start teaching her to do a few things for herself and others. Teaching compassion begins by exposing kids to the real needs of others. Service projects are a great way to teach kindness with the added benefit of boosting your child's self esteem. I have witnessed my young children and other preschoolers serving people in life-changing ways. I've seen slumped-over, disheveled elderly folks suddenly sit up straight and light up like a Christmas tree when a child simply shares their space. Don't wait until your child seems old enough to reach out. Even a baby can give warmth, with smiles and the gift of touch. Sometimes they turn out to be the most beautiful and treasured gifts.

Character

Teacher's Conference

Teachers and schools today are taking a bigger role than ever before in encouraging their students to serve others and their community. My daughter's elementary school holds a campus beautification day every year. The administration asks families to participate in cleaning, maintaining playground equipment and planting shrubs and flowers. Both of my high-school students are involved in the "lunch buddies" program at school. In this program, a regular education student is paired with a mentally handicapped student for lunch once a month. Counselors have found this to be a good way to break down social barriers and foster compassion for students with special needs.

In years past, service projects and community service were predominantly thought to be the responsibility of parents, churches and civic groups. But today, many states are taking on a much bigger role in teaching their students to serve others and give back to the community. In 1993, the Maryland Department of Education went so far as to implement a statewide community service graduation requirement for all public high-school students. It is still in place today, and receives rave reviews from students, parents and the community.

The state of Maryland has found that some of the most popular student projects include working with senior citizens, restoring parks and playgrounds, and helping care for toddlers in a local daycare center. Service projects can also relate to the student's academic studies. A group of middle-school math students put their knowledge of proportions, division and calculations into action and implemented a successful fundraiser for a homeless shelter in their community.

One group of sixth graders, upset over a classmate's serious bicycle accident, organized a service project to help teach other students safe biking practices. The students' work led to the passage of a statewide bicycle safety bill. It is a powerful gift for a child to realize that they can make a real difference in their world.

Service to others has so many benefits:

- It gives everyone some perspective. When your family members witness the poverty, loneliness or hunger of others, they are sure to count their blessings.

- It builds your child's confidence. When he sees how his talents help others, he feels great!

- It teaches compassion and tolerance. When your child meets someone with a physical challenge, learning difference, or someone from another culture, she will see the similarities they share, too.

- It brings the family together.

- It can be educational. A trip to drop off cookies at a fire station is a great way to teach how firefighters stay overnight in the firehouse and use their equipment to fight fires. Your little one might even get to climb on the truck!

47

answerkeys

Mom Tips

Start small when teaching children about acts of kindness and service to others. Service projects don't necessarily require committee meetings, big budgets or galas. Show your child the power she has to change lives in simple ways.

Keep in mind that serving others should come from the heart. Children should never be dragged or coerced into service. Passing out cookies at a retirement home or delivering food to a shelter should be fun. If your child isn't comfortable doing that, find a different worthwhile project. It is best to model service until they are ready. What's important to you will also become important to your children. When you share the good feelings you have serving others, it will have a contagious effect.

Develop your own family approach to service. Melissa has taught her children the special saying, "we help those that cannot help themselves," because it can be applied to so many situations and helps children grow up with a genuine desire to help others in all capacities of need, of age, economic circumstances or background.

Homework

Assignment #1
Commit to a family service project.

Decide you will perform a service project together as a family, rather than sending your child out to do one by himself. Set a date and commit to it. You may even want to commit to volunteering on a regular basis so you can protect this special time. Assign different family members to be in charge of planning each upcoming service project.

You want their memories of serving others to be positive, so think of creative ways to make the project more fun. Encourage your children to invite a friend to join along in the fun.

Assignment #2
Match your child's talents and personality to the project.

What are your child's gifts and talents? Maybe it's art or organizing; perhaps he has a musical talent or love showing off the family pet. What makes him light up? Is he very shy? Maybe a "behind the scenes" project is best, such as sorting food at a food pantry.

Gathering a family meeting is another way to discuss and celebrate everyone's gifts. Write down three gifts that each family member possesses. Next, discuss how best you can share them with others.

For example, here's what we learned at our family meeting and how we used those gifts to serve others:

Child's talent	Child's service
John Henry easily talks with adults, is good in math and enjoys one-on-one contact.	He tutors men in a half-way house on math skills in order to pass the GED.
Murphy is a good teacher, loves soccer and is good with children.	She and her friends put on a soccer clinic at a park in a low-income neighborhood.
Whitley likes to cook for others, has a big smile, and is good at sharing.	She bakes and passes out cookies with a smile at the local retirement home.

Assignment #3
Teach your child that while her situation might be different,
the people she serves are just like her.
For example, ask your child to tell you how it must feel to share a bedroom with four other children or not have a place to keep your toys. Talk about what it means to have an attitude of humility. When talking about what it means to be humble, I tell my children, "You never want to wear a fur coat to work in a soup kitchen." Teach them to consider the feelings of the people you will meet at this difficult time in their lives. Explain that we are all human and we all have the potential to face hard times in our life.

Cafeteria Line

Here are some ideas for service projects for you and your children to enjoy. Service can even start with a party! These are a few tried and true party ideas that can also be tweaked for any holiday or occasion.

Mommy and Me Cookie Bake. Have your child invite her friends with their mothers to bake or decorate cookies. Whitley makes her invitations and ties them to a wooden spoon with special ribbon. She hand delivers the invitations and asks all the guests to bring their gently used toys. After our cookies are baked (and we sample a few), we load up our toys and the children, and we deliver the gifts to the local Goodwill or Salvation Army.

Ornament Exchange. Have each child bring an ornament to exchange as a gift and then bring another gift to give to others. Murphy invites about ten her friends over for brunch and an ornament exchange each year. This year, all the guests were asked to bring art supplies to the party. After the girls drew numbers and exchanged ornaments, they enjoyed hot chocolate and brunch. We loaded up the art supplies and delivered them to the front desk of the emergency room at the local charity hospital. These supplies will be much appreciated by parents and children that have many hours to wait before seeing the doctor.

Stuffing Stockings. Invite your playgroup or neighbors over for an easy meal and to decorate stockings. One year when my children were in preschool, we had our playgroup over for chili, and the children decorated and stuffed pre-made stockings with candy and little toys. I bought glitter, snowflakes and buttons for the children to glue on the front. After they dried, we delivered them to our church for distribution to needy children in the community.

More ideas for fun service projects for young and older children:

Preschoolers
- Make play-dough or bubbles for a children's shelter.
- Host a lemonade stand or bake sale for a children's charity.
- Make cards—Get Well or Holiday.
- Perform a song or dance at an elderly community.
- Plant a tree.
- Make care packages for soldiers.
- Make a neighborhood flyer publicizing a project, such as collecting coats and blankets.
- Make a "bedtime boosters": snack packs that include a toothbrush and toothpaste for children living in homeless shelters.

Older Children
- Read a favorite novel to the blind.
- Play board games with children at a hospital.
- Help prepare food and serve at a soup kitchen.
- Volunteer at the Special Olympics.
- Take a friend to church or youth group.
- Share your skills by putting on a sports clinic in a low-income park.
- Sort through and organize donations for relief agencies.
- Tutor your favorite subject at an after-school program.
- Have lunch with the new kid in school.
- Play with pets at a local animal shelter (call first, there may be an age restriction)
- Volunteer at a local road race or sporting event.
- Coupon Collecting: Clip weekly coupons for the elderly or homebound. Offer to shop for or pick up groceries.

You can also find out if your child's school is already planning a service project and involve the whole family. If they aren't, you may want to create a service project for the class. What a great way to teach leadership skills and get your child excited about serving others!

Continuing Education

The Search Institute reports that youth who volunteer just one hour a week are 50% less likely to abuse drugs, alcohol, and cigarettes or engage in destructive behavior. I can tell you that I have witnessed the positive impact of service in my own children.

My seventeen-year-old son, John Henry, and sixteen-year-old daughter, Murphy, are typical teenagers that complain about cleaning their rooms and doing laundry. Last summer they went on a mission trip to Mississippi. They spent a week rebuilding local homes and a church that had been destroyed by Hurricane Ike. The work there was hot, hard and dirty. They slept in tents at night after long exhausting days in the sun. John Henry spent most of his time shingling roofs and doing carpentry, while Murphy spent time putting up sheet rock and spreading dirt.

These typical teens loved every minute of it, telling anyone that would listen that it was one of the most amazing experiences of their lives. When teens learn to serve others they become empowered. They made lifelong friends and felt deep camaraderie with their fellow workers. They experienced genuine gratitude from the community they helped. This was a truly life-changing experience for my teens.

Words of Wisdom

I believe we were uniquely designed to serve others. Growing up, I enjoyed service projects as a way to do something positive and make new friends. Our church youth group gave us opportunities each Christmas and several times throughout the year to serve others. But it wasn't until much later in life, during dark times, that service took on a much greater meaning for me. Serving others truly does feed the spirit.

Sources

Friedman, Susan. "Community Service for Kids." Family Education.
http://life.familyeducation.com/volunteer-work/community-life/29595.html

Oliveri, Denise. "Service Projects for Kids." Suite 101.com. (August 18, 2007)

http://baptist-church.suite101.com/article.cfm/service_projects_for_kids

Rogers, David. "A Vision for Renewal—at Work and at Home." Laity Connections. (Summer 2009)
http://www.laityrenewal.org/pdf/1267635851.pdf

Today's Lesson:
Your Family's Mission Statement

While we try to teach our children all about life,
Our children teach us what life is all about.

– ANGELA SCHWINDT

Chalk Talk

Corporate mission statements, family mission statements and a teacher's lesson plan all have the same objective. They begin with the end in mind. They each set the expectation for the company, family member and student. Here are a few examples of some well-known corporations' mission statements:

"To solve unsolved problems innovatively"

~ 3M

"Saving people money so they can live better."

~Wal-Mart Stores, Inc.

"To make people happy"

~ The Walt Disney Company

A teacher's lesson plan is a tool designed to help her teach with a goal, and this allows her students to achieve success. Being intentional is crucial to covering material for grade-level expectations. The purpose of your family mission statement is to protect and promote your family's core values, while also serving the needs of each individual member.

Teacher's Conference

If you are anything like me, you spent countless hours picking out just the right shade of pink for your baby's room. Not too purple, not too bubble gum. I made at least three or four trips to the paint store to retrieve more swatches, knowing that each trip would be the last. I was sure the elusive pink swatch would be in the next pile.

In retrospect, I wish I would have known about the importance of a family mission statement before my children were born. A family mission statement at this stage is nothing more then a declaration of all your hopes and dreams for your new baby. This is where you can be very romantic and write a love letter of sorts to your newest family member. This is where you also talk about why you fell in love with your husband. You can list the great qualities he and his family have. He may have character traits that you wish you had and strengths that you hope your baby will inherit.

Have your spouse write the same love story about you and your strengths. Include people, activities, and beliefs that the two of you hold dear. This is a precious first gift, and I would encourage you to make this the first page of your child's baby book.

As your family grows, and your children become older, it is time to involve them in crafting the family mission statement. Each family member possesses unique gifts, qualities and temperaments. How are you going to shape these things? What is your plan for teaching them to be honest, hardworking, resilient, self-reliant and kind to others?

A family mission statement can give your family a sense of purpose and unity. It's like a road map that helps keep everyone on track. It's more difficult to begin teaching family values when your child is older. Even the best teenager has a hard time thinking of anything other than "Where are the car keys?" and "Can you give me some money?" It is this teenager you should be thinking of when your child is young. Who is the young adult, spouse and father you want your child to become, and how do you get there?

The truth is the minute we arrive home from the hospital we hop on the treadmill of life (it goes fast!), and if you don't decide on your family's direction, the world will. Well-intentioned friends, family members and neighbors will want to tell you what is important and how you should spend your time. I encourage you and your spouse to decide that for yourselves.

Examples of "well-intentioned" advice I received for my children:

- My son should attend preschool for (X) days a week.
- My two-year-old should already be working on a second language.
- If my daughter didn't start taking gymnastics by age three, she would never make the cheerleading squad in high school.
- My toddler should learn to play the violin in order to make important connections in his brain development.

That's the treadmill, and it's not just exhausting, it's very expensive. At a certain point you will wake up and ask, "Does synchronized swimming really fit into our mission as a family?" It helps to learn to say "no." Or, better yet, "No, thank you." This is where a family mission statement can pull you out of the ditch and guide you back to where you want to be.

Homework

The process of writing a family mission statement doesn't need to be complex or time-consuming. It does, however, need to be deliberate and authentic. Bear in mind that your mission statement will also change and need to be updated as your family grows and changes.

Guidelines when writing a family mission statement:

- It should be a collective effort.
- It should encouraging, uplifting and obtainable.
- The writing process should not be rushed.
- Both parents should agree on the basics before bringing it to their children.
- Families should celebrate their uniqueness.

Assignment #1
Establish Priorities

Using ten index cards, you and your spouse write one of your family's core values on each card. Have your older children put the cards in order of importance. By starting with the parents' values, you establish what matters, get the discussion started and avoid blank stares from your kids.

Assignment #2
Include Children's Priorities

Next, have each of your children write down five things that are important to them as part of your family. For example, when my daughter was four, she sat in the kitchen and dictated to me, "We pray. We share. And we do what mommy and daddy say." Frankly, I was pretty impressed. I told my husband, "Wow, that's pretty much it in a nutshell."

Expect more complex answers from your older children, and challenge them if they try to wimp out. My teenage son wrote: "1. Know and share the gospel 2. Be the hands and feet of God. 3. Love each other 4. Spend time together 5. Education." My teenage daughter's were: "1. Be kind and giving to others 2. Live for the Lord 3. Educate ourselves 4. Family fun 5. Make safe choices" What a comfort it was to see the overlaps in their answers.

Assignment #3
Put It All Together

Next, look at what was written, and as a group answer these questions: What is important to our family? What do we want our focus to be? In our family, the mission statement has three parts.

- Family as a whole. We will provide a safe place for each person to live and give them unconditional love. We will regularly do family service projects, plus do some independent projects. We will work to be fully educated and support each other's dreams. We will make choices that keep ourselves and others safe. We will be part of a spiritual community.

- Our older children will:

  - Develop in our religious life.
  - Grow spiritually into people who enjoy using their talents to serve society.
  - Fully educate their minds so that they can take advantage of all opportunities that come their way.
  - Learn to be satisfied when their needs are met.
  - Spend time together having fun and making memories.

- Our preschooler will:

  - Grow in her religious development.
  - Share with friends and family.
  - Be kind and include others.
  - Never argue with adults or be disrespectful .
  - Always say "please" and "thank you".

I would not normally suggest having different statements for your children, but in our home, eleven years separated my teens and my preschooler when we wrote our mission statement. These two groups clearly have different expectations and objectives. You can use the guidelines above, but craft your statement to meet the needs of your family.

Words of Wisdom

As mothers, we have many physical and emotional demands on our time, and often we can really be hard on ourselves. As a result, we sometimes lose sight of what's really important. The bad news is that parenting is a 365-day-a-year job with no overtime pay and no vacations. The good news is that because it's a 365-day-a-year job, you will have many opportunities to get a lot of things right.

Sources

"The Mission Of Your Marriage and Family." Marriage Missions International. (July 23, 2009), http://www.marriagemissions.com/the-mission-of-your-marriage-and-family/

"Developing a Family Mission Statement." New Life Community Church. http://www.new-life.net/growth/parenting/developing-a-family-mission-statement/

"How to Write a Family Mission Statement." Ehow. http://www.ehow.com/how_2043790_write-family-mission-statement.html

staying sane

"Calmness is power."

– JAMES ALLEN

(H) eather

Do you ever have days that your life feels turned upside down? When having one of those days, it is easy to feel overwhelmed. I find humor is a good way to deal with unimportant stress that can weigh me down. It is important to use any tricks you have to pull yourself back to reality and put things into perspective. Laugh out loud, talk yourself through it, call a friend or just take some time to find peace. Situations beyond our control are going to occur. Be proactive by getting your life in a good working order where days are running smoothly- establish routines and systems that work for your lifestyle. Recognize accomplishments and always strive for an even better tomorrow. Most importantly, stop, take a breath and don't miss the moments that really matter.

(M) elissa

One of the greatest gifts you can give your family is the gift of a loving home. The memory of your comforting hug, an all-healing boo-boo kiss, or your bold words of encouragement before the big game are fond memories you want your children to remember when they're older. If you want to truly enjoy their childhood while instilling in them attributes like time management and personal responsibility, you need to take action in your own life first. I think we've all heard some variation of the saying, "You cannot be good to others if you're not first good to yourself." Start now. Turn over a new leaf today. Become the best "you" possible so that your children and spouse will retain warm, cherished memories of a loving home.

(J) ennifer

When I became a mother, I quickly discovered that I needed to redefine many things I once took for granted. Clean = a lack of visible bodily fluids. A full night's sleep = five hours. Privacy = only one child watching you go to the bathroom. My understanding of sanity was another thing that changed a great deal. Mom-sanity is very different from regular sanity. The worry, the repetitive mundane tasks and the sheer endlessness of motherhood are enough to drive even the most grounded woman a little crazy. There is so much that we can't control and yet so much at stake. We can't control our children or their choices. We can't control what life throws at us. But we can control how we respond. Life is much better for me as a mother and a teacher when I choose to be grateful, rather than grumble, and proactive, rather than pessimistic. I find my sanity in laughter, flexibility, planning and structure. I find peace in community, creativity, acceptance and forgiveness. Deciding to fight for and embrace a sense of balance and wholeness in your own heart is an incredibly powerful way to love your family.

(P) atina

Sanity is a relative term. For me, it's controlled chaos. The controlled part is faith, family and fun….the chaos part is everything else. At forty-something, I am wise enough to know that I cannot control everything. In fact, most of the wisdom I have gained has come from suffering. I learned a long time ago that no one is promised tomorrow, so I had better live in the moment and enjoy life's simple pleasures. Comparing myself to others or striving for perfection will surely steal my joy. At the end of my life, I assure you that my children will not say, "She never left a dish in the sink," but they might say, "She always made life fun." My sanity comes from knowing my family's values and what is most important to me. My comfort comes from knowing there is laughter, love and human imperfection in my home.

Today's Lesson:
Balance

What I dream of is an art of balance.

– HENRI MATISSE

Chalk Talk

Balance evokes a sense of equilibrium, mental and emotional steadiness, and stability. We all want it, seek it, dream of it or at least think we should have more of it. Balance. It is an elusive concept.

Teacher's Conference

As a teacher with strenuously high expectations for my students and myself, I soon learned that periods of rest were necessary for all of us to sustain a high level of effort and activity over the course of a school year. I knew that what I was asking of my students, middle schoolers with learning disabilities, was borderline ridiculous: to face their greatest weaknesses head-on for eight hours a day. Meanwhile I was supposed to create a space where this was not only possible but probable. A safe space for the fragile and thunderous egos of children on the cusp of adolescence. Thinking of rest as a composer would—as an interval of silence in a piece of music—I planned moments of silence and independence for my students and myself throughout the day. Time to read, draw, think, choose, or just be. Seeing the fruit of these quiet moments in the classroom had a huge impact on my approach to motherhood. Daily time for myself is imperative. It is a gift to my children as well as to myself. But how can I find that place of balance? Of enough rest when there is so much to accomplish? It's a challenge for all of us.

As parents juggling kids, jobs and catastrophes of all kinds, finding that perfect point of balance seems unrealistic and even ridiculous. A few years ago, at a staff retreat, I had an experience that radically changed my idea of balance. Now this wasn't a transcendent, spiritual experience- just a tiny moment. A small "Aha!" Our entire staff had gathered to bond at our annual retreat, and the chosen team building activity was yoga. None of us were yoga experts. I was mostly happy that my mom uniform of yoga pants and hoodie was actually being put to use. We gathered—awkward, wobbly and giggling. Standing in the candle-lit dimness, trying to focus, breathe and balance I heard one of my friends mutter in frustration, "Are we supposed to be holding perfectly still?!"

"Oh, absolutely not," our patient yoga instructor replied. She went on to explain how balance is not at all static. It is about making a series of small (or large) adjustments to keep you from falling flat on your face. This was a revelation for me. Every time I wobbled or touched my toe to the ground, it felt like a failure. Seeing these movements as necessary adjustments was very liberating.

Balance is active and dynamic. I had often thought of it as a fixed point, a place or a single moment when I had a clean house, a clean self, a happy family, enough money, a fulfilling career, enough time …There was relief in realizing that true balance has nothing to do with perfection and absolute stillness, two things that seem to be at complete odds with motherhood and life in general. Oh, how I longed for it to be a destination. Balance is work. I am learning more and more each day that in much of life, there are no finish lines. There is progress, there is movement, and there is rest. And yes, there is balance.

Homework

For me, the keys to finding balance as a mother are intent and proactivity: choosing my life instead of letting it all just happen to me. I can be a victim of the chaos, or I can celebrate the wonderful mess of parenthood and make choices to structure my home and my day so that things are more likely to go well.

Assignment #1

- Write down a typical daily schedule. Yes of course you don't have time for this, but I believe it is critical and potentially life-changing. Write it as if you were journaling, rather than carving it in stone. Take just a few minutes while you're in the carpool line, at the car wash, or can't sleep at night. Write about your day to find hidden pockets of time, to realize how much you are actually doing when it feels like you're getting nothing done. You have two goals with this assignment: to discover and to choose. Discover what a typical day (or week) actually looks like. Seeing it on paper may make things seems less out of control. Make choices based on these discoveries. There will be some unavoidable things (school, work, appointments), but there will also be some opportunities to create space and rest for you and your children.

Assignment #2

- Fill in the blank: If my life were perfectly balanced, I would finally be able to _____. (take a nap, play tennis, learn to speak Italian, go on a date with my spouse…)

Find a way to do the things you are waiting to do. Take baby steps toward your dreams. You will likely find that this brings more balance to your life. Taking care of yourself makes parenting sustainable. These are the adjustments that keep us from falling down and falling apart.

Today's Lesson:
Fostering a Positive Attitude

A happy person is not a person in a certain set of circumstances,
but rather a person with a certain set of attitudes.

– HUGH DOWNS

Chalk Talk

Being a positive or negative person is a choice. Choosing to be positive doesn't mean you are happy all the time, or that you are fine with whatever life throws your way. In most cases, positive people have developed and committed themselves to using a set of skills to focus on the good things in life, and not dwell on the negative. Upon further inspection, you will find that most joyful, contented people give credit to a parent or role model for setting the example and teaching them how to live a positive fulfilling life.

At twenty-eight, I was a happy wife and mother of two beautiful children: my son John Henry, age two and my daughter, Murphy, age five months old. My life was turned upside down, and my world shattered, when my super fit, young husband died of a heart attack. After this sudden devastating loss, I found myself flat out, face down in the emotional dirt. The only thing that saved me was my dedication and love for my children. They were watching me, and they had to be okay no matter what. Actually, I wasn't satisfied with okay, I wanted them to be great, just like their dad and I had planned for them.

You can't teach your child something that you don't know yourself. That's why I'll never try to teach my children Russian, the piano or how to become a pastry chef. But teaching my children to have a positive attitude was as important to me as teaching them to swim—and just as important a survival skill.

The journey to sustain and teach a positive attitude was a process for me. The truth is that I had to fake it until I made it. When my spirit was too broken to get out of the bed and care for my children, I did it anyway. For months on end, I made the mental choice to get out of bed everyday for my children, and my body followed.

answerkeys

Teacher's Conference

Personal experience and years in the classroom have shown me that a positive attitude is born in the subconscious mind. It is as if a movie plays whenever we consider our circumstances or think about the future. For example, your friend says, "Hey, let's go to the rock-climbing gym tomorrow." You may see yourself in a cute outfit, climbing with ease to the bell at the top. Or you might see the movie where everyone on the ground is looking up thinking, "Wow she has a big behind! I wonder if she is ever going to make it to the top." Then you see yourself frozen with fear as they send someone up to get you down. No matter what answer you give your friend, it has been influenced by your mental movie.

The same thing happens with our children when they are asked to do a school assignment. They may picture themselves as knowing the material, doing well on the test, and appearing smart to their friends and teachers. Some children see a different movie—one in which they don't know the answer, fail the test and look stupid in front of their friends and teachers.

A student with a negative outlook can be a huge challenge for a teacher. Even an average student may feel defeated and unwilling to try a simple task. An experienced teacher can easily recognize the signs of a child caught in his own negative mental movie:

- They seem unconcerned about their grades.
- They isolate themselves from the group.
- They want to appear too cool for school.
- They sit in the back of the class and never raise their hand.

These behaviors are how children, and even some adults, protect themselves from disappointment. Our attitude, whether negative or positive, has a direct effect on our perspective and our response to other people.

Homework

Assignment #1
Create your positive mental toolbox

As far back as John Henry and Murphy can remember, the majority of their childhood was spent with just one parent. This was not easy, but it was our reality and a circumstance that we could not change.

Living in suburbia was often a painful reminder of our great loss. John Henry and Murphy were the only children in their classes without a father. All children suffer from the everyday bumps and bruises of growing up, but at certain times throughout the year, it became particularly difficult to keep their chins up. Every father-son camping trip, "Dad and Me" boxcar derby race, doughnuts with Dad event or father-daughter dance reminded us of what we were missing. But before I could work on their state of mind, I needed to get mine in order. My mother told me that my children would be as happy as their mother. My job was to find happiness for myself, and set the example of a life lived with a positive attitude.

With this in mind, I created a mental toolbox—a first-aid kit of sorts—to construct a better emotional place for myself.

Here are some ideas based on my positive mental tool kit; maybe it will spark your thoughts as to what should be in yours. Everyone's toolbox is different.

- Call a friend or family member who listens well with no judgment. A true friend finds ways to shine a light on your strengths and remind you of the positive things in your life.

- Create something with your hands. I would sew a dress for Murphy, paint or hammer something.

- "Count your blessings" is more than a cliché. I would name them one by one until I fell asleep.

- Breathe deep in a warm bubble bath.

- Spend twenty minutes (kid-free) picking out a new lipstick in the drugstore. It's the poor girl's form of retail therapy.

- Whack a tennis ball. Fresh air and exercise were a good combination for me.

- If you cannot change your circumstance, it always made me feel good to change someone else's in some small way. I would make a meal for our neighbor who was going through chemo, or do a little fun service project with my children. (See lesson on *Promoting Service Projects & Volunteer Work*, page 46, for more ideas.)

Once your toolbox is in place, you can start making one with your child. Take notice of all the things that lift your child's spirit. This could include people, places or things. Remember, every child is different and will need different tools.

Assignment #2
Create a Happy Box

Find or build a special box with your child, and talk to him about what special items you can put in his box. Explain that the box will have a special place right by his bed. Allow your child to share special things that make him smile and lift his spirit. Through your daily activities with your child, you will discover all sorts of things that are positive and affirming to put in his box.

Examples of things to include in a child's box:

- Pictures that bring back fun memories like a family trip to Disney World, a special birthday party or neighborhood friends.

- First-place ribbon from swim team.

- Special collectibles or trinkets like rocks or seashells.

- Write out positive comments that were said about your child. "Mrs. Shields, your teacher, said you were her best classroom helper. You are the first one to help pick up the toys and get her room in order. Mrs. Kimberly said you were such a good friend to Megan even though she was having a bad day."

- Young children also love to see baby pictures of themselves.

- You may also want to put that special "lovie" stuffed animal in the box.

Assignment #3

Practice positive thinking. Before your next family vacation or trip to Grandma's house, send your mind to your positive outcome first. Talk about how excited everyone will be to see you drive up or arrive at the airport. What will their faces look like? Talk about how good the cake that Grandma bakes just for you will taste. Talk about how the warm water feels on your toes as you splash in Grandpa's pond. This is a helpful exercise to prepare children for their first day of school, a new team or other situations in which they're a bit nervous.

Cafeteria Line

Take heart. Parents are the most influential "screenwriters" for a child's mental movie. There are ways to teach a positive attitude.

- **Limit your criticism.** Excessive criticism can break a child's spirit. Children believe what their parents say about them and their lack of abilities. If you tell your child she is slow, lazy or worthless, you are mentally programming her with a negative attitude towards herself.

- **Help your child control her internal dialogue.** Children need to be taught that they do have control over their thoughts. Teach them that if they start thinking negatively about themselves they can stop and think of something positive. For example, if she forgets the steps in her dance recital she may think, "I am a bad dancer; I should just quit dance." She needs to be taught to replace that negative thinking with a positive attitude and thoughts like, "I may have missed a few steps but next recital I will practice harder and do great."

- **Encourage your child to learn something new that interests him.** The excitement of learning something new helps a child feel proud of himself. This could be a sport, music, chess or just being a good friend to others. The only thing that matters is that you recognize and value their skills.

- **Teach your child to say "I tried" instead of "I can't."** Remind your child that no one is good at everything, but you are proud of her for trying. Trying new things is a great way to uncover special strengths and hidden talents. Let your child say "no" at times, too. Being able to take control of a situation is a good thing.

- **Assure your child of your unconditional love.** This is the best way to build your child's self-esteem. A child that feels loved and safe will be less likely to allow negative thoughts to take root. Be generous with your affection, especially after disciplining him. For some kids, this may be the best time to assure them of your love. Children that do not get love and affection in their home may act out or seek attention in negative ways.

- **Teach your child to be grateful for what she already has.** She should not have a running list of the latest and greatest things she wants. Children who are never satisfied with what they have grow up to be unhappy adults.

- **Teach your child that no matter how bad the situation may seem at the time, the outcome may be good.** Talk to your child about all the lessons you have learned through difficult situations.

- **Seize the day.** Find as many reasons as you can to laugh and smile each day. Laughing actually changes your brain chemistry and makes you feel better. Play jokes, tell funny stories, and take the whole family to see a family movie. A house full of laughter is a happy house.

Specifically for older children and teens

Text a High Five. Older children and teens stay connected by texting, even more than by voice. Send your child an unexpected, uplifting text. Wish him a super day or specifically comment on how you liked something he recently did or said. For example, *I liked the way you volunteered to help your dad with the car. You Rock! Mom*

Create a positive or affirming scrapbook. Leaving home and making your way in the world takes courage. A little positive reinforcement will help ease their way. I have been working on a positive or affirming scrapbook for John Henry, who will be leaving for college in about four months (sniff, sniff). Children never get too old to be reminded by their parents that they are special and loved. The first page is where I wrote a three-part love letter of sorts. First, I wrote about his strengths, the ones he was born with, and those he has developed over the years. Second, I wrote about how very proud and thankful I am to be his mother, and lastly how excited I am about his future. The scrapbook will then be filled with some of his accomplishments, meaningful pictures and things that make him laugh and fill his spirit when needed.

answerkeys

Words of Wisdom

I taught my children to believe that we would be great. We would be great because daddy wanted us to be great. On particularly difficult days, I would ask John Henry in my most upbeat voice, "What does daddy want?" And he would always say "Daddy wants us be happy". In fact, that was the first complete sentence he learned to say....and it was Murphy's too.

Fostering a positive attitude was my mission as a mother overcoming a devastating tragedy. But all children need to feel they have the confidence to handle whatever comes their way. Children with a positive attitude understand that while some outside events are out of their control, they have the skills to get through the rough spots and live largely free of fear.

Sadly, some teens decide early on that becoming pessimistic about the outcome of situations is a good plan. This is their way of ensuring that they will never be disappointed. Developing a positive attitude towards life and the future is an important way for older children and teens to cope with the stresses of growing up. Teach your child early on to choose to take a positive view. This will help him to keep trying even when the going gets tough. Soon he will gain self-confidence and realize the value in working hard and not giving up.

66

HIGH FIVE to **Rita Graves**, Principal, Roberts Elementary, an International Baccalaureate World School in Houston, TX and mother of two; and to **Mary Hollis**, Executive Director Cornerstone United Methodist Preschool, Houston, TX. and mother of three.

Sources

Teresa, The CuteKid™ staff, "Developing A Positive Attitude." Thecutekid.com. http://www.thecutekid.com/parenting/positive-attitude-children.php

Harness, Ken. "Positive Attitude: How to Have A Positive Attitude In 7 Simple Steps." Healthandgoodness.com. (2006) http://www.healthandgoodness.com/article/positive-attitude-tips.html

"Happy Boxes." Stitch links. (November 2009), http://www.stitchlinks.com/pdfsNewSite/Health%20Matters/Happy%20box.pdf

Today's Lesson:
Healthy Lifestyle

Those who think they have not time for bodily
exercise will sooner or later have to find time for illness.

– EDWARD STANLEY

Chalk Talk

As a child, my mom would have to drag my brother and me into the house when it was time for dinner. In the winter, we would bundle up like Ralphie and Randy from "A Christmas Story" and sled down the hill for hours. It did not matter that the one inch of snow had long since melted away and left us with only a steep path of mud. In the summer, we would play tennis for hours, soaked with sweat and always armed with an enormous thermos of ice water. No matter the season or the weather, we were going full force, playing as hard as our little bodies would allow until the dreaded call from our mom to come inside for the night. We were never forced to exercise, and we didn't have to sign up for an organized event to get moving. There was always a good old-fashioned game of kickball, "kick the can," freeze tag or climbing trees, bike riding and tumbling in the backyard. We weren't parked in front of the television for hours. We were socializing, learning new skills and burning energy through unstructured free time and organized activities too.

Promoting and modeling a healthy lifestyle could be the best gift you give your child. Think of all the benefits of living a healthy life: positive self image, maintaining a healthy weight, decreasing possible illnesses, reduced blood pressure, strong muscles and bones, reduced stress, a healthy heart and healthy habits for a lifetime. You are doing your child an incredible disservice if you aren't encouraging him to exercise and promoting a healthy lifestyle.

answerkeys

Teacher's Conference

Teachers understand the importance of allowing students to move around, and they don't expect them to sit in a chair the entire day. Children need time to get their wiggles out. They will be better prepared to learn if they aren't anxious, fidgety and feeling caged. Experienced teachers take advantage of classroom time to get students moving through music, exercise or stretching. As part of our daily routine, my students and I would dance and sing along to learning songs. It was a great way start to the day. My students were on task, following specific directions and actively moving. Some of my favorite CDs were from Dr. Jean and Jack Hartmann.

Unfortunately, parents can no longer count on schools for exercise programs that truly benefit children. Many of today's schools are cutting back on physical education time and recess, or eliminating them altogether. It is our responsibility as parents to make sure that our children are getting the proper amount of exercise for their age.

From the time they become mobile, children are natural explorers and love to be active. Let them have fun being active while learning new skills and socializing. Children continue to learn new activities that build off of previously learned and mastered skills. It is important to make sure they are having fun and not feeling too much frustration. Exercises and structured play should be challenging, but not above their skill level. Regardless of the child's age, there are skills that can be developed through exercise. Physical activity is important for all ages as it promotes balance, coordination, hand-eye coordination, and gross large motor skills, just to name a few.

Homework

Assignment #1
Get moving!

Think about your child's amount of daily activity time. Is she getting enough activity time?

Give your child time and opportunity to play through free time and structured activities. Enroll your child in an organized sports activity. Your favorite sport may not be hers. Accept it and be glad she is enjoying learning a new sport and working with others.

Let your child see you being active on a daily basis. If you do not have time for scheduled exercise, you can take some extra steps by taking the stairs, or parking in the back of the parking lot. Participate in activities with your child or in a hobby you enjoy. If you have a young child, there are programs including strollers that allow you to exercise while interacting with your baby. My favorite way to exercise soon after Maya was born was walking. I put her carrier in my jogging stroller, looked at my watch and would not head home until I had walked for an hour. This was a great way to exercise, clear my head and get out of the house with a little one. Maya still loves to go for walks, although now we stop for playtime at the park. Additionally, as your child gets older, let him choose the ways he would like to be active. It is not the actual activity that matters. The important part is making sure your child is getting exercise and the benefits that go with it.

On rainy days, don't let the gloom get you down! Go outside and play in the rain, or organize indoor activities, such as dance, yoga, exercise videos, a trip to the children's museum or an indoor play place.

Assignment #2
Eat Right!

You should model good eating habits and make sure your child is eating a balanced diet. If you have concerns about your child's eating habits, talk to your pediatrician. If you think your child won't notice that you are eating an enormous piece of chocolate cake while they are nibbling on broccoli for dinner, think again. Your child will notice and will want to eat the same thing you are eating.

It is often a challenge to prepare healthy meals for our families. If you don't have the time or energy, take advantage of healthy prepared meals from the grocery store or choose wisely at restaurants. I would like to cook beautifully colored healthy and fresh meals, but that has never been my cup of tea. My brother would tell you that I burn water. I do try though, especially now that I have a child, and I can take pride in my attempt to provide nourishment for my family and be a good role model. Trust me when I say, I am not a glowing example of a health nut. My friends would tell you that my freezer resembles the ice cream section of the grocery store. We are big on variety in my house, so rest assured I could make you an incredible sundae at any time. Treating yourself is not a bad thing, but it should be done in moderation.

Pediatricians are kid experts and offer the following dietary recommendations:

- Eat a healthy, well-balanced diet including at least four servings of fruits or vegetables.

- Make at least one serving a vegetable and no more than one should be fruit juice.

- Strive for at least three servings of a calcium/Vitamin D-rich food or drink.

- Milk, cheese and yogurt are best.

- Sugary treats, including sodas and sugary drinks like Gatorade, should be reserved for special occasions.

- Milk and water are the best things to drink.

- Eat lean meats, including fish (for a good source of Omega-3 fatty acids), and try to limit red meats to fewer than three times per week.

Assignment #3
Make bad habits a thing of the past.

If you smoke, look into the best option to help you stop. This is not only for your health, but also for the health of your family. Second-hand smoke can cause cancer, pneumonia and bronchitis as well as being a risk factor for developing asthma.

answerkeys

- **Do more than eat an apple a day to keep the doctor away.**
  Make sure you and your children have yearly check-ups, including your general medical exam as well as dental (for all over the age of three) and ophthalmologic (for all older than six). Get your child's shots on time so that she won't get a serious disease that is vaccine-preventable. The American Academy of Pediatrics now recommends yearly flu shots for all kids from six months to eighteen years. Adults should also consider getting vaccinated in order to protect themselves and avoid spreading infection to others.

- **Put safety first.**
  Use appropriate safety equipment. Too many children every year are injured due to accidents involving cars, bikes, scooters, skateboards and similar equipment. All wheeled recreational equipment should be used with helmets at all times! Follow the advice of the National Highway Traffic Safety Administration on proper use of car seats, and consider having car seats checked for proper installation. Way too many young kids are allowed to sit in the front seat. It is not worth the additional risk. Visit www.nhtsa.gov for specific guidelines regarding rear-facing seats, forward-facing seats, booster seats and seat belts, as well as state/local installation stations.

- **Be sun sensible.**
  Protect your child's skin from the sun. More than 80% of lifetime sun damage to our skin occurs in the first eighteen years of life so now's the time to slather on the sunscreen and put on a big hat.

Are you drinking excessively? There is no one definition of moderate drinking, but generally the term is used to describe a lower risk pattern of drinking. According to the Dietary Guidelines for Americans, drinking in moderation is defined as having no more than one drink per day for women and no more than two drinks per day for men. This definition is referring to the amount consumed on any single day and is not intended as an average over several days

Assignment #4
Keep a healthy perspective.

Don't obsess about your weight. This can cause kids, especially girls, to become self-conscious and develop a poor body image. This could also set the stage for disorders, such as anorexia or bulimia. We want our children to be beautiful from the inside out. Let's promote a healthy mind, healthy attitude and healthy body!

Cafeteria Line

- **Unplug your life.** Chose one day each week and turn everything off—the TV, computer, phone, Blackberry, iPhone, Wii (you get the drift) and engage in a healthy family activity.
- **Park & walk.** Park further away from your destination than normal. Take the stairs instead of the elevator or escalator. A little movement goes a long way toward building healthy habits.
- **Dance party.** Put on some music and go nuts. Many American families enjoy shows like American Idol or Dancing with the Stars. Get up and dance during the performances or play your own music during the commercial break. Have your own family competition.

- **Do chores and burn more.** Did you know that vacuuming your house or weeding the garden for thirty minutes burns over 100 calories? Clean the house and get some exercise with your kids. Not only will you teach them healthy habits, but you'll also encourage them to learn responsibility by doing chores around the house.

Mom Tip

Be mindful of always rewarding positive behavior, good grades, etc. with food or sugary treats. Likewise, be careful not to use food to cheer up your child or make up for something negative. An occasional treat is just that, a treat. However, constantly associating happiness or success with food may lead your child to develop an unhealthy relationship with food.

Words of Wisdom

Participating in sports can have a multitude of positive effects as kids get older. Kids participating in team sports are more likely to develop a strong work ethic and enjoy being part of a team. Practicing healthy lifestyle habits during the teenage years can carry over into the independence of young adulthood. Start early, set a good example and hope it sticks!

HIGH FIVE to **Dr. Erin Holsinger,** Houston pediatrician and mother of three for health and safety recommendations.

Today's Lesson:
House Rules

Rule #1: Use your good judgment in all situations.
There will be no additional rules.

Chalk Talk

Rules are everywhere. Stop. Go. Wear your seatbelt. You must wear clothes to eat here. Don't shoot others. Drive on the right side of the road. Stay out of the dryer. Walk in the hallway. Don't run at the pool. Where would we be without rules? Our homes, schools, businesses and society would be completely chaotic if there were no rules to follow. Rules are designed to keep us safe and let us know what is expected of us. They help everyone get along better and prevent conflicts.

Teacher's Conference

Teachers have a classroom full of children, raised with different philosophies and varying rules at home. At school, teachers expect children to follow the same rules and accept the same consequences. Modeling and relaying a message of respect is one way the teacher gets her students on board to follow school rules. Teachers show respect to students and share expectations of learning, safety and kindness in of the hope that students will reciprocate those values. Teachers get students to "buy in" to the rules and take ownership by allowing them to help create those rules. Children will better understand the importance of following rules and think they are fair if they help create them. Teachers make sure the rules set clear expectations. They model the rules and allow for plenty of practice, and the payoff is a calm sense of order in the classroom.

Teachers usually spend the first few weeks of school primarily focusing on rules. It takes time, patience and lots of practice to help students understand limits and follow school rules. She reads books about following rules, plays games involving specific rules, lets students practice making good decisions and following rules through role playing. The teacher also explains the consequences of breaking rules and how that may look in her classroom. I have tried many techniques in my classroom, such as having a stop light. Everyone begins the day on green. After a warning, if a student breaks a rule, he needs to slow down and think about the behavior and he moves his name to yellow. If the student breaks another rule, he needs to stop, move his name to red and talk to me about the behavior. I ask the student what he can do to turn his day around to make it better. After lunch, I would make sure all students started on green again. I think it is important for children to have a chance to work toward improving a difficult day.

Children will not automatically follow the rules you put in place in your home, especially if you are implementing new house rules and consequences. Children need reminders of the rules and plenty of practice following them. It takes time.

Homework

Assignment #1

Have a family meeting to discuss the importance of house rules and why they are necessary. Tell each person to make a list of some rules they think are needed in the house. For young children, they can verbally tell you as you write them. Let each person read from their list. Because it would be impossible to think of every "do" and "don't" that could be created for your house, and a mile-long list would never be remembered, create three to five broad rules under which will fall more specific rules. Some examples of these rules are:

- Show respect to others and to belongings.
- Be kind.
- Be safe.
- Use a polite and inside voice.
- Listen.
- Always do your best.

Using broad rules will promote moral and ethical behavior. Revisit each family member's specific rule list, and discuss how they would fit under the broad rules. Modeling these rules is essential in letting your child see that everyone in the house is following the same rules. Once you have agreed on your house rules, write them down and have each family member sign them as a contract they agree to uphold. Post these rules, maybe in a snack cabinet or pantry, to serve as a gentle reminder of expectations in your home.

Assignment #2

Talk to your spouse and other caregivers in your household about consequences. Do this together so you are on the same page when you discuss consequences with your children. After you agree about how to handle different situations of rule-breaking in your house, discuss the consequences with your child. Give your child situations in which house rules are broken, and let him tell you the consequences he thinks would be fair in that situation. Use consequences that make sense for the rule that's broken. If your child chooses to throw a toy at the window, the logical consequence would be to take the toy away. It is so important to remember that we are human and will make mistakes. When your child does break a rule or make a mistake, use it as a teachable moment.

Assignment #3

Talk to your kids about having friends over. Make sure your children understand they are responsible for letting their friends know about your house rules. It's important to remember that all children may not have the same rules you do. For example, if you expect your child to take shoes off at the door, you will need to tell her playmate to do the same and not expect that she will do so automatically.

Assignment #4

Play board games together. This is a great way to let your child practice following rules while having fun as a family.

Words of Wisdom

Focus on the behavior you want, not the behavior you don't want. Keep your statements positive. Instead of saying, "Don't put your feet on the table," say to your child, "Please keep your feet on the floor."

Today's Lesson:
Chores

[My mom] was big on cleaning stuff, which is actually a disservice in a way. Because when I got my first place I had pizza boxes and Coca-Cola bottles all over the place. I just didn't have those skill sets. I was like, "Wow, this is weird because usually I put this down and tomorrow it's gone, but this thing ain't going anywhere."

– VINCE VAUGHN, ACTOR

Chalk Talk

Do you find Tupperware in the dryer? Barbie in the dog's bowl? The dog, who still hasn't been fed breakfast, trapped in the toy box? Is your child hidden under a pile of clothes when you wake him for school? Is that the horrible, unidentifiable smell of moldy socks in your child's backpack? If these examples resemble situations in your life, it is time for your children to help.

Chores are a way for your child to give back to your family. Lifelong habits, organizational skills, character building and a sense of responsibility are a few of the traits your child can develop through chores.

Teacher's Conference

Throughout their school career, children are expected to be good classroom citizens. Each child must work together to maintain a clean and organized shared space. I have had some fantastic helpers in my classroom over the years. I wished I could take them home to help me clean and organize my house. Anytime

answerkeys

I would comment about this to one of their parents, they would look at me like I was crazy. "My child? I cannot get him to clean his own room at home, much less help with any other responsibility in the house. How do you get him to do it?" From talking with other teachers, this is a common conversation between teachers and parents. It is not a teacher's job to clean up a child's mess, and she can't spend valuable teaching time picking up after twenty-five students. The teacher gets and keeps children excited about cleaning and personal responsibilities by assigning classroom duties/jobs, acknowledging a job well done, and giving positive praise. Clear expectations are set and the children are accountable for their job. Kids want to help. They want to feel useful and successful. They want a job that makes them feel important and in charge. This same behavior can and should happen at home.

When giving children directions, be specific and say exactly what you want accomplished. Instead of saying "Clean your room," you could say "Make your bed and put your dirty clothes in the hamper."

A good place to start with chores is in your child's room. Encourage your child to take pride in his own space and talk about it. Ask, "How does it feel to have a clean room?" Make sure to lead by example. If you don't make your bed, don't expect your child to make his.

Homework

- Have a family meeting to discuss things that need to be accomplished. Work together to find a schedule and routine that will meet your needs as a family. Encourage team building.
- Give jobs fun names!

A few examples that may work in your home are:

Postman	brings in mail/newspaper and puts in designated spot
Environmentalist	in charge of recycling. This is a great job for kids.
Horticulturist	waters plants
Chef	helps in preparing meals
Pet Pal	takes care of pets (food, water, walking, brushing...)
Toy Manager	makes sure toys and games are properly put away

Get creative. If some of these jobs do not work for you, find and name chores that do. Some important jobs may require an application and interview that can help to develop public speaking skills. Remember to make the job sound important, appealing and less of a demand. Always reward good work with positive praise.

- If you want a job done a specific way, make sure to properly train your child for the task but also allow your child to develop their own technique and routine of getting their job done. It is okay for your child to do it differently than you, as long as the job is accomplished. And don't fall into the trap of doing the chore for your child because it would be easier to just get it done. Your goal is to have your child do their chores independently.

- You can help the process of putting away toys and clearing clutter by having easy access storage. Many toys and games today have a thousand tiny pieces. Kids have a way of taking things apart, but many times lose interest before putting them back together. Make sure bins, tubs or baskets are accessible and place where your child can reach.

- Let your kids pick out storage bins where they would like keep belongings. Color code the storage bins by child.

- Take pictures (bed, bookcases, etc.) to show how certain areas of your house should look. Post them for your child to reference.

- Use chore charts to show your child their "to-do" list. Charts can help with self-discipline by showing what has been accomplished and the chores that still need attention.

Cafeteria Line

Make chore time fun. Wouldn't it be great if your child enjoyed helping the family while also developing important life skills?

Some of these suggestions can energize chore time:

- Rock out with some great tunes. Encourage your child to speed clean and have his job accomplished before the end of the song

- Make up "clean-up" songs to sing together. There are a variety of songs you can find online under "clean up songs."

- Practice counting or the alphabet to learn a skill while cleaning

- Use an egg timer

- Put out a trash bag and tell your children whatever is not picked up in the set amount of time goes in the bag and they will have to earn the items back

- Give your child a big shopping bag and let her "shop the house" for her toys, books, shoes, etc, that need to go back to her room

- Let children pick out stickers or stamps they would like to use with their chore chart

Continuing Education

As your child gets older, you may choose to have your child help with household jobs for an allowance. Establish the difference between chores and jobs for an allowance. An allowance should be used for jobs that are completed above and beyond your minimum family standards. Try not to bog your child down with too many responsibilities. It is quality that counts, not quantity. Kids need to learn responsibility and do their share, but also enjoy being kids!

Cheat Sheet

Modeling: setting an example for your child to imitate. You are your child's most important teacher. They will learn many skills, reactions and traits by watching you. Be a positive role model.

Words of Wisdom

Do you love cleaning the toilets? Probably not, but you can still model a good attitude while doing household chores for your family. Taking care of your house helps take care of your family and that is something to be proud of.

Today's Lesson:
Separation Anxiety

The most important thing parents can teach their children is how to get along without them.

– FRANK A. CLARK

Pop Quiz

Have you ever.....

A. Had the babysitter distract your child so that you could run out the back door while she wasn't looking?
B. Snuck out of your child's classroom when she turned her head in the opposite direction?
C. RSVPd "no" to an event rather than endure your child's crying, screaming and grabbing at your legs as you left the house?

Chalk Talk

If you answered "yes" to any of the above questions, then you have dealt with separation anxiety. You are not the only mother to ever ask herself, "Why can't my child just wave goodbye like little Gracie?" And, you are not the only mother to consider sneaking out an upstairs window to get a night out with your husband.

We've all been there, and you can rest easier knowing that your child's behavior is totally normal; in fact, most children will experience separation anxiety at one or more stages in their development. But with love, empathy, some firmness and a calm, consistent routine, you can teach your child to be independent and enjoy new experiences.

answerkeys

Teacher's Conference

For classroom teachers, separation anxiety is as much a part of each new school year as boxes of sharp crayons. When I taught kindergarten, I had a darling student named Stanley, who refused to come out from underneath the table for the first two weeks of school!

Teachers deal with separation anxiety by employing several tricks of the trade, or simply put, by applying a bit of psychology and a lot of common sense.

Teacher Toolbox Tip

Do not discuss this or any issue while the behavior is taking place. Do not tell the teacher, "I just need a minute," and then launch into a laundry list of issues you're dealing with at home. Do not ask for advice regarding separation anxiety during drop-off or pick-up time. An experienced teacher will want to devote the time and attention necessary to come up with some solutions. Make an appointment and come prepared with examples and questions. If you think there might be a simple answer, send an email.

- **Teachers are loving.** They don't yell at children who show anxiety; they give hugs and wipe away tears.

- **Teachers are empathetic.** They get down on the child's level to hear her woes, nod their heads and let the child know they understand.

- **Teachers are consistent.** They provide a routine. Even from under the table, Stanley knew what came when during the school day. There is comfort in knowing what to expect next.

- **Teachers are calm.** Contributing to the drama will only create more drama! Without embarrassing or drawing attention to the child, teachers model grace under fire and comfort everyone involved by being a calm voice amid any hysteria.

- **Teachers are firm.** Teachers cannot stop their day because one child is experiencing fear or anxiety. Even though a child may cry out for mom, throw herself on the floor, cry, stomp, threaten and cajole, a strong teacher is ever firm in reinforcing her routine and bringing that student back into the group through positive reinforcement, and not with hollow threats, bribery or begging.

Parents can gain some great information from how teachers handle classroom situations. With a loving, empathetic, consistent, calm, firm approach, parents can learn to tackle separation anxiety head-on and avoid many of the pitfalls that accompany this issue. It is important to understand that children may experience separation anxiety for a whole host of reasons. The majority of reasons, however, have to do with a child's developmental stage.

Words of Wisdom

Keep your anxiety under cover. Thank goodness my daughter was only nine weeks old when I went back to work. I sobbed so hard the first day I left her that I couldn't breathe. Children take their cues from us. If we're calm, they stand a much better chance of being calm, too. Wait until you get back into the car, and then go ahead and lose it.

- Prepare yourself. Talk to a friend or your spouse. Don't be afraid to express your fear to another adult (it's never appropriate to share your anxiety with your child). Remember why you chose the care-giving environment or school for your child.

- Parent with the end in mind. Remind yourself that part of preparing your child for a fabulous future of self-confidence and success is to let her go (for a few hours at least).

- Avoid the meltdown trap. Children are smart and will resort to all kinds of manipulation in order to get you to stay with them. Be loving. Be kind. Be empathetic. Above all, however, be firm. Leave when you say you are going to leave, and do not participate in her outburst. Return when you say you are going to return, and act as if the separation was no big deal.

Homework

Baby (birth to 24 months)

- Go on a "date night" with your spouse or enjoy a night on the town with friends. If you have a busy schedule, make an appointment.

- Find a caring neighbor, babysitter or family member with whom to leave your little angel.

- Plan a routine for your actual departure. At approximately ten months, a time when his language is developing, plan to say something like, "You're going to play with Grandma for a while. Have fun! Mommy always comes back."

- Get into the car and drive away, even if your child begins to fuss. It is important that you teach your child to get along with others and develop a sense of self. If is also important that your child learn you'll be back after your time away.

- Enjoy yourself! Resist the urge to call home every five minutes. Relish the fact that babies at this age do not understand time. Being gone five minutes or two hours is not going to make a huge difference. Sit back. Relax. Order a glass of wine. Rediscover adult conversation.

- Do all of this knowing that you are actually providing your child with building blocks toward becoming an independent person. There is a very good chance your child is having fun with her new play partner.

answerkeys

Toddler (ages two to four)

- Repeat the above instructions.
- While children in this age group do not have a firm grasp of time, they do know the difference between five minutes and five hours. Do not tell them you'll be back in a minute to simply avoid tears. This is a valuable "teachable moment" for you to develop trust between your child and you.
- Explain to your child that you are going out. Feel free to give her a few details about your outing. You can tell her you're having a "play date" with daddy.
- Utilize "car talk" time (can be done at all ages) to talk through drop-off procedures, what will happen while your child is away from you and pick-up.
- Again, remind her she will have fun while you're away and say those comforting words "Mommy always comes back."

School Age (ages four-and-a-half and older)

- Tell your child what to expect from her day at school or time with a caregiver, and show her your enthusiasm for all the fun things she gets to do.
- Rehearse by actually visiting the school or daycare center ahead of time to get the "lay of the land."
- Time your departure carefully. Do not trick your child so that you can run away while she's not looking. Again, this does not build trust.
- Say good-bye when it's time to leave.
- Say your usual good-bye words, stressing, "Mommy always comes back." Remind her how much fun she'll have while you're away.
- Leave.
- Don't hang around or peek in the windows.
- Don't overdo the reunion. You want your child to believe that school or any "non-mom & dad" care is routine. A grand entrance may backfire and cause her to dread separation even more.
- Ask follow-up questions at pick-up. Get your child to engage with you and talk about her day. This can help to get her pumped for next time she'll be away from you.

Cafeteria Line

- For a bit of comic relief, have your child "push" you out the door when it's time to leave. This will add some levity to a potentially explosive situation and give your child a sense of control.
- For children between approximately eight months through first grade, a comfort item is a great way to help her transition to a new school or day care environment. Always check the school's policy, but many will allow children to keep a comfort item in their cubby or backpack.

Staying Sane

- A "mommy and daddy love you" note for older children is a wonderful comfort item.
- Place a sticker or "lipstick" kiss on your child's hand. She can look at it and be reminded of you.
- Take your child out to lunch or dinner so she can talk about her anxiety. Address her fears and walk through them with her. Just because your child is young, doesn't mean she can't grasp certain mature concepts. Talking and walking through it with her will help ease her anxious mind.
- Start counting down the days on a calendar (one to two weeks before school begins).
- Learn your child's schedule in advance and plan to attend any school meetings or orientation.
- Focus on the positive aspects of school and how much she'll learn.

Cheat Sheet

Developmental Age: This is the age at which a child is behaving as a total person. It may or may not be the same as the child's chronological age and is viewed as the composite of the various domains or aspects of development—physical, social, emotional and academic. Developmental age is the age at which a child can sustain a function with ease.

Car Talk: This is a discussion of expectations or any important issue before you get out of the car. While in the car, your child is a captive audience. It's a perfect time to role-play different situations and check for understanding.

Words of Wisdom

Separation anxiety is not necessarily an indication that the environment in which you are leaving your child is bad, unhealthy or unsafe. Children tend to do what is comfortable, and they thrive in a routine. If you are dropping your child off at a new activity, daycare center or school, it is natural for her to feel uncomfortable and want to leave with you. While nothing is more desirable to a four-year-old than spending time a parent, it is important that your child be encouraged to engage in new activities. This is the only way she'll form new relationships and learn to venture out on her own.

Sources

Parents.com. (for preschoolers) http://www.parents.com
HelpGuide.org. http://www.helpguide.org

Today's Lesson:
Playgroups

Friendship doubles our joy, and divides our grief.

– SWEDISH PROVERB

Chalk Talk

As a young mom in my twenties, I was scared to death. I couldn't believe they were going to let me walk right out of the hospital with a perfectly good baby. Were they crazy? Didn't I have to take a test or something? After all, the state requires you to get a license just to go fishing.

My mother came to stay with me the first week after John Henry was born. I will never forget how I broke down into a hysterical mess in the front yard after she drove away. I had a very similar reaction when my husband, John, left for work that first day. Even though I was sleep-deprived, I was clear-headed enough to understand that hanging onto his bumper was only going to delay the inevitable. I knew I was going to have to muster up some confidence, even if it was purely manufactured.

Three or four long weeks later, I was invited to my first playgroup. Shari, my new neighbor, had given birth to a little boy in the same hospital one day after me. She and some of her college friends had started a playgroup, and they invited me to join. I had been a part of many groups throughout my life, Girl Scouts all the way through a college sorority. None have been as meaningful to me as my first playgroup.

My playgroup answered questions like: Will he ever sleep? Is his poop supposed to be yellow? And is the extra screw from the stroller really that important? These new friends also offered support on topics like: How could I have fat on my back? Can you die from bleeding cracked nipples? How do I hold the stall door closed, pee and keep his hands out of the toilet all at the same time?

Being a mother is a tough job, and can leave you full of self-doubt. Unfortunately, there is no manual. It's more of an on-the-job training experience. For me, there was nothing more helpful than the friendship and support of my playgroup. As our children grew and thrived, so did our friendships and confidence as mothers. Husbands are great, but when you are complaining about your C-section scar, no one can understand you better than a friend who just had one six weeks earlier. She really does feel your pain.

I am happy to say that my first playgroup has now been together for seventeen years. Since our children are now older, we do not meet once a week anymore. We do take at least one vacation a year together, spend many holidays together, and celebrate our birthdays together over lunch. We have experienced many ups and downs over the years. We celebrated when Kelly adopted her foster child, Faith. They were there for my children and me after John died (I needed them more than ever!). We recently rallied around Shari after she was diagnosed with breast cancer. We all organized around-the-clock prayers, meals and emotional support through her fight.

Now many years later, we have a collection of sixteen wonderful children. We all recently gathered for Kelly's son, Taylor's, high-school graduation party. That was a real shock for me. I could have sworn that just last week he was drooling and hanging on his mother's leg. Time sure does fly when you're living a full life.

Teacher's Conference

Learning to get along with others is one of the greatest benefits your child will receive from participating in a playgroup. Interacting with other children close in age helps to prepare your child for school. Most teachers will say that social skills are as important as academic skills when starting Kindergarten.

Heather had a student enter Kindergarten with a significant lack of social skills. He had never been in a structured social setting, and he didn't know how to interact with others, share or follow rules and directions. His lack of social experiences and awareness made it very tough on him as well as the entire class. Children need to be taught how to behave and interact with others. They also need opportunities to practice their emerging social skills. Playgroups can provide a way for you to observe your child in a social setting and teach him how to get along in a group.

Research has found that:

- Infants need lots of physical play to help them reach milestones like sitting up, crawling and takings their first steps.

- Toddlers and preschoolers need play to develop their newly learned motor skills.

- Weekly playgroup time can significantly help a child's ability to develop social skills, gain independence, and build self-confidence. These tools prepare children for school.

- Creative play helps children become better problem solvers.

- Preschoolers need to develop skills, such as sharing, negotiating and patience.

Playgroups give parents much-needed opportunities to get down on the floor and play with their children. Floor time with your child facilitates creativity and helps promote higher-level thinking.

answerkeys

"I think many families are much too focused on trying to teach children concrete memory-based things like their letters and numbers. Those things are important, but memorizing doesn't teach you to think, writes Stanley Greenspan, child development expert and author of *Playground Politics* and *The Secure Child*. "Play-what we call floor time, which is getting on the floor and being imaginative with your child-this is what teaches your child to be creative. It teaches them to think."

In order for you and your child to get the most out of your playgroup experience, he should participate in the appropriate developmental age grouping. The developmental differences between an eight-week-old and a ten-month-old are much greater than the differences between a four-year-old born in January verses another four-year-old born in September. The developmental gap between children shrinks as they get older.

Examples of Developmental Groupings
- Babies younger than one-year-old
- Walkers and toddlers (for children from one to three years old)
- Preschoolers (for children ages three to five)

Homework

Attending Playgroup Etiquette
- Have a positive attitude. You may visit a playgroup and feel like you have nothing in common with the other moms. Don't be too quick to judge. Give the new group at least two more chances. You will probably find out that you have many more things in common than you first thought. If it just doesn't work out, try another group or start your own.

- Reach out. Introduce yourself to everyone and try to remember names. Also try to associate the children with their parents. It will take a few visits.

- Get involved. Volunteer to host the group and provide snacks. Pass your email address out to anyone who might be interested in getting together. Make a list of interesting places to visit that the members may find fun.

Hosting Playgroup Etiquette
- Make a date. It is helpful to set up a regular date and time for playgroup each week. Moms like to plan ahead. Before you know it, your toddler will be saying "It's Wednesday, playgroup day!"

- Get organized. Email all new friends with a list of members, their children's names, and numbers. Also don't forget to ask about any food allergies.

- Give them what they need. Provide the children with healthy snacks and drinks. Parents will also appreciate a snack as well.

- Have enough toys. Whenever possible, provide more than one riding toy and have several balls. This will help prevent conflicts. You can purchase most of this at your local Goodwill store or any discount store. You can also ask the members to bring any extras to share with the group.

- Finish big. Always walk your guest to the door and have your child thank them for coming to play. Model a proper good-bye.

Mom Tips

- If your child is not feeling well, skip the playgroup until the following week or until he is feeling better.

- If your child is misbehaving, don't ignore the bad behavior. Give him a warning. If your child doesn't heed the warning, leave and try again next week. People will respect your decision and appreciate that you took care of the situation.

- Try not to know it all or brag about what your child can do. You can jeopardize friendships this way. We are all in life's journey together.

- A good playgroup rule is: First touch, first turn. The child that has the toy first, gets the first turn to play. After a few minutes he will be reminded to give the toy to the next child. This will take parental involvement at first, but around the age of three-and-a-half, the children will get the hang of sharing soon. Use lots of praise.

- Do not allow your child to bring toys that she isn't ready to share with the group.

- Always take five minutes before you leave someone's home and pick up. Encourage your child to do his part. The hostess will appreciate you and your child not leaving her house a wreck.

- Every time, before you leave have your child say "good-bye" and tell the hostess "thank you for having me." You should also give your hostess a proper good-bye. As I have always said, "modeling isn't just for Cindy Crawford." You must model the behavior you want from your child. You are her first and most influential teacher.

- Have your child put away any lovies or special toys before the guests come to play. Make sure he understands that all the rest of his toys are to be shared and that no one will take them home.

- As the children get older, it is fun to do crafts or have theme day, such as Farm Animal Day. Bring your favorite stuffed animal for show and tell. Arts and Crafts can include pig stick puppets, games and "guess the animal sounds." For a snack, try Purple Cows (milk and grape juice).

answerkeys

Words of Wisdom

For working moms: Don't give up on a playgroup just because you work outside the home. You and your child deserve the social interaction and support as much as other mothers. Your playgroup may just look a little different and that's okay. You might meet on Saturday afternoons at the park or Friday night for dinner. You could start a neighborhood stroller-walking group. Or you can meet on Sunday after church for lunch with the whole family. Soon, you will find that it is well worth the extra effort.

Sources

"Young children need active play, experts say." *Jet.* (March 18, 2002) http://findarticles.com/p/articles/mi_m1355/is_13_101/ai_84184929/ (Accessed via findarticles.com on August 24, 2010)

"Playgroup USA Tips." Playgroup USA. http://www.playgroupusa.com/playgrouptips.php

Today's Lesson:
Tattling

Cindy, you know by tattling on your friends, you're really just tattling
on yourself. By tattling on your friends, you're just telling them
that you're a tattletale. Now, is that the tale you want to tell?

– THE BRADY BUNCH MOVIE

Chalk Talk

Have you ever felt like if you hear one more tattle your ears may fall off? A tattletale is an informer or a gossip. His job is to get others in trouble, and he takes this job seriously! Some kids seem to make a habit of tattling, as they tattle on anything and anyone around them. "He hit me!" "She is looking at me!" "Socks scratched me!" "That tree dropped a leaf on me!" For your own sanity, you do not want your child to be a tattletale. At school, you should not want your child to be known as a tattletale because no one wants to be friends with the tattletale.

Teacher's Conference

Imagine twenty-five kids all reporting every little detail that passes through their brains. The teacher would not only need therapy, she wouldn't be able to teach. Teachers encounter tattling everyday, often many times a day. One of the hardest parts of teaching kids not to be tattletales is helping them understand when to tell and when to find another way to deal with the situation. At the beginning of the school year and throughout the year, teachers can spark discussions about tattling and reporting important information by reading related books and role-playing with the class. Role-playing in a variety of situations can help children understand when it's both appropriate and necessary to tell. Children must understand that reporting important news to an adult isn't tattling. Tattling happens when one person is trying to get another person in trouble; telling is used to get someone out of danger and to keep others safe. Kids need to know that if they sense danger, they should report the news right away. Many teachers refer to the three Bs: blood, barf and being hurt. If any of these things are involved, tell an adult.

In my first-grade classroom one year, I had some professional tattlers. I had talked with the class repeatedly about tattling and telling. We read books. We role played. I talked one-on-one with the biggest informers to find out what the payoff was for this behavior. Nothing seemed to help, and each tattle seemed to trigger another. I was losing valuable teaching time. I had another discussion with the class about tattling to get others in trouble and ended this discussion by explaining that a new tattle tool was going into effect in our classroom. I was going to start keeping a tattle tally. Each tattle earned a tally mark on the board and each tally mark took one minute off free time or recess. Every time I would put a new tally on the board, you'd hear, "Uh," "Oh," "No," "Why?!" Grunts and moans came from all areas of the room as the students began to see how much of their time would be wasted. I explained that every tattle took away from learning time, and now it was going to take away from their personal time. The number of tattles in my classroom fell dramatically. During our daily review and recap, I would reinforce the importance of telling important information by saying something like, "And I would like to thank the student who came to me with a situation that helped keep another student safe. Your responsible behavior should make you feel proud, and I am proud of you."

In many situations that don't need adult intervention, the child is really looking for attention. Many siblings tattle in hopes of more attention from mom or dad. Some examples: "Mary won't play with me." "Henry stepped on my shoe." Children need practice dealing with these types of situations and using words to work out the problem. Once again, role-playing and practice are key. Give praise when you hear your child working out a problem on his own to encourage this behavior.

Role play example:

If Sam says, "Henry stepped on my shoe." You should tell Sam that it was Henry that stepped on his shoe so it is Henry that he should talk to about the problem. Walk Sam through a practice round of working out the situation before going to Henry.

"Henry, you stepped on my shoe. It hurt my toe and got my new shoe dirty."

"I'm sorry Sam. I didn't mean to step on your shoe. Is your toe okay?"

Of course, not all kids will react as kindly as Henry. If this is the case, tell Sam that you are proud of the way he talked to Henry, and try to keep the focus on the positive way Sam handled the situation.

Tattling is going to happen, but the key to keeping your sanity is making it manageable and dealing with it in an effective way.

Homework

Assignment #1

- Talk to your child about the difference between tattling and telling. Give your child specific examples in which he should always tell. When he does tell, be supportive. If your child tells you about a situation, think before you react. You want your child to always feel he can talk to you without the fear of you overreacting or giving him a lecture.

Assignment #2

- If your child continues to tattle, help him get it out of his system by:
  - ◎ Having him write the problem in a tattle tale folder or notebook. Tell your child that you will read it at a certain time each day and everything in the folder will be discussed at that time.
  - ◎ Having him tell a favorite stuffed animal.
  - ◎ Making a tattling tally chart at home to show your child how many times he was tattling that day. After a given number of tallies, take a privilege away, or count the number of tallies together and using a timer, give your child that many minutes of think time to find other ways to deal with problems.

Assignment #3

- Make a tattletale game to play with your family. Write situations on index cards. One member of the family draws a card and shows how she would handle that situation. Let other members of the family show how they would deal with the same situation. This will show that there are many ways to work out problems and not just one right way. It is also a good way to talk about serious situations and ways to handle them. Some examples for the cards could be: "You saw your friend take a cookie out of the class jar without permission. What would you do?" "Your brother accidentally knocked down your fort. What would you do?" "Your friend told you she was going to hurt herself but not to tell anyone. What would you do?" Guide and direct answers in the beginning if necessary. Practice will help.

Continuing Education

As your child gets older, it is important to continue your discussion of situations that should be reported to adults. Middle- and high-school kids are going to be put in tough situations and will need guidance in learning how to handle them. We must help them understand that if lives are in danger, it's their responsibility to talk to an adult they trust. Let your child know you are on his side and are there for help.

(See lesson on *Decision Making*, page 16.)

answerkeys

Put to the Test

When Patina's son was a junior in high school, a friend passed a note to him during class saying she was thinking of committing suicide. He was torn about how to handle this situation. His friend made him swear not to say anything to anyone. But he knew if he didn't, she would not get the help she needed and could possibly take her own life. John Henry realized the serious nature of this situation and decided it was better to lose a friend because he told an adult about the note than to lose a friend to suicide. Lucky for his friend, John Henry had many discussions with Patina that helped him understand the importance of telling a trustworthy adult about serious or harmful situations. In John Henry's case, his friend got the help she needed and was grateful to him for being there for her. Adolescence is a tough time, and kids need guidance and support to get through it.

HIGH FIVE to **Jill Ivey**, third grade teacher in Nashville, TN and mother of two.

Today's Lesson:
Time Management, Organization & Study Skills for Children

I find it helps to organize chores into categories:
Things I won't do now; Things I won't do later; Things I'll never do.

– CARTOON CHARACTER "MAXINE"

Chalk Talk

I love my children, and there is a part of me that wants them to stay young, sweet and impressionable forever. However, I also want them to grow up one day, graduate from college and forge their own way in the world. My husband and I both know that our desire to feel wanted and needed by our children is less important than their need for independence and success. Therefore, we are doing our best to instill in McKenna Kate and Mac the skills they need to grow up to become mature, independent, responsible adults. And if we succeed, we'll end up with a serious case of empty nest syndrome.

It is important that as parents, we create positive learning environments in our homes. Instilling strong time management, organizational and study skills within our children will benefit their development, enhance their school experience, and put them in a stronger position to develop important life skills.

Teacher's Conference

When I taught middle school, I noticed that many of my students had difficulty managing their time effectively. Throughout the years, they had been taught various study skills and strategies. However, many of them struggled to form a meaningful connection between how they learned and how they could best implement strategies that complemented their learning style. This disconnect, in turn, negatively impacted their ability to develop sound study skills.

answerkeys

In response, I chose to write my Master's thesis on the relationship between study skills development and academic achievement. After conducting a semester-long experiment, researching past literature on the topic and interviewing students, I came to a few strong conclusions. Students were more likely to improve their skills and grades if they:

- Understood how they learned.

- Could apply that knowledge to time management, organizational and study skills strategies.

- Could effectively sort through and choose strategies that worked for their schedule, learning style and comfort zone.

In a nutshell, students performed better when they could engage in a process called metacognition, a fancy term for "thinking about thinking." Simply put, students who engaged in the process of evaluating how they learned and how they could use certain strategies to enhance how they learned, were more likely to perform well in school.

There are several strategies I used with my students to help them develop the ability to think about how they learned:

- I set a good example by being organized and following through with my commitments to them.

- I allowed my students to employ various study methods that worked most effectively for them.

- I encouraged them to use an assignment notebook/calendar for time management.

- I held them accountable for their words, work and actions.

- I talked and walked them through the learning process.

- I taught them to have their own voices and to use them respectfully and responsibly.

A recent study by the University of Pennsylvania goes so far as to say that self-awareness and an ability to engage in the metacognitive process are better predictors of school success than IQ. That's a pretty bold statement, but one I am inclined to agree with for a few key reasons:

- Simply being intelligent doesn't indicate that one knows how to process, sort or use information effectively or efficiently.

- As the information one encounters in school becomes more difficult, a child's normal coping skills may become exhausted. If she hasn't been systemically monitoring how she learns, she will be unable to apply new management, organizational and study skills to difficult concepts.

- Engaging in higher-level thought processes, such as metacognition, promotes the movement up from one developmental stage to the next.

However, you don't need to read the research or seriously study the subject of time management to create a positive learning environment in your home. Addressing four key areas—Time Management, Organization, Study Skills and Perception—with your child can help her reach her full potential in school and develop important life skills.

Teacher Toolbox Tip

The younger children are when they learn the value of consequences, the better they will fare in life. When children are in elementary school, the stakes are pretty low. Allowing them to "take their lumps," so to speak, will teach them how to avoid similar pitfalls as they get older. Forgetting an assignment or bombing a test in sixth grade is of much lower consequence than doing so in college.

Homework

I found that students responded well when I coached them through all aspects of the study skills development process. This homework reflects how parents can utilize a similar approach to create a positive learning environment at home.

- Set a good example.
  - Get and keep yourself organized. (See lesson *Staying Organized: How to Handle the Paper Chase*, page 100.)
  - If you make a commitment to your child, keep it. You want to build a trusting relationship with your child. Parent with your child's future in mind.
  - Don't pay lip service to outside commitments. Keep apointments and attend events, appointments, etc. to which you respond 'yes.'

- Allow your child to discover through trial and error what strategies work well for him.
  - If it works, don't fix it. Our children do not necessarily learn the same way we do. If taking notes in the margin of a textbook works for your child, support him by purchasing a home copy for his use.

- Encourage your child to use an assignment notebook/calendar for time management.
  - Using some form of calendar system will allow your child to view what's on his plate, but will also allow him to stay organized and on top of his commitments.

- Hold your child accountable.
  - Again, when children are young, the consequences are minimal. Allow your child to make mistakes in order to learn important life lessons.
  - Work with your child to come up with consequences for negative behavior or bad habits. Make sure he understands the consequences and then consistently enforce them. Your child will soon learn that he is responsible for his actions.

- Talk your child through the learning process.
  - Talk to your child about how he learns best. What strategies are most comfortable and easy for him to use?

- If your child asks for help, do your best to meet his needs. I am all about "teachable moments," and if we can teach our children to ask for help when they need it, they are more likely to do so in the future.
- Provide your child with strategies for test-taking, homework, time management and organization. Give him opportunities to see what may or may not work for him.

• Teach your child to advocate for himself.
- People, including teachers, make mistakes. Helping your child develop a strong, respectful and polite voice will help teach him to stand up for himself.
- If a child is graded unfairly, he should have the skills to be able to discuss the issue with his teacher. Our children will be better off if they can learn to fend for themselves. We won't always be there to save them.

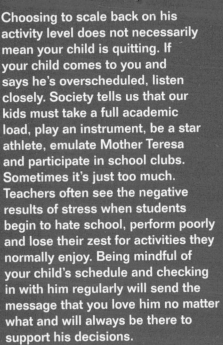

Teacher Toolbox Tip

Choosing to scale back on his activity level does not necessarily mean your child is quitting. If your child comes to you and says he's overscheduled, listen closely. Society tells us that our kids must take a full academic load, play an instrument, be a star athlete, emulate Mother Teresa and participate in school clubs. Sometimes it's just too much. Teachers often see the negative results of stress when students begin to hate school, perform poorly and lose their zest for activities they normally enjoy. Being mindful of your child's schedule and checking in with him regularly will send the message that you love him no matter what and will always be there to support his decisions.

Cafeteria Line

We cannot assume that our children learn the same way we do. If we try to make them "highlight" or use "sticky tabs"" and neither falls within their comfort zone, it's as though we've taught them nothing. Allowing her to discover through trial and error what works best will lead her to take greater ownership and responsibility for her actions and decisions.

In the Homework section I outlined what steps you can follow to set up a positive learning environment and support your child's efforts to develop strong study skills. This section addresses different strategies, tips and hints, all of which you can use.

Organization—Without this skill, everything else is lost.
- Stay informed. Be in the know regarding assignments, tests and outside activities.
- Create and use a Study Station. (See lesson on *Creating a Study Station*, page 135.)
- Check your child's backpack on a consistent basis.
- If possible, visit your child's locker with him. Help set up an organized space and check in with him to see if his locker system is working effectively.
- Encourage your child to use an assignment notebook and calendar system.

- ◎ If your child chooses an assignment notebook, have him employ the following steps to stay on assignments and tests:

- Check it three times a day—end of school day, after homework, before bed.
- Put down something for each subject area. If there is no homework, write "nothing" in the blank. This will ensure you really know if work has been assigned in that area or not.
- View it day-to-day, week-to-week and month-to-month. The earlier you learn to see the bigger picture and understand how to view larger chunks of time, the better able you'll be able to keep yourself organized.
- Take large assignments and give yourself smaller chunks to address each day. Write those smaller chunks on your assignment notebook to help with time management and planning ahead.

Time management—There are only twenty-four hours in a day.
- Help your child estimate how long it will take to complete each assignment.
- Work with her to use a calendar and plan ahead.
- Make sure your child understands her textbooks.
- Space out studying for tests over several sessions.
- Make "to-do" lists each night for the following day. This will keep schoolwork and activities in perspective.

Study skills—Your child doesn't have to be the smartest, just the best prepared.
- Help your child set realistic performance goals.
- Keep homework time consistent. Try to complete homework in the same place and at a similar time each day. (See our *Creating a Study Station* lesson, p. 135 for more homework tips.)
- Assist your child as she reviews class notes. Back away as she becomes more proficient and independent.
- Insist that your child proofread and check all work for accuracy and grammar/spelling.
  - ◎ I used to circle errors, but would not give the student the correct answer. It was her job to find the answer on her own.

Perception—Help your child understand that school is a game, and that she needs a game plan to succeed!
- Appearance makes a difference.
  - ◎ Your child should look like she wants to be at school.
  - ◎ Your child's assignments, projects and papers should be of the highest quality she can produce.
- Be proactive versus reactive.

- This is part of teaching your child to advocate for herself.
- Students should go to teachers when they do not understand material or performed poorly on an exam.
- Students can use rough drafts and tests as opportunities for free feedback. Teachers appreciate students who make the extra effort.
- Students who are proactive are more likely to be seen by teachers in a positive light.

- Student/teacher relationship
  - Your child is her own best advocate.
  - Having a good rapport with her teacher can help her on subjective tests. If a teacher believes the student is working/studying hard, she will be more likely to grade assignments with a positive outcome for the student.

- Parent/teacher relationship
  - It's your job as a parent to establish and maintain a positive relationship with your child's teacher. When teachers are treated with respect, they are more likely to view the relationship as positive.

Teacher Toolbox Tip

Avoid acting as your child's tutor. I have found that the parent/child dynamic rarely works well together in tutoring situations. It often creates tension, causes arguments and leads the child to dread learning new concepts. If your child needs a tutor, get a reference from her teacher, look into local tutoring programs, or hire an older student from your neighborhood or local university. It is worth the extra effort and expense to keep your relationship with your child intact.

Words of Wisdom

It's far more powerful to be encouraged than discouraged. Children aren't perfect, and they shouldn't be expected to be. They will make mistakes and poor choices. Forgetting assignments, bombing a big test and failing to budget one's time are all part of growing up. Give your child wings to fly by acting as her coach, her advocate and her biggest fan.

Challenge yourself to step away from utilizing negative reinforcement to train your child to be organized, manage her time and study effectively. Nagging, bribing, commanding and begging might all work in the short term. However, you will find that these strategies fall flat as your child ages and the workload becomes tougher.

99

HIGH FIVE to **Evan Weinberger** of Houston, founder of the student coaching center, www.stayingaheadofthegame.com.

Sources

http://www.pbskids.org

http://www.bhg.org

http://www.greatschools.net

http://staffweb.peoriaud.k12.az.us

http://school.familyeducation.com

http://www.howtostudy.com

http://www.teachersandfamilies.com

Today's Lesson:
Staying Organized: How to Handle the Paper Chase

Organizing is what you do before you do something,
so that when you do it, it's not all mixed up.

– A.A. MILNE

Chalk Talk

Having moved one husband, two children, a dog, a fifty-year old piano and an entire household from California to Florida to Minnesota to Texas AND back to California in four-and-a-half years can be considered quality street credibility in the organization department. Add that to my background as a teacher and you can imagine how hard I've worked to create, maintain and consistently refine my approach to organization.

In order to organize your own life, however, you don't have to share my passion for all things systematized. Aside from helping you clear your head, one thing I can tell you with certainty is that learning to categorize, manage and store important paperwork and related items can help you achieve many of your goals. A few examples:

- Considering and evaluating the "bigger picture" will allow for increased time with family, friends or for pursuing a passion or hobby. The "smaller picture" is that you will actually get out the door on time with the knowledge of where you're going and how to get there.

- Appropriately prioritizing activities and events will result in less stress and confusion,

- Increasing productivity will allow you to gain the ability to better manage commitments and projects,

- Modeling the appropriate behavior for your child will help him become more organized, too.

Teacher's Conference

Let's face it....successful teachers are organized. You won't last long in the profession if you send students to PE when they are supposed to be at the library. The questions is: How does the teacher develop a sound system for organization?

From where to store toys and educational items to where students hang their backpacks, structure, routine and consistency are three key ingredients to having an efficient classroom. A teacher also encourages students to file their papers, keep their desks free of clutter and use a daily classroom planner. Lastly, a teacher models the appropriate behavior by sending home assignments in a timely manner and keeping communication with parents open, current and relevant. Parents from last year's class would certainly not appreciate being called to chaperone this year's field trip!

A strong teacher adopts a system that works for her personality, learning environment and for the classroom space she uses on a daily basis. You, too, can develop and apply an organizational system to your everyday life. Start by evaluating your home environment and answering these important questions:

- What is the general flow of your household? Is the major dumping ground for backpacks and other items in your kitchen, the mudroom, etc? Where does clutter tend to collect?

- What type of workspace is available to you? To other members of your household?

- How much time do you have to spend on keeping yourself organized each day, week, etc.?

- Do you have a tendency to avoid getting organized? Do you simply shut down and just throw it all out or into a box? Do you procrastinate?

Answering these questions will help you create a system that works best for you. Just as every teacher has a different way of organizing her classroom, parents need to find a system of organizing paperwork that works for their particular needs.

When I taught Language Arts, 120 middle school students moved through my classroom every day. At the end of each quarter, I was responsible for giving out over 900 grades in three separate subject areas. From homework assignments and tests to book reports and special projects, I had a ton of information to keep organized. I would spend several days setting up and arranging my classroom before the beginning of the school year, and I'd come up with a plan that allowed me to begin and end the year organized. I would also make adjustments and improvements to my plan throughout the year. What did my system look like?

- I kept one inbox per grade level on a table along the far end of the classroom, far from the entrance/exit. This allowed for good flow and kept the main areas of the room from clogging up with student traffic.

- I also kept several inboxes in my office labeled "take action", "file", "office", "take home" and "reference". This let me sort items every day and put them in a spot where I could respond to each one appropriately.

answerkeys

- I would address the "take action" and "office" inboxes everyday, making a "to-do" list for the following day. I also made sure that I went through the "reference" and "file" inboxes twice a week. This allowed me to maximize my time and become more efficient with my filing system.

- I kept current "reference" material in a file folder that I could easily stick in my briefcase for faculty meetings, to read at appointments or to forward to colleagues.

- My "take home" file consisted of items I did not need to keep in my office at school, but wanted to retain for future reference. If you're a working mom, this is an efficient way to move papers to and from your office.

Homework

Assignment #1
Tackle the mountain of paper
- Take a deep breath, and tell yourself that you can do this.

- Start small. No one is asking you to clean out every closet in one day.

- Make a list of each school activity and after-school activity (for every family member).

- Go through that horrid pile of "stuff" sitting on the corner of your desk or on the kitchen counter.

- Divide your paperwork (phone lists, schedules, etc.) into piles first by child, then by activity. Even if both of your kids play tennis, keep their schedules separate unless those schedules are identical.

- Sort through mail as soon as you receive it. Place each piece into its appropriate place ("trash," "shredder," "take action," "file," "references," etc.). Letting mail pile up will lead to another horrid pile you'll certainly avoid.

Now that you have paperwork and schedules organized by family member, activity or task, you can move on to developing an effective system for storing that information.

Assignment #2
Develop a system
- Tackle the "toss" and "shred" piles first. It's instant gratification.

- Now label a file folder for each item on your list (think about using a different color for each member of the family, file, reference and any other categories of paper you receive and keep.) Place each item into its correctly labeled folder.

- Place "take action" items within whatever calendar system you use. This is an effective way to stay on task in addressing those items in a timely manner. Choose one that best fits your lifestyle.

- ◎ Large desk calendar.
- ◎ Day planner.
- ◎ Blackberry or electronic calendar system.

- Use this calendar to record family events, important school dates and activities.

- Label a file folder for each item on your list. Place each item into its correctly labeled folder.

- Depending on the amount of paperwork and the size of your workspace, purchase an organizational tool or combination of tools that works best for your lifestyle.

  - ◎ Three-ring binders. These are good for small work/storage spaces, cars and work offices.
  - ◎ File bin. These are good for small home offices.
  - ◎ Stand-up fan file folders are great in small spaces, too.
  - ◎ Filing cabinet. These are effective for larger workspaces or for long-term storage. Many filing cabinets can be kept in closets if they're used on a sporadic basis.

- Consider a fireproof cabinet or small, bolted floor safe for vital records (birth certificates, social security cards, etc.) and important documents (deeds, wills, etc.).

  - ◎ Use a calendar to record important dates.

- Use your calendar every night, and make a list of what is happening the next day.

- Make a date with yourself. Set up a specific time each day, week or month to review all paperwork, and keep your filing system up to date. This will ensure that you have the latest and greatest list of phone numbers, the most current calendar, and will allow you time to purge items you no longer need.

103

Mom Tip

If you are updating a list from the current year, replace the list completely each time it's updated. But do keep lists from past years so that you can find old numbers or addresses if you need them down the road. For example, I copy my Christmas card list every year, and make a new file with the current year (Christmas Cards 2007, 2008, 2009). So I always make a new list, but I keep the old ones in case I need to access previous contacts.

answerkeys

Assignment #3
Organize information on your computer

- You can follow a similar system to what you created for paper copies of important information.

- If you prefer to store items on your computer, you can purchase mini-copy machines that allow you to scan items, such as receipts, schedules, etc., and store them as documents on your computer. Check out local office-supply stores to see who carries the kind of machine you need.

- Sort through your email inbox everyday. Try to limit the number of items in your inbox. Just as you moved paper to set folders, create and utilize email file folders on your computer.

- Don't want to print everything? Save class lists, phone lists and other important documents on the desktop of your computer; not just in an email file. This way, if your Internet connection goes down, you will still have access to this information.

Mom Tip

Even though going green and paperless is all the rage these days, I would be careful of paperless filing systems. Unless you back up your computer files on a regular basis via online or external methods, this system is only as effective as your computer and your Internet connection. My advice is to print a copy of every document that is important or save it to a desktop file. You don't want to be caught with your Internet down, no directions to the big game AND no phone number for the coach.

Assignment #4
Organize your child's work...trash or treasure?

- Gather all of your child's work. If you have more than one child, make a pile for each child.
- Establish three areas and label them: "keep," "throw away" and "re-purpose."
- Go through the pile with your child and ask her if she is attached to any specific piece of artwork, etc. Allow her to advocate for her work and also choose pieces to "throw away" or "re-purpose."

For the items you choose to keep:

- Add names and dates to back of each piece.
- Create a Time Capsule Box. For work that you want to keep for a long time, find a large plastic con-

tainer with a secure lid in which to store it. Have your child help you decorate and label it.

- Artistic Storage. Mount items in a scrapbook or artist's notebook.

- Create Your Own Art Gallery. Choose certain pieces to display. Buy frames that can be easily changed out on a consistent basis. Then encourage your child to host a "showing" of his work for relatives or close friends. You can make it a festive occasion by serving punch and cookies as your child explains his work to others. Artwork that comes down can be put in the time capsule container or discarded.

- Find Another Use. Artwork can be easily laminated and used as placemats or surface covers for painting, for using Play-Doh™ or for working with a substance that might damage a tabletop. Artwork also makes great wrapping paper and homemade cards. Smaller pieces can also be laminated and used as bookmarks or gifts for grandparents.

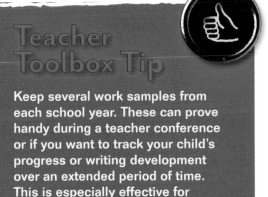

Teacher Toolbox Tip

Keep several work samples from each school year. These can prove handy during a teacher conference or if you want to track your child's progress or writing development over an extended period of time. This is especially effective for students with learning differences.

Cafeteria Line

As I mentioned earlier, part of staying organized involves creating and using a system that works for you, your needs and space constraints. Here are several options you may want to consider when organizing your home for ultimate productivity and organization.

- Post a wall-sized white board calendar (you can either get these at office stores or make your own) in a common area of the house. Use different colored dry erase markers to list the activities of each family member.

- Post a wall-sized bulletin board in a common area of the house. Pin current activities, party invitations, etc. to the board, and make sure they are in plain view. You can pin current activities under a heading, such as "now playing" and upcoming activities under something like "coming attractions."

- Limited space? Cover the inside of a closet or pantry door with corkboard. You can purchase it in rolls at a local home improvement store. You can also cover the inside of a child's closet with cork so that she can post important notices or a calendar of activities.

- Large desk calendars can also be hung inside a closet door or on the wall.

- If you are a working parent, adopt a much smaller version of your master filing system from home. Make copies of class lists, phone lists, calendars, etc. and organize them in a smaller binder (no more than 1 inch think so that you can put it in a briefcase) by activity and child. This will allow you to stay organized on the go.

answerkeys

Words of Wisdom

Try not to compare yourself to other moms who seem flawless or overly organized. Even though I consider myself to be pretty well schooled in structure and order, I have my bad days, too. There are going to be those times when none of your children will follow directions, the mail will sit on the counter until it screams for your attention, and dinner will come out burned. Smile, laugh, take a deep breath, and forgive yourself. Nobody ever said parenthood was easy, and there's no such thing as a perfect system.

HIGH FIVE to **Nancy Mendez**, fellow Houston MOPS mom, freelance writer and mother of two.

Sources

http://sbinformation.about.com/

http://www.20somethingfinance.com

http://www.thefrugallife.com

academics

An investment in knowledge pays the best interest.

– BENJAMIN FRANKLIN

(H)eather

Through life's twists and unexpected turns, an education will remain with and benefit a child for a lifetime. Even in trying times, we must strive to instill a love of learning and make our children's education a positive experience. Learning really can be an ongoing adventure, one that our children look forward to every day. Let's be their proof that you are never too old to learn and that we can use our world as a classroom. I hope that Maya will use what she has learned in her life to be productive and successful in what she enjoys, and use her knowledge to help make our world a brighter place. What do you want for your child?

(M)elissa

Giving our children the gift of an educated home where they are challenged to meet their full potential is very important to my husband and me. And while we understand that we'll never be able to control what McKenna Kate and Mac choose to do with their lives after they leave the nest, we can ensure they receive the support and guidance they need to develop the confidence to fly on their own. I believe that wanting your child to succeed and setting your child up to succeed are two completely different things. Simply wanting it fails to involve the action needed to help a child reach his academic goals. Create a positive learning environment in your home so that your child feels celebrated, respected and, above all, confident enough to tackle life's challenges and emerge triumphant.

(J)ennifer

I believe the way to a child's brain is through his heart. As a teacher, I would never expect a student to show me what he thinks or how much he knows until I have earned his trust. A strong self-concept is more important to me than a strong grasp of academic concepts. If a child struggles in school, then shame, frustration and self-doubt are likely to follow. As a parent, you are your child's first and most important teacher. Being equipped to encourage, support and advocate for your child throughout his academic career is important. Loving and accepting your child with his strengths as well as his struggles is essential.

(P)atina

When John Henry and Murphy were just toddlers, I wrote "college degree" on their to-do- lists. It was in permanent ink just below "personal relationship with God." Sure, it was a short list, but I had just learned firsthand how these precious things could prepare them for anything life might throw their way. Never in a million years did I expect to come home one evening to find my healthy, athletic twenty-eight-year-old husband had collapsed and died a mile from our house. After paying off our debts, selling his car and our home, I was left with my infant and toddler, what was in my heart and what was in my mind. My faith and my college degree got us through those difficult years and taught me that I had to be sure my children were prepared for whatever life had in store.

Today's Lesson:
Developmental Readiness: Is Your Child Ready for School?

The greatest gifts you can give your children are the roots of responsibility and the wings of independence.

– DENIS WAITLEY

Chalk Talk

As the inexperienced mom of a six-month-old, I was thrilled when my sister-in-law, Shannon, invited me to join my first playgroup. The boys and girls ranged in age from about six- to eighteen-months, and in kid years, that's a pretty big spread. Spending time with children of this age range allowed me to witness a wide span of behaviors and competencies.

It was easy to observe that children do not develop, grow or mature at the same rate. There were children in the group who walked as early as nine months and others, my daughter included, who did not walk until close to fourteen months. By eighteen months, however, every child in the group was off and running. Because of my background in education, I wasn't too anxious when my daughter, McKenna Kate, took her time learning to walk. She is a very deliberate child, one who closely observes and evaluates her surroundings. I can never get away with grabbing an extra cookie or skipping a page of her favorite book when she is watching. To this day, I believe she was just taking her own sweet time to walk. Even with teaching and administrative experience, however, I can relate to any parent's pang of concern when their child does not hit a specific developmental milestone at the same time as his siblings or peers.

Now that I have two children, I have been blessed with the opportunity to watch them grow and develop at their own pace. Coincidentally, my son, Mac, walked at almost the same age as his sister. However, he developed a desire to be read to at age two, much earlier than she did. In fact, McKenna Kate did not enjoy being read to, nor did she exhibit the desire to write her name, until she was close to four years old. In a nutshell, children travel through myriad ages and stages as they grow and mature. Really, it's a gift that no two children —not even twins—are exactly alike when it comes to their development. It's their way of saying, "Look out world, I'm my own person!"

answerkeys

Teacher's Conference

German philosopher and teacher Friedrich Froebel originally conceived Kindergarten in the 1800s. The direct translation from German to English is "children's garden." He saw it as, literally, a place to fill with plants and flowers and nurture children's curiosity. It was not meant to be a functional classroom. Clearly times have changed. And with many children beginning their formal school experience at ever-younger ages, our societal expectations of what a child should grasp have increased drastically. Last time I checked, however, the human brain hadn't changed all that much.

Children actually possess two ages—one chronological and one developmental. A child's chronological age is easy to determine…just check the calendar for his birthday! Determining a child's developmental age is a much trickier undertaking.

A child's developmental age can be determined by evaluating several areas of development—academic, social, emotional and physical. Children enter and exit different stages of development approximately every six months from birth to the age of six, and then about every year from age six until they reach adult maturity. This may explain why your extremely cooperative four-year-old begins to defy and mystify you with his knack for answering "NO!" to everything you ask of him when he hits four-and-a-half.

Assessing each of the four areas is a reliable method that teachers and administrators use to determine both a child's developmental age and whether or not he is ready for school. Combining the developmental age of a child in each of these areas allows educators to come up with an average age at which the child is functioning as a "whole person."

For example, a five-year-old child may possess a developmental age of five for social, five-and-a-half for emotional, four-and-a-half for academic and five-and-a-half for physical. Put more simply, this child's developmental age is roughly five years of age. In other words, the child is functioning as a "whole person" at a five-year-old expectation level. This can understandably sound confusing to parents. But they should understand that while their child may show strength in one area, he may lag a bit behind in another. Not to worry. Most kids don't exhibit the same developmental age in all areas at any one time; after all, they are individuals and will follow their own timeline. This is why it is paramount that teachers and parents work together to give children well-rounded opportunities for development—and it's why a school program should always focus on all four areas of the developmental sphere.

Here's where I pause to emphasize how important it is for parents to understand how children advance from one developmental stage to the next. Lev Vygotsky, a foremost expert in the field of psychology and child development, says that people move through the stages of development by scaffolding, or building upon information previously learned through personal experience and formal/informal instruction.

In order for children to be able to apply previously learned information to new encounters, they first have to absorb that information through a host of different experiences. For instance, children learn what a farm is through the following sources:

- having a teacher or parent read to them about farms
- learning about the animals that live on a farm
- becoming familiar with the items one might find on a farm (tractor, barn, crops)
- looking at photos of these items
- watching "Charlotte's Web" or another movie that takes place on a farm
- visiting a farm
- milking a cow and smelling the scent of hay

Without pictures, props, books, vocabulary and, above all, personal experience, it would be nearly impossible to teach a student what a farm is. Strong teachers are well versed in what is considered age appropriate for all aspects of student development and are trained to provide students with opportunities and experiences that support the child's current developmental stage. They also present new, more advanced material to encourage students to move to the next developmental stage.

Teacher Toolbox Tip

It is typical for a child to be developmentally ahead or behind his chronological age by up to nine months without cause for concern.

DEVELOPMENTAL MILESTONES BY AGE GROUP
Many children begin preschool at the age of three. Being able to evaluate a child's developmental age and stage can help parents make better informed decisions about when their child is ready to begin school.

For more information on developmental readiness see The Gesell Institute:
www.gesellinstitute.org

Homework

At first glance, you may find that many of the following homework assignments mirror those in other lessons. This probably makes sense since you've now learned that children use personal experiences to create meaning, and build on previous knowledge to process important concepts. Some of the common threads between this and other lessons (specifically *Chores, p.75, Fostering Independence, p. 210* and *The Importance of Routines, p.168*) include creating a consistent routine and organized environment, engaging your child in activities that increase his environmental knowledge base, setting expectations that are developmentally appropriate, and fostering a home setting that promotes learning.

Build environmental knowledge (academic, social, emotional and physical)
As previously mentioned, children learn new information by building off their past experiences. Giving your child the opportunity to experience life's offerings is a wonderful way to support her development as a well-rounded person.

answerkeys

- **Take a field trip**
  - The zoo
  - A local farm
  - Museums
  - Local attractions, such as state fairs and church carnivals
  - Sporting events
  - Turn everyday events into field trips by focusing on a specific topic. When you go to the grocery store, talk about fruits and vegetables. How are they grown, what do they need to grow, why are they healthy, etc.

- **Use your home as a classroom**
  - Science in the backyard
  - Math in the kitchen
  - Predict the weather
  - Plant a garden
  - Take a nature walk, even in the city

Exercise mental muscles (academic, social, emotional)
- Ask your child about his day. Discuss all aspects of the day—positive and negative during bath time, at dinner or before bed.
- Address the positive parts of his day before delving into problems. It's easier for children to open up about the good stuff that happened.
- Be specific. Don't simply ask yes or no questions.
- Be an active listener. Pay careful attention to what your child says, and make sure he knows that his thoughts and opinions are important to you.
- Be conversational. Talk to your child, not at him. Sometimes you need to give instructions or discuss something important, but letting him have center stage will develop his conversational skills.
- Make your home an extension of school. If your child wants to discuss his day or show you something he did in school or at day care, encourage him to do so.

Ease the transition from home to school (emotional, social)
- A few weeks before school starts, move bedtime back to an earlier time.
- If your child is attending a new school, pay a visit ahead of time. Help your child become more familiar with his new surroundings.
- Talk about any anxiety he may be feeling. Read books about going to school and play out school-type scenarios (how to make friends, etc.) ahead of time.
- Put a positive spin on going to school. Share a funny story from when you were in school.
- Don't take a big trip right before school begins. Children do well with routine, and the earlier you start one, especially with younger kids, the easier the transition will be.
- Establish a schedule before school begins. Practice it, and get used to it.
- Start making connections. Set up play dates, or invite a few families over before the first day of school.
- Make sure your child's school records are up to date (including immunizations and emergency contact information).

Get physical (physical, social, emotional)
- After visiting the zoo, ask your child to gallop like the horse he just saw.
- Let your child chase you around the backyard or in the park.
- Play tag or other fun games.

Cafeteria Line

Remember that you can encourage your child's development, but you can't rush it. Just as with walking and talking, children engage in certain behaviors when they're ready. The following activities will provide you with more strategies to help your child navigate new developmental challenges.

- **Social**
  - Encourage positive behaviors, such as sharing, allowing a guest to have first pick of an activity and practicing conversation skills.
  - Promote good manners and a healthy respect for authority.
  - Engage in "show and tell" activities. Ask your child to share, and then you share something with him too. By listening and then asking questions, he will learn to be a good listener, absorb information and broaden his understanding.

- **Emotional**
  - Help your child become more self-aware. How do his actions affect other people?
  - Prepare your child for transitions, including time away from you.
  - Share your frustrations (minor ones like forgetting your keys) with your child, and explain how you deal with certain emotions (fear, loss, anger, sadness). By sharing these experiences, you'll teach your child that you aren't perfect either, and that it's okay for him to reveal his personal emotions to you. He will also takes cues from you regarding how to react when life throws him a curve ball.

- **Academic**
  - Teach concepts informally by counting together in the car or singing the alphabet song together.
  - When unloading groceries, ask him to put the cans in order by size or in groupings by color.
  - Ask him to tell you what's the "same" or "different" about two leaves or pieces of fruit. Who is sitting in the front, middle or back of a car? Include concepts such as bigger/smaller and taller/shorter.

- **Asking your child questions that challenge him to "think outside the box" and come up with his own answers (not just 2 + 2 = 4) will help him graduate to a level of higher thinking**
  - Ask him to describe the differences between characters on a TV show or in a book.
  - Have your child re-tell stories or make them up from viewing picture books.
  - Encourage him to play with objects to learn basic concepts: first/last, front/behind, up/down, same/

different, close/far and other comparisons.
- Let him complete his own sentences, even if the answer is incorrect. Help him develop his own voice and opinion.

- **Physical**
  - Activities geared toward strengthening a child's small and large motor skills.

- **Small Muscle**

  - **Bead Stringing**
    In any order, by colors, by shapes, in a pattern, with a certain number of each type

  - **Cutting**
    Begin by cutting on short, straight lines and then progress to curved lines and then shapes.
    Begin with thicker paper or brown paper shopping bags. This helps with stability.

- **Playing with Clay/Play-Doh™**
  - Mold it
  - Pound it
  - Cut it with scissors, a knife (a play one, of course) or a cookie cutter

- **Coloring**

- **Easel Painting**

- **Large Motor**
  - Running
  - Jumping
  - Skipping
  - Throwing
  - Climbing

- **Ball Bouncing**
  - With one hand
  - Hand to hand

  - With another person
  - In a group
  - Throwing the ball to a partner or around a group

- **Tag, Simon Says or Red Light, Green Light**

- **Playing with Blocks or Other Manipulatives**
  - Stacking
  - Sorting
  - Repeating an object built for them by memory

- **Hitting a Ball**
  - Tie it to a tree branch
  - On top of a tee
  - With slow pitch

- **Monkey Bars**—working on the bars or practicing climbing on a play structure can help develop upper arm muscles and general agility.

- **Balance Beam**—a fun gymnastics class is a great way for children to hone their large motor skills. Walking, skipping and jumping on a low (usually about six inches off the ground) beam can help with balance and coordination.

- **Tether Ball**—aside from the fact that it's just plain fun, engaging in tether ball or kick ball can help your child alleviate stress while developing his large motor skills.

Academics

Cheat Sheet

Developmental Age. This is the age at which a child is behaving as a total person. It may or may not be the same as the child's chronological age and is viewed as the composite of aspects of physical, social, emotional, and academic development . Developmental age is the age at which a child can sustain a function with ease.

Developmental Readiness. The point at which a person possesses the skills—social, emotional, academic and physical—to accomplish a given goal with ease within those four developmental areas.

Environmental Knowledge. A person's understanding of concepts and information in the surrounding world.

Milestone. A standard level of achievement of the average child at a particular stage.

Imaginative Play. When a child uses toys or dolls to act out events and interactions.

Small Motor Skills. Skills that involve the hands or fingers directly—cutting, writing and drawing.

Large Motor Skills. Skills that help develop hand-eye coordination and involve more of one's body, such as bouncing a ball, throwing/kicking, balancing and skipping.

Teacher Toolbox Tip

Remember that when it comes to art projects, it is important to focus on process instead of product. Resist the urge to have your child create something specific or to direct him too much. Ask your child to describe his handiwork when he's finished. Don't label it or comment negatively if he decides to paint the sky purple. Allow your child to create his own meaning for the project. This promotes creativity and an imaginative mind.

HIGH FIVE to Mrs. Pomerantz and Mrs. Hale, Kindergarten teachers at St. James Day School in South Pasadena, CA.

answerkeys

Words of Wisdom

As a former Kindergarten teacher, school administrator and as the mother of a Kindergarten student, I am pretty familiar with the concept of developmental readiness. Nevertheless, I still ask the same questions as other parents. "Will my daughter be able to keep up with her peers?" "Did I pick the right Kindergarten environment for her?" "Am I doing enough at home to help my son acquire the skills he needs to do well in school?" It's okay to have questions, and it's okay to ask for help.

Be open to the advice, wisdom and guidance of those who also know and love your child. That said, keep in mind that you are your child's primary educator, and no one can take that gift away from you. It's easy to get caught up in the comparison game and sucked into the "my child is doing this or that" trap. Rise above the fray, and remember that your child is a beautiful, unique and exceptional young person. Make decisions with his best interest in mind. Supporting his individual growth and development is a tremendous gift you can give him as you steer him toward adulthood.

Teacher Toolbox Tip

Focus on the program, not the teacher. Students aren't always assigned to their favorite teacher, and many schools do not take requests for class changes.

Sources

The Gesell Institute-http://www.gesellinstitute.org

"Teaching Our Youngest: A Guide for Preschool Teachers and Child-Care and Family Providers." Early Childhood Head-Start Task Force U.S. Department of Education, U.S. Department of Health and Human Services. http://www2.ed.gov/teachers/how/early/teachingouryoungest/index.html

Understanding Your Child: A Parent's Guild to Starting School-The Gesell Institute

Brazelton, T. Berry. *Touchpoints Birth to 3*. New York: Perseus Publishing, 1992.

Copple, Carol & Sue Bredekamp, eds. *Developmentally Appropriate Practice in Early Childhood Programs. Serving Children from Birth through Age 8*. 3rd ed. National Association for the Education of Young Children, 2009.

Academics

Today's Lesson:
Letter Recognition

My father told me once that words and letters hold the secrets
of the universe. That in their shapes and sounds I could find everything,
could see beyond myself to something special... perfect.
My father told me once that I could reach the ear of God.

– ELIZA, IN THE MOVIE "BEE SEASON"

Chalk Talk

Letter recognition is an important pre-reading skill. It helps children understand how letters and sounds connect. It's important to expose children to letters, sounds and words at an early age; most respond enthusiastically because most are naturally curious about reading. Fostering this curiosity should be a positive process as you give your child the tools and opportunities to develop letter recognition skills. We read to our kids from before they are born, but we don't expect them to read as soon as they're born. By the same token, we should encourage and promote our children's natural curiosity, but not expect them to master concepts right away. Young children learn at their own pace and when they're interested. So while your child should be familiar with upper-case letters, lower-case letters and sounds by the time she enters Kindergarten, she shouldn't be forced to master these skills or be a proficient reader before starting school.

Just as children do not all walk at the same age, they will not all learn at the same pace or in the same way. It's important to remember that each child is an individual and should not be compared to her siblings or other children. There is no right or wrong. The right time is when your child becomes curious and excited about learning a new concept.

answerkeys

Teacher's Conference

Teachers, especially Kindergarten teachers, begin the year with a classroom of students with varying levels of letter recognition skills. I have begun the year with students with no letter knowledge and with students who have mastered all their letters and sounds. It was my job to help all students master all skills and challenge those who had already mastered them. One learning game could have several different objectives in order to meet all ability levels. On more than one occasion, students who began the year with little or no pre-reading skills quickly caught up to the students who knew all letters and sounds, and could read just as well by the end of the year. They learned the skills at their own pace. It's all too easy to compare your child with another child the same age, and to feel pressure to push your child academically. She will get it when she's ready; if you push her before then, you'll only stress yourself out. Think of her brain as a light bulb that will turn on when it's ready to absorb new skills and information.

Reinforce skills being taught in the classroom by working with your child at home. This is key not only because it's important for children to practice the skills they are learning in school, but also because it enables you to monitor whether your child has a firm grasp of new concepts. There are many fun ways to let her play while she's learning beginning reading skills – and she won't even know she's learning. Ask your child's teacher for suggestions. Ask your child what she is doing in the classroom. You may want to recreate her favorite classroom learning center at home. (See lesson on *Learning Centers*, page 185.) Make learning fun through play and games, and your child will develop a love of learning.

Homework

Assignment #1
- Don't make it feel like homework!

Assignment #2
- Read to your child. You can never read too much. Let your child just enjoy the story; at the same time, however, you can also make him aware of book concepts and letter recognition. Suggestions for things to say when reading together are: (Point and read the title together on front cover.) "Let's open the front cover of the book. This is the title page." (Read the title, author, illustrator and publisher) "The title is the name of the book. The author is the person who wrote the book. The illustrator drew the pictures in this book. The publisher is the company that puts the book together and sends it out for us to be able to read." (As you read, track the print with your finger. Your child will get used to the left, right progression and reading top to bottom.) "That was the end of the story. Let's close the back cover of the book. Look at this page again. This is the letter 'e.' How many 'e's' can you find on this

page. Why does this 'E' look different from this 'e?' Look at this page again. Let's count how many letters are made with straight lines. Look at this word. How many letters are in this word?"

Assignment #3

- Ask your child's teacher for letter recognition activities. One fun example my students enjoyed was a letter treasure hunt.

Letter Treasure Hunt

Use what you have at home to make a buried letter treasure for your child. Fill a tub or pot with rice, beans, noodles, packing peanuts etc, and bury magnetic or foam letters. Let your child go on a dig for the buried treasure. Depending on your child's level, have him/her match the same letters, match capital to lower case, put letter or words in ABC order, match the letters to pictures you have set out to represent the beginning or ending sound.

Another fun activity is to dig for small toys or figurines beginning with targeted letters and have your child match them to the letter.

A less messy or on-the-go letter treasure hunt is to put wooden or plastic letters in a bag. Have your child reach in and feel the shape of the letter trying to identify it by feeling the shape without peeking. This is a good activity for older children.

Words of Wisdom

If you are using sand for letter practice, beware! Model the way you would like for your child to dig in the sand. Put the tub on a sheet or tarp or do this one outside.

Assignment #4

- Talk about letters that have curves and letters that have straight lines. Sort the letters by attribute. A good place to start with young children is discussing the letters in their name. Let your child pretend to be the teacher. This is a fun way for you to see how much information she's retaining.

119

answerkeys

Cafeteria Line

You can practice alphabet recognition with your child just about anywhere.
Here are a few examples:

- In the car, identify letters on signs, sing alphabet songs, ask what letter begins with given sounds, practice writing the letter in the air with a "magic air-writing finger"

- In the store, identify letters and find objects that begin with specific letters

- At the doctor's office, use a highlighter to find letters in magazines, newspaper, or junk mail.

- At home, glue objects on letters. For example, glue marshmallows on the letter 'm': glue popcorn kernels in the letter 'p'

- Use bendable wax sticks or Play-Doh® to make letters

- Paint letters with pudding or shaving cream

- Sidewalk chalk

- Letter BINGO

- Concentration: Make this game by writing one letter on each card. Each letter chosen needs to be written on two cards. Focus on just a few letters at a time. Place the cards face down. Take turns flipping over two cards, looking for matching letters. You could also play matching capital and lower case letters.

- Play hide-and-seek with magnetic or foam letters

- On a walk, look for objects shaped like different letters.

- Draw large letters on paper or on the sidewalk with chalk and have kids drive small toy cars on the "letter roads" to learn the shapes of letters.

HIGH FIVE to **Susan Waterstreet**, Kindergarten teacher in Atlanta, Georgia and mother of one.

Today's Lesson:
Reading Readiness

To learn to read is to light a fire; every syllable
that is spelled out is a spark.

– VICTOR HUGO, FROM *LES MISERABLES*

Chalk Talk

I love to read. For me, it is a soothing, healing, and deeply comforting activity. If I don't read a little bit every day, I am noticeably cranky. Many of my students, however, have had the exact opposite experience with books. Words have become insurmountable obstacles. Rather than providing an escape, the pages of a book are a prison, holding them back and weighing them down with shame and frustration. As a teacher, one of the greatest gifts has been to be present when something shifts inside a reluctant reader. There is a moment of discovery, hope and excitement when the power of the written word begins to come alive. You'll find that it's a great joy and a privilege to take those first few steps toward reading with your child and to continue with her along this incredible journey.

Teacher's Conference

Before there were written stories, there was storytelling—tales shared across a community and handed down through generations. Just as speaking preceded writing in history, telling and listening to stories is one of the best ways for your child to start to learn to read. Many stories, especially those developed for children, have a noticeable rhythm and pattern. The poetic feel to children's stories not only makes them pleasant to read aloud, but also serves a valuable educational purpose. Hearing rhythmic stories and nursery rhymes helps your child learn to enjoy and play with the sounds of language. One of the most important skills a reader must possess is the ability to manipulate or "play with" language. The most common barrier to literacy is the inability to process language phonologically: in other words, understanding how words are made of sounds and how to change and manipulate sounds to make new words. As a parent, you can help lay much of the groundwork necessary for your young child to become a successful reader simply by reading aloud to her every day. Reading to your child teaches her that reading is fun and worthwhile. As you read, help your child discover that:

- The symbols on the page are letters, and letters make up words.
- Words have meaning and come together to tell a story.
- When we read, we move from left to right.
- The author created the story and wrote it down in a book to share with other people.
- The illustrator drew or painted the pictures in the book.
- A book has a title.
- Stories have different characters.
- Stories have a beginning, a middle and an end.
- Books can teach us things we did not know before.
- Anything can happen in a book, whether it's make-believe, fantasy or adventure .

If you are losing sleep worrying about whether or not your child is ready to read or how you will know when to start, then put those worries aside for a moment. The most important things you can do to help your child get ready to read are things you are likely already doing: reading aloud to your child, singing songs, and playing games. Teaching your child beginning reading skills should be fun and natural, not boring or stressful. Babies, toddlers and young children do not need to look at flashcards or watch reading videos. What they do need is to watch and listen to you read and have rich life experiences to give them a strong vocabulary base and a love for learning.

Homework

Assignment #1
- Read aloud. Reading aloud to your child is extremely important, so make it a part of each day. Reading before bedtime is often a natural choice and a good part of a soothing evening routine. Try to find other times to read aloud to your child. Read to your child while waiting at the doctor's office. Read for fun in the middle of the day. Take a trip to the library or bookstore together for story time or just to browse. Read things like cereal boxes, street signs, letters and postcards, recipes, menus, receipts, and lists. Help your child to see that words are everywhere.

Assignment #2
- Sing songs and play games. Some of the most significant work you can do to prepare your child to read is to sing songs. Help your child notice and anticipate the rhyming parts. i.e. Row, row, row your boat gen-

tly down the stream. Merrily, merrily, merrily, merrily, life is but a dream. (Stream and dream rhyme.) Mother Goose and other nursery rhymes provide perfect opportunities for playing with sounds. When your child becomes familiar with these songs and rhymes, try leaving out a key rhyming word and see if your child can fill in the blank. For example: "Hickory dickory dock, the mouse ran up the _____. (clock)." Even very young children can begin to have fun with the sounds of language.

Assignment #3

- Provide opportunities to enrich vocabulary and comprehension. Decoding is a significant part of reading, but strong readers must also be able to understand what they read. Providing your child with varied and rich experiences is the best way to build her vocabulary and world knowledge. This doesn't need to be expensive or time-consuming. For example, spend a little extra time in the produce section of the grocery store allowing your child to touch, discover and learn the names for things like artichoke, kiwi and endive. Take a trip to the zoo so she can see how big an elephant really is and to watch how a sea lion glides through the water. Going to the art museum can show your child much more about "sculpture" and "collage" than you could ever explain in words. If your child loves trucks of all kinds, point them out and name them as you see them on the road: excavator, hook and ladder truck, cement mixer. You can also make connections between what your child is reading to what you see in the world around you. Help your child find the places mentioned in her book on a map. If the main character in your son's favorite book loves lasagna, make it for dinner. Try to connect life and books as much as possible.

Cheat Sheet

- **Phonological Awareness:** the understanding of different ways that oral language can be divided into smaller parts and manipulated. For example, a sentence can be broken into words. A word can be broken into syllables or onset and rime (beginning and ending sounds i.e. "truck" = /tr/ and /uck/). A word can also be broken down into individual sounds.
- **Phonemic Awareness:** the ability to recognize that a spoken word consists of a series distinct sounds as well as the ability to manipulate or "play with" these individual sounds (for example, rhyming = changing the beginning sound in a word). Phonemic awareness is the most complex and sophisticated level of phonological awareness.
- **Phonics:** a method of teaching beginning readers to read words by learning to associate letters with the sounds they represent.
- **Decoding:** the ability to read individual words.
- **Fluency:** smooth, quick, efficient reading.
- **High Frequency Words:** the words that occur most frequently in books and other texts. These words often don't follow regular spelling patterns and therefore can't be "sounded out." Some examples include: of, do, are, is, said.

123

answerkeys

Questions for the Teacher

What if my child...

...wants to read the same book over and over again? Wanting to hear a favorite story again and again is not only normal, it is a very good thing. Becoming familiar with a story can help your child remember and anticipate its sounds, rhythm and rhyme as well as its plot and characters. Repetition is a proven method of reinforcing a new skill. Familiar stories are comforting and sometimes even funnier the third, fourth or fiftieth time around. Be patient and know that by humoring your child's many requests for *Goodnight Moon*, you are accomplishing something wonderful: engendering a love of reading in your child's heart.

...uses her finger to keep her place while she reads? Using a finger, bookmark or pointer to track the print while reading is a developmentally appropriate step toward becoming a successful, independent reader. When you are reading aloud to a very young child, it is a good idea to point to words as you say them to show that the squiggles on a page have meaning and that we move from left to right when we read. Allow your child to use her finger if it makes her feel more comfortable. Ask her to read aloud to you, and listen to see if she is struggling with certain words or has slow, hesitant, or "choppy" reading. Part of becoming a good reader is having good fluency. Your eyes can move across the page faster than your finger can, so eventually you will want your child to be able to read unassisted. Talk to your child's teacher if you have any concerns.

...has no interest in reading? Encouraging your child to read is not the same thing as forcing him to read. You do not want reading to be a source of stress or disconnect between you and your child. Before you worry about your child's reading habits, make sure that you are taking time to read. Modeling the kind of behavior you want to see from your child is always a good place to start. Encourage any small steps that your child takes. If he enjoys comic books, graphic novels, or books that seem a bit too "young," don't despair and don't criticize his choices. Have other books readily available at home, but support any effort your child makes to read. A subscription to an age-appropriate, high-interest magazine can be a great way to get him reading. It is also important to make sure that your home environment is conducive to reading. Expecting your child to read when the TV is on, music is blaring or video games are going is unrealistic. Set aside quiet time for the whole family can read. Even older children enjoy hearing stories read aloud. Ask your child's teacher for book suggestions.

Academics

Words of Wisdom

Illiteracy locks people out of higher education, job opportunities, and even things many of us take for granted like following a recipe, making a grocery list, or understanding the labels on a medicine bottle. In our information-driven society, many people still struggle to learn to read, while in our children's schools, heightened expectations and increased pressure to learn to read are evident as early as Kindergarten. It is understandable, then, that as parents we are very anxious to help our children learn to read. As your child's first teacher, know that getting your child ready to read should be playful, natural and fun. Make your home a place where reading is a joy, a privilege, and a source of excitement and wonder.

Sources

"Big Ideas in Beginning Reading." Big Ideas in Beginning Reading. http://reading.uoregon.edu (accessed July 17, 2010).

Mohler, Geri. "Stages of Reading Development: The Major Qualitative Characteristics and How They are Acquired." California State University, Bakersfield.

Today's Lesson:
Writing Readiness

Writing became such a process of discovery that I couldn't wait
to get to work in the morning: I wanted to know what I was going to say.

– SHARON O'BRIEN

Chalk Talk

Children begin writing at a very early age. In the beginning, they can write by making marks on paper, scribbling or drawing pictures; they're just beginning to connect written symbols to spoken language. During this stage of writing, encourage your child to tell you about what she has written by asking open-ended questions like, "Tell me about what you have drawn or written," or "Tell me about this part." Don't assume that you know what's on the paper. It is always sad to mistake what you think is a picture of a dinosaur for a picture of Dad.

Although inventive spelling is a widely debated topic among educators, it allows children to write freely without worrying if the words are spelled correctly. Inventive spelling is used with beginning writers in Kindergarten and first grade. Many parents worry that their child won't learn to spell correctly if they allow him to make spelling mistakes. As students progress, they begin to learn and use rules for spelling and writing. Activities, such journal writing, can also be a time for children beyond Kindergarten to use inventive spelling, as the focus is to express thoughts— not spelling mechanics— on the paper.

As children progress in their writing, they experiment with letters and sounds, trying to form new words and relay a message. An example of inventive spelling could look something like this: *i lik tu et trke* (I like to eat turkey.) The child writes the sounds he hears in the words. Allowing a child to use inventive spelling can help to avoid frustration and build confidence as a beginning writer. By not focusing on the mechanics and rules, a child can liberally express his thoughts on paper without the fear of doing it wrong. He can be creative as he grasps new skills. To build self-confidence, it is important to praise your child and his efforts. Note the things he did correctly, such as representing the sounds in the correct order or using individual words to make a sentence. Writing is a complex task, and mastery of the steps involved should be celebrated.

Teacher's Conference

Oftentimes, students enter class with the attitude that they can't do it. "I can't write." "I can't spell." "I don't know how to write." Some kids will even shut down and forego attempts to write. Teachers have to get students to make an effort to write through lots of encouragement and praise. Children need to feel successful and encouraged for their efforts and a job well done, and teachers can motivate students by reminding them that they are authors and illustrators telling a story. The child is communicating his story on paper, regardless whether or not we can read it.

Personally, I have found that if I focus too much on the structure of the sentence, many times I will lose my thought. If I write without worrying about proper grammar, I can get my thoughts on paper and go back later to work out the details. Children should also have the opportunity to write without worrying too much about the rules. They will go through stages of writing, and we, as parents and teachers, have to be patient and supportive. Moreover, teachers don't teach all components of writing at the same time; those are taught separately and integrated as children become developmentally ready. Children begin by orally expressing thoughts because they don't make the connection between their language and their "writing." The marks on paper and scribble writing turn into recognizable shapes and patterns; eventually, kids develop letter recognition knowledge and start connecting letters with sounds. Print awareness skills, such as left to right progression, can be picked up during read aloud books. In addition, children spell words in isolation using the sounds they hear. When they write using inventive spelling, they're actually using all but one of these skills— and they integrate the final skill (spelling words correctly in sentences) once they are comfortable with the entire writing process.

Words of Wisdom

Wondering where to begin in writing? Start with your child's name. This is often the first word she learns to write. Do not get fancy with aspirations of teaching your child to write in cursive. You can point out that her name begins with a big letter (introduce the words capital and upper case) and the other letters that follow are little (introduce the word lower case).

answerkeys

Homework

- Expose your child to print. It's all around you! Talk about the environmental print on street signs, restaurants, cereal boxes, etc.

- Encourage your child to write. Provide different kinds of paper and writing utensils.

- Model writing for your child. Write letters or your grocery list while your child is writing. She'll enjoy doing the same thing as you and feel like a big kid while doing it.

- Build her self-esteem by giving specific praise. "I like the way you wrote the letter 'G'." "Wow! That was so smart of you to put that word next to your picture."

- Ask open-ended questions about your child's writing like, "Tell me about what you wrote."

- Tell your child she is an author or illustrator. You can't imagine how motivating it is for a child to hear that.

- When reading with your child, talk about the print—the spaces between the words, left to right progression, punctuation, capital letters

- Have your child practice fine motor skills to strengthen the muscles used for handwriting: stringing beads/macaroni, using a large thumbtack to punch holes in paper, using tweezers to pick up objects, etc.

Continuing Education

Children move beyond "learning to read," and begin "reading to learn" in approximately the third grade. Basically, what this means is that teachers expect students to comprehend reading material they read themselves, as opposed to that material being read aloud to them.

This process, in turn, leads to a greater expectation when it comes to a child's ability to write. There are four types of writing that students are expected to master by the time they graduate from middle school. Being able to identify and understand all four types of writing can help you prepare your child for success in school, even before she is old enough to write on her own.

Expository Writing—gives facts or directions, identifies terms or clarifies ideas. Expository writing includes:

- Definitions
- Cause and effect relationships
- Comparisons and contrasts

Examples of Expository writing include research reports, how-to speeches, newspaper articles and glossaries.

Narrative Writing—tells a story. Narrative writing includes:

- Accurate ordering of events
- Conflict that generates action
- A climax or turning point in the action
- A satisfying resolution

Examples of Narrative writing include stories, skits and plays, personal experience essays and plot summaries.

Persuasive Writing—expresses an opinion and attempts to convince the reader that this opinion is correct. Persuasive writing includes:

- A clear and direct opinion statement
- Specific facts
- Examples or statistics to back up the opinion and disprove opposing opinions

Examples of Persuasive writing include essays, editorials, book reviews and debate preparation essays.

Descriptive Writing—gives a clear and vivid picture of a person, place, thing or event. Descriptive writing includes:

- A clear focus on the subject
- Significant details that appeal to the senses
- Specific, lively and interesting words
- Figurative language, when appropriate

Examples of Descriptive writing include poetry, character descriptions, book reports and science observations

Sources

http://catalog.instructionalimages.com

Today's Lesson:
Multisensory Learning

I never teach my pupils. I only attempt to provide
the conditions in which they can learn.

– ALBERT EINSTEIN

Chalk Talk

My strongest memories of school and early childhood are tied to my senses. I remember making ginger-bread with my mom and watching the molasses mixture froth and steam, filling the kitchen with spice and heat. I remember the mysterious and strangely sweet smell of my great-aunt's house and the disillusion-ment I felt upon discovering, years later, that the magical scent was really just mothballs. I can feel the thick, brown shag carpet from my grandparents' ranch that I secretly snipped and used for my sock puppet's hair. I can still taste the flavor-dipped cotton swabs that we touched to our tongues in science class to learn salty, sweet, sour and bitter. Engaging the senses unlocks powerful memory-laden portions of the brain, causing it to be awake and eager to learn.

Multisensory learning is just what it sounds like—involving and engaging multiple senses in the learn-ing process to maximize attention, understanding and memory. While multisensory strategies are an essential component of programs for students with learning differences and special needs, engaging different senses enhances every student's ability to learn. Stepping outside the box of paper-and-pencil teaching can be messy and unpredictable; but it's also incredibly effective as well as fun for both the teacher and her students.

Teacher's Conference

When I was teaching in the classroom, multisensory instruction was an integral part of every one of my lessons. These creative experiences have given me a supply of fun and engaging learning activities to

Academics

use when working with students and with my young children at home. Using a combination of senses can facilitate learning regardless of your child's strengths or learning style. Multisensory learning experiences activate multiple pathways of the brain at the same time; over time, this actually creates and repairs neural pathways, thereby making new or difficult tasks more manageable. What a powerful gift it is to know that it's possible to strengthen and shape your child's brain!

As a teacher, my favorite classroom memories are of when my students were fully engaged, often elbow-deep in a mess. One of the best geometry lessons happened while using rubber bands stretched around geo-boards to make rectangles, trapezoids, octagons and parallelograms. I should have known that passing out rubber bands to fifth-graders must be done after a thorough and serious discussion of their appropriate use. Once we had collected hundreds of rubber bands from around the room (and in my hair), my students discovered things about shapes that I never could have taught them through a lecture or written assignment. What they learned was well worth the extra work. In the long run, the more time I put into creating hands-on activities in the classroom, the less time I spent correcting and cajoling my students. Enabling them to learn in fun and creative ways reduced behavior problems. When students are actively engaged in the learning process, they are much less likely to resort to non-productive and disruptive behavior.

Learning through hearing and speaking

Being a good listener is key to being a good student. Much of what your child learns at school will come from listening to his teacher; but there are other things to hear, besides a teacher's or parent's voice, that can help your child learn. He may need to "say it to himself" or move his lips as though talking to himself to process new material efficiently. Have your child read a passage from his textbook aloud to you or listen to an audio book. He may also enjoy explaining a science or math concept to you as if he were the teacher and you the student. Something as simple as singing songs can be fun and effective when learning certain things like the days of the week, state capitals or math facts. If your child has trouble concentrating on a difficult task, try turning on some soft music or white noise—it may help him focus.

Learning through seeing

Watching, observing and reading are also key skills for school success. A great deal of information in the classroom is presented visually. Maps, graphic organizers, pictures and charts are important and useful study tools. When retelling a story, have him draw pictures to illustrate the sequence of events. When working on a math word problem, use real objects so that he can "see" what is happening. Having a supply of small objects, such as coins, buttons, checkers, beans or even macaroni, can be useful for counting or for tackling a difficult, abstract concept.

Learning through doing and moving

While most gross motor activities like running, jumping, and climbing are reserved for the playground or PE class, children often love to involve their whole bodies in the learning process. Stepping or hopping on a giant, floor-sized map to learn geography or tossing a ball while reciting math facts are engaging and refreshing ways to move both their brains and their bodies. Often young children will "skywrite" —trace giant letters in the air, moving their entire arms to engage larger muscle groups and larger parts of their brains.

Learning through touch

Many students understand things better by touching them. Tracing letters in sand or shaving cream and using small objects to solve math problems are a great way to involve multiple senses and increase understanding and retention. Puzzles and blocks are also ideal tools for problem solving, planning and reasoning.

Learning through smell

Even though sense of smell is often overlooked in the learning process, it is a sense that's deeply tied to emotion and memory. Encountering a familiar smell— a certain perfume, baking bread or freshly sharpened pencils—can transport you to an early memory. And there is nothing that can drive you from a room faster than an awful smell. Smells can give you clues about what something is and how it works; the results of chemistry experiments can be determined by a particular odor. Positive scents can affect the mood and comfort level of a classroom or home.

Homework

Engage Your Child in Multisensory Learning

- **Engage your baby from the beginning.** Babies naturally explore the world with their senses. There are an abundance of toys and games designed to stimulate and soothe the very young. You'll probably discover that your child will have more fun with a random piece of string or cardboard box, than any battery-powered gadget. One of my favorite things to do when my children were babies was to let them play with things with their toes while they were in their ExerSaucer®. Many things that were unsafe to touch were fabulous for their feet. Things that worked well: feathers, silk scarves, water, bubble wrap, and tissue paper. Things that did not: Styrofoam peanuts (she mashed them into tiny, airborne pieces) and baby lotion (too slippery).

- **Read together.** Books for young children often engage multiple senses with peek-a-boo flaps, different textures and pop-up pages. Don't be afraid to let your children touch, explore and flip the pages of their books. Be animated as you read books aloud to your child. Even older children like to listen to you read their favorite stories. You can also let your child read to you or into a recorder, and then play it back to him. Encourage him to use a funny voice or act the way a certain character might when reading aloud, especially when doing repeated readings. This can transform the activity from torture to talent show.

- **Write together.** Tracing letters on sandpaper or textured fabric, such as velvet or corduroy, can be fun and stimulating for children learning their letters. Picking up objects with tongs, children's chopsticks

Academics

or large tweezers can help develop the muscles necessary for handwriting. Encourage your child to write with different tools and on various surfaces; chalk works well on an individual-sized mini chalk board, a wall covered with chalkboard paint, or on the driveway or sidewalk. You can also "paint" the sidewalk or back fence with brushes dipped in water. Cotton swabs dipped in water work well on paper—read your message quickly before it disappears. A varied supply of markers, pens, and crayons are also fun and effective writing tools. Dip a toothpick in lemon juice for invisible ink. Hold the paper in front of a light bulb (with adult supervision) to heat the lemon juice and watch the message appear.

- **Create a kitchen classroom.** There are endless opportunities for discovery and learning in the kitchen. Smelling, tasting and touching are involved in each step of the cooking process, as are measuring, counting and reading. Using measuring cups and spoons as well as slicing pizza or brownies provide a crash course in fractions. Telling time, following multi-step directions, and sequencing are all critical school skills as well as essential parts of following a recipe. Allow your child to help you cook dinner or prepare a special treat. You might have a larger mess to clean up, but the lessons they learn at every step along the way are well worth it. Plus, veggies taste better when you help prepare them yourself, and your child will be very proud to tell her friends that she helped make the cupcakes for the class party.

- **Conduct backyard science experiments.** Whether you are a complete novice or a veteran scientist, exploring and experimenting in the backyard with your child can be a great learning opportunity. Young children can play in a wading pool and learn about sinking, floating, liquid volume, and cause and effect, all while having fun and cooling off. Birdfeeders can be low-cost and low-maintenance biology projects. Work with your child to build your own, either from a kit or by simply covering a pinecone with peanut butter and rolling it in birdseed. Hang the pinecone from a string, and watch the birds (and squirrels) feast. Much can be learned simply by being outside and quietly observing clouds and weather patterns, a spider web, a bird's nest, frost on the window, or plants growing in the garden.

- **Find success with spelling words.** Calling out your child's spelling words and having her write them on paper is good practice, since it mimics the format of the real test. For variety, try having your child write on a dry erase board or easel, or even use sidewalk chalk. Colored paper and markers or crayons can also be fun. Patina bought her daughter a used overhead projector and let her shine her words on the wall.

- **Reinvent the flashcard.** Play Concentration, the classic matching game. Instead of writing information on the front and back of the cards, have your child (you can do this step for a younger child) make a deck of cards with math facts, vocabulary words, or rhyming words. Spread the cards out on the table and take turns finding matching pairs. Play Twister. Use construction paper or large index cards and write words or numbers on them. Lay the cards on the ground and call out a question and a body part (i.e. left foot 4x6). Your child must put the correct body part on the right answer. Create your own Bingo game to practice sight words, vowel sounds, math facts or vocabulary words.

answerkeys

Teacher Toolbox Tips

- **Improve the way your child outlines and organizes information.** While I believe that outlining is an important skill for students to learn, it isn't always the most efficient or effective pre-writing and organizational tool for students, especially younger ones. Graphic organizers can be a great way to collect, organize and interpret information. There is also amazing, easy-to-use software that produces beautiful charts, webs and diagrams, and converts them to classic outline form with one click.

- **Help your child study smarter.** Many of us can remember trying to cram for a big test and spending hours staring at our class notes, only to realize thirty minutes later that our minds were far away from the page. If your older child has the same trouble, try giving her colored pens or markers. Highlighting can be a useful tool for textbooks, but actually tracing over the letters, essentially rewriting key words in a bright color can be more effective when reviewing class notes. This introduces a tactile/kinesthetic element to a predominantly visual task, which can help "wake up" the brain and improve retention. Having your child say the key words aloud as she traces them makes it even more effective. Try photocopying and enlarging pages of a textbook, worksheet or novel to use this same technique.

- If your child is blessed with a teacher who encourages hands-on learning, do your part to help by dressing your child in play clothes that she can get dirty. School is not meant to be a fashion show. Encourage your child to have fun while learning without the pressure of trying to keep her best clothes clean and spot-free.

- When creating multisensory learning opportunities for your child at home, be prepared for a bit more mess but a lot more fun.

- Planning ahead and clear communication are essential for actual learning to take place. Playing and learning fit together well. Chaos and learning do not.

- The benefits of multisensory learning experiences definitely outweigh the extra preparation and mess. It is easier to clean up shaving cream off the kitchen table than it is to convince an unwilling child to practice his spelling words one more time. Odds are, he'll be more likely to remember them if he was interested and engaged while studying.

Academics

Today's Lesson:
Creating a Study Station

Before anything else, preparation is the key to success.

– ALEXANDER GRAHAM BELL

Chalk Talk

You can picture it in your head. A huge pile of papers. Folders everywhere. Bits of an art project lying around. Pencils, broken crayons. And underneath the entire pile is…a desk…perhaps? Who really knows and honestly, who really wants to find out?

Getting and keeping children organized in today's fast-paced society can be daunting, frustrating and enough of a pain to make any parent throw her hands up in defeat. Rest assured that you are not the only parent to gnash her teeth in frustration when it comes to study time. The thought of helping your child stay on top of his schoolwork, however, doesn't need to leave you in a cold sweat.

Setting up a Study Station with your child will allow you to accomplish several different goals, all with the same end result: a more responsible, confident and independent child. These are just a few of the benefits of having a child who's organized for homework and study time:

- You will have fewer arguments.
- You will need to intervene less and less.
- Your child's self confidence will improve.
- Your child will develop a higher level of personal responsibility.
- Your child will take greater ownership of his academic success.
- Your child will become more independent.
- Your household will run more smoothly.
- Your stress level will drop.
- You'll be able to step back and stop hovering.

World peace? Perhaps not, but peace at home is a start.

Remember, parent with the end in mind. What does that mean? Here's a thought: Who do you want your child to be when he grows up? If you asked me want I want for my two children, I would tell you that my husband and I want McKenna Kate and Mac to grow up to be responsible, mature, respectful adults who take advantage of the all the wonders this world has to offer. So, as difficult as it is to be consistent, I always parent with that thought in mind, knowing that I want my kids to leave the world the better place than it was when they got here. Creating a Study Station provides your child with an opportunity to exercise his responsibility and organizational muscles.

Teacher Toolbox Tip

The best place for a study station is in a common area of your home. I don't recommend that students in lower school or middle school study alone in their rooms. While there may be circumstances in which this works well, many children aren't developmentally ready for this challenge until high school. Be patient when working with your child. Spend time explaining and guiding him toward independence.

Teacher's Conference

Teachers know that students require age-appropriate tools to achieve success in the classroom. Teachers also know that students need guidance when choosing these tools. Successful classrooms and organized teachers regularly have learning centers or an area of the classroom designated for project work. By modeling your Study Station after these proven systems, you set your child up for success at home, too.

Children do well when they understand what is expected of them. They also thrive when they're put in situations where they are set up to succeed. Therefore, work together with your child to set up the Study Station. Explain why it's important to be organized and how put together you feel when your things are in their proper place. Head to the office or teacher supply store together and make it fun! He'll have a sense of ownership over the space and will be less likely to let "his" space get chaotic if he has a part in putting it together. Besides, if left to their own devices, many children will simply put crayons in their station and nothing else.

In addition to bringing a level of organization and harmony to your home, creating a Study Station will help your child adopt these positive behaviors, among others:

- Independent work habits
- Organizational skills
- Time management skills
- A greater sense of personal responsibility

- A larger sense of control over his work environment
- Ownership of his performance in school
- Improved creativity and concentration

Homework

So what goes into the Study Station? Of course, not all age groups will use all materials. A fantastic place to start is with your child's school-sanctioned supply list.

The most opportune time to create a Study Station is at the beginning of the school year or the start of a new quarter, trimester or semester. However, you can help your child build an appropriate Station at any point during the school year or the summer. Go shopping with your child. Make it a fun outing where he gets to take control of his own learning. This endeavor can be used as a bonding activity for and the two of you.

Basic tools

- Separate work area (an office desk or even the kitchen table. However, the space should only be used as a Study Station while your child is working).
- If you are using a common area space as a Study Station, purchase a tool caddy or similar holder. This will allow your child to store all of his materials in one place.
- Writing instruments (pens, pencils, crayons, markers)
- Paper
- Stapler/staples
- Tape
- Hole puncher
- Scissors
- Glue/glue sticks
- White-out
- Protractor, calculator or other subject specific tools
- Desk dictionary/thesaurus
- A shield or barrier your child can put around himself if he's easily distracted or desires privacy. You can use a couple of regular file folders. Open them completely and make a half box around your child's work area.
- Egg timer to monitor study time or give practice time tests

Teacher Toolbox Tips

I also suggest creating an area for storing graded assignments and tests. Reviewing previous assignments and tests will allow your child to pinpoint his mistakes (carelessness, for instance) and learn from them. Reviewing these materials yourself will also help you learn more about your child's strengths and weaknesses.

answerkeys

Teacher Toolbox Tip

Resist the urge to bail out your child. Although you need to assist your child and help keep him on track, especially when he's young, you should not rescue your child when he makes a bad choice or fails to fulfill his responsibilities. Mistakes and minor failures are *good* for kids. If your child doesn't tell you that he's out of pencils, don't run to the store and buy more when his assignment calls for them. He runs the risk of developing a sense of learned helplessness if you always bail him out. Parent with the end in mind.

Continuing Education

As your child gets older, you may want to encourage him to become more independent by allowing him to "manage his Study Station". Have him make a list of all of his supplies and how much he needs of each. Keep this with his Study Station materials and ask him to monitor when he needs new items. Encourage him to notice when he's down to, say, two pencils. This will allow you ample time to re-stock. If he waits until all the pencils are gone, he may not have the appropriate tools to complete a project. This helps to foster a sense of personal responsibility.

Questions for the Teacher

When is it appropriate to begin using a Study Station?

- Students can build a Study Station at any age. However, I suggest that parents begin working with their child during either pre-Kindergarten or Kindergarten. Although they usually have little to no homework at these grade levels, practice makes perfect. The more your child can engage in the behavior of becoming and staying organized, the more likely he is to develop and maintain healthy study and organizational habits.

- Building and maintaining a Study Station is also a great way to entertain younger siblings while the older one completes homework. Younger children can complete make-believe worksheets or color. Jennifer's daughter, Katie, loves to play "school" when Jennifer tutors her neighbor.

- A Study Station can be fun! Make sure you add plenty of crayons, markers and creative items, especially for young children. Like teachers, parents should promote a love of learning in their child and a desire to explore new learning adventures.

What do I do when it "all goes south" and the mess takes over again, despite my best efforts to keep him organized?

- Don't panic! Nothing ever goes smoothly the first time around. Remember, practice makes perfect. Watching your child descend into chaos can be frustrating, but resist the urge to yell and scream.

- Listen to your child. Talk to him about what's not working and why. Take the time to understand how your child learns and what makes sense to him. We all organize ourselves in different ways. Believe me, the more involved he is in the beginning, the more independent and successful he will be later on.

- Start over. Build a Study Station together and develop a plan for its storage and upkeep. You may need to check its contents on a regular basis and spend more time supervising your child until he gets the hang of it.

- Help him create a "re-order" form he can fill out and give you when supplies are running low.

- Build a team. Ask teachers to sign off on his assignment notebook (this is especially helpful for students with learning differences). Inform them that your child is having trouble keeping on task and staying organized at home. If it's happening at home, it's probably happening at school too. Strong teachers will welcome the opportunity to form a partnership with you. CONTINUED ON NEXT PAGE

139

answerkeys

Do you have any helpful hints for homework time?

◎ Provide support and praise for homework completion.

◎ Be available to provide non-critical assistance with a positive and helpful attitude.

◎ Encourage her to complete homework well enough that she has a sense of pride and control over her own learning and levels of competence.

◎ Help your child understand what types of homework they enjoy, and encourage her to choose assignments accordingly. When given a choice, some students prefer written reports; others prefer hands-on projects.

◎ Use homework preferences to develop a homework schedule. Some children like to get their least favorite assignments over and done with, while others want to do their favorite work first.

◎ If a child dislikes a subject, find ways to make it less frustrating. For example, set a goal of doing five math problems and then taking a stretch, listening briefly to music, or playing with a preferred game or toy.

◎ Encourage your children to participate in study groups with friends. Research shows that children who form study groups perform better than children who always study alone. This is particularly appropriate with middle and high school students.

◎ Encourage your child to have fun—eat a snack, call friends, start an activity, play a computer game, or watch a favorite show—when homework is finished.

◎ Never use homework as punishment.

◎ Be a good listener, and encourage your child to ask questions about things she doesn't understand.

◎ Set aside time for your children to share the skills and information they are acquiring with you.

◎ Help your child study for tests by quizzing him on the material in a friendly manner. Engaging in "car talk" is a great setting for this.

CONTINUED ON NEXT PAGE

140

Academics

How do I know if my child is getting too much, too little, or just the right amount of homework?

There are entire books dedicated to the argument for and against homework, so giving a "simple" answer is simply impossible! However, I can give you some general guidelines and tips based on my teaching experiences in both elementary and middle school. I also encourage you to visit our website, www.theanswerkeys.com, for a complete resource list.

◎ Children up to Kindergarten age do not need paper and pencil homework. They need to gain knowledge through experience-based learning. Learning to tie one's shoes or bringing in a household item that begins with a certain letter are fun ways to introduce young children to academic concepts.

◎ A large body of recent research indicates that children in elementary school really do not need homework either. That being said, if there is homework, it should consist of pleasure reading (or being read aloud to), long term projects, test preparation, completion of homework originally assigned yet not completed during class, and review material such as math facts or spelling words. Some amount homework assigned with a specific purpose can teach students skills such as time management and setting priorities.

◎ Children should not be learning new material at home. If you (or a tutor) are repeatedly teaching your child new material sent home by the teacher, schedule a conference to review the school's homework policy.

◎ Children should be able to complete the majority of homework independently. If your child requires constant attention or help during homework time, you need to speak with his teacher to see why he isn't learning the information in class.

◎ Middle-school students need free time too! Even though the homework load will increase as your child gets older, tweens and teens need a break too. If your middle-school student cannot participate in after school or pleasure activities because of his homework load, you need to review the homework policy with his teacher.

◎ Just say no! Good teachers use homework as a gauge to see if students are retaining what they learn in class. If your child cannot get his work done in the expected time frame, draw a line under what he has finished and send a note to the teacher letting her know the load is too much.

◎ Talk to other parents to see how much time their children are spending on homework. If you find that a majority of students in your child's class are spending way too much time on homework, talk to the teacher or principal. Homework should be used to enhance the classroom experience and not to hinder your child developing a love of learning.

141

answerkeys

Cheat Sheet

Learning Center: an area of the classroom where students can complete independent work and projects. These centers can be divided by interest or subject area, but can also be general areas where children can complete projects or other work that cannot be completed at one's desk.

Experience-Based Learning: using personal experience to learn as opposed to one-dimensional worksheets. **Example:** learning to count by placing fruit in a bag at the grocery store as opposed to counting pictures on a worksheet.

 HIGH FIVE to **Nancy Mendez**, fellow Houston MOPS mom, freelance writer and mother of two.

142

Sources

Kohn, Alfie. *The Homework Myth: Why Our Kids Get too Much of a Bad Thing.* De Capo Press, Philadelphia, PA. 2006.

Bennett, Sarah and Nancy Kalish. *The Case Against Homework: How Homework Is Hurting Our Children and What We Can Do About It.* New York: Crown Publishers, 2006.

http://www.teachersandfamilies.com

http://www.adprima.com

http://www.stayingaheadofthegame.com

http://www.campushealth.unc.edu

http://www.childdevelopmentinfo.com

http://www.schwablearning.com

Academics

Today's Lesson:
Test Preparation and Anxiety

Neither comprehension nor learning can take place in an atmosphere of anxiety.

– ROSE F. KENNEDY

Chalk Talk

We have all heard the saying, "The only certainties in life are death and taxes." Well, I think we can add one more to the list: standardized testing. Your child will take one or more of these tests every year until she graduates from high school. If you are lucky, she'll have no trouble with these exams; but for many students, the very thought of breaking out the number-two pencils can keep them awake at night.

Veteran moms will tell you that the number of children you have probably equals the number of different personalities and learning styles in your home. It certainly makes things interesting. My two older children have taken dozens of standardized tests over the years, and each of them handles this type of assessment differently. My son, John Henry, is perfectly comfortable with it. He is an auditory and visual learner; he's also very bright and a bit lazy. Even so, he's able to listen intently in class, manage his work and perform well. Given a choice, he'd opt to never do another science fair project or build another clay-and-baking-soda volcano, and that's okay.

My daughter, Murphy, is the exact opposite. She hates standardized exams—and any other paper-and-pencil method of evaluation. Tests cause her a great deal of anxiety, so much so that the atmosphere in our house becomes thick with worry a night or two before a big test. A kinesthetic learner, Murphy is incredibly creative and prefers to be evaluated through projects where she can utilize all of her senses. She can write and present a beautiful play about the first Thanksgiving, design a board game on fractions, or take a box of popsicle sticks and build a model of Jamestown fit for King James himself. It's how she demonstrates her understanding of what she has learned, and that's okay, too.

No two children see the world in the same way, process information in the same manner or perform well under the same conditions. However, standardized tests are designed to be one-size-fits-all and to measure all students with the same tool. While these exams are unavoidable, test-taking anxiety doesn't have to be a constant part of your child's life. Helping him prepare for the stress—and how to deal with it effectively—will serve him well now and in the future.

Teacher's Conference

Standardized testing is an important part of your child's education that begins early on and continues throughout her entire academic career. Sometimes starting as early as preschool, these tests measure a student's abilities and help determine placement, even promotion. It isn't easy to accept the fact that significant educational decisions can be made based on how your child performs in a limited amount of time and under very specific circumstances. Throughout the year, teachers often use many different methods to informally assess students, carefully evaluating their strengths and weaknesses. When looking at your child's past test scores or preparing for an upcoming exam, bear in mind that the results are only one piece of your child's overall academic performance.

Test anxiety is actually a kind of performance anxiety. It's the feeling a child gets when he knows his performance really counts. For some students, taking a test can feel like singing a solo in the school talent show or stepping up to bat with two outs in the ninth inning. He may experience a stomach ache, butterflies or sweaty palms, or he may feel his heart beating a little faster.

A little test anxiety isn't necessarily a bad thing. Not only is it normal to feel a little stressed out before a big test, but a bit of nervous anticipation can actually work to your child's advantage. It can get him revved up and keep him at peak performance during a test. Too much anxiety can have the opposite effect, however, causing him to flounder just when he needs to shine. If your child exhibits any of the following symptoms before a standardized exam, it may be necessary to seek the help of a professional:

- Headaches
- Diarrhea
- Light-headedness
- Shortness of breath
- Becoming shaky and sweaty
- Difficulty sleeping
- Dizziness or nausea

In addition to ruling out any physical causes of these types of symptoms, you may want to set up a conference with your child's teacher to learn how she prepares the children for testing. Reinforce those strategies at home—but make it more fun and pressure-free. Use this teachable moment to share with your child ways in which you remember successfully dealing with test-taking anxiety as a student.

Homework

Assignment #1

- Gain a better understanding of how your child learns. As your child progresses through school, his primary learning style should become apparent. Once you know your child's learning style, you can help him capitalize on his strengths and navigate his weaknesses. Ask his teacher for insight into how your child performs best in the classroom setting.

The three main learning styles are: auditory, visual and kinesthetic.

- *Visual learners* retain information better by seeing and reading. They account for about 55%–75% of the population.
    - Children who favor this learning style are more likely to take notes on their reading material, enjoy charts and graphs where they can see the end result, and often enjoy reading aloud to their parents.

- *Auditory learners* learn better by hearing or speaking. This group includes about 20%–30% of the population.
    - Children who favor this learning style prefer lectures and often take detailed notes when a teacher is speaking. They love to listen to stories, and do well with books on tape and related audio tools.

- *Kinesthetic learners* absorb information best through doing and touching. Approximately 5%–15% of people fall into this category.
    - Children who favor this learning style love to touch, feel and visualize their way through a project or task. They often build or assemble items without directions and will sometimes use musical rhythms .and melodic acronyms to remember information.

Assignment #2

Teach your child strategies to help manage anxiety and stress.

- Harness nervous energy and use it in a positive manner, whether through exercise, journaling, art or a favorite hobby.

- Encourage positive study habits. Suggest to your child that he study over time rather than "cram" the night before.

- Foster a good attitude towards school and learning—there is no benefit to negative thinking

Assignment #3

Set your child up for success on the day of the big test.

- Get enough sleep. Sleep is brain fuel, make sure your child gets the recommended eight hours of sleep at night.

- Start the morning with a healthy breakfast. A combination of protein and complex carbohydrates will stick with your child longer and prevent a midday sugar crash.

- Get to school on time. Make sure your child is there before the first bell and has all her necessary materials. Rushing to get to school on time will cause her undue stress.

Teacher Toolbox Tips

For parents:

- Make sure your child is in school each day. Good attendance is key, as your child must be in class to learn the material and perform well on exams.

- Complete and review homework with your child each night. Help her prepare for weekly and quarterly content-area assessments in order to build confidence and test-taking skills for standardized exams.

- Communicate regularly with your child's teacher. Be aware of what tests your child is expected to take each year and when they will occur. The teacher can also let you know if your child seems unusually anxious before regular tests or if there's anything that you might need to work on at home.

- Encourage daily reading. Good reading skills make a big difference during timed tests. If your child is a reluctant reader, try magazines, newspapers or even comic books.

For students:

- Listen to all test-taking directions given by the teacher, and ask questions about anything that's unclear.

- Relax and count from one to ten, taking deep, slow breaths to relieve tension before or during the test.

- Take one question at a time, rather than worrying about the entire test.

- Don't panic if you have a memory lapse or mental block. Take a slow, deep breath, and move on to the next question. Come back later to the trouble spot.

- Don't expect to know every answer. Some questions may to be too hard.

- Avoid unnecessary clock-watching.

- Ignore other test takers.

- Think positively. Remind yourself that you are prepared and will do well.

- Don't give up!

Academics

Words of Wisdom

Standardized tests alone cannot assess a child's abilities. A paper-and-pencil test doesn't always reveal what or how an individual student thinks or learns. Tests have their limitations, and no one test is a perfect yardstick to measure all students. Keeping this in mind can help lower your own anxiety about your child's performance, and allow you to help your child manage her stress as well. It is perfectly normal to be a little nervous about your child's performance, but be cautious about transferring that to your child.

Remember that your home should be a place of refuge. Your child's self-esteem or self-worth should never be tied to a test score. Remind her that her test score has nothing to do with who she is as a person or how much you love her. Taking the pressure off will allow her to maintain her focus and perform to the best of her ability.

Question for the Teacher

My child earns virtually all A's in all her classes, but consistently scores poorly on standardized exams. How should I deal with this discrepancy?

- First and foremost, don't panic. Remember that standardized exams, while important, are only one component of your child's overall performance in school.
- Schedule a conference with the teacher. Bring work samples that show your child has performed well in class, but has underperformed on the equivalent skill on a standardized test. Ask the teacher to explain why your child may perform well on one assessment and not on another.
- Evaluate how important standardized testing is toward your child's advancement in school. The importance of exam scores varies by state, district and school (especially if your child attends a private or parochial school).
- Consider enrolling your child in a program that can boost standardized exam scores. Keep in mind, however, that placing her in a score advancement program might increase her stress level. Get her thoughts and input before moving forward with an outside program.

answerkeys

Sources

Narang, Shama. "Standardized Test: What you should know before your child sharpens his #2 pencil." Scholastic.
 http://www2.scholastic.com/browse/article.jsp?id=1403

"Eleven Tips to Help Your Child Prepare for Test." Family Education.
http://school.familyeducation.com/educational-testing/teaching-methods

"Test Anxiety." KidsHealth.
http://kidshealth.org/teen/school_jobs/school/test_anxiety.

Shanks, Lorna and Pat Shank. "Spectacular Content- The Learning Modalities of you market." Ezine Articles.
 http://ezinearticles.com/?Spectacular-Content-Marketing-Tips---The-Learning-Modalities-of-Your-Market&id

"Ways to De-Stress and Help Your Child Do the Same." Family Guide. (September 4, 2003),
http://family.samhsa.gov/talk/destress.aspx

Academics

Today's Lesson:
Attention Deficit Hyperactivity Disorder (ADHD)

> "The task of the educator lies in seeing that the child does not confound good with immobility and evil with activity."
>
> – MARIA MONTESSORI

Chalk Talk

Attention Deficit Hyperactivity Disorder (ADHD) is a controversial, often misunderstood and misdiagnosed, but very real disorder. Although it is often portrayed as a recent, technology-induced disorder, ADHD was actually first described in 1845 by Dr. Heinrich Hoffman, a German psychiatrist and poet who began writing for children when he was unable to find suitable books for his young son. One of his books, *The Story of Fidgety Phillip*, along with its vivid illustrations, could be describing a scene out of many dining rooms, with Phillip leaning back in his chair and ultimately pulling the tablecloth and the family's dinner down on top of himself. Although we have known about ADHD for more than 150 years, there is still much confusion and controversy about its causes, treatment and even its symptoms.

It is a common misconception to say that those who suffer from ADHD are unable to pay attention to anything. Individuals with ADHD all have a hard time managing their attention, but the challenge manifests itself in many different ways. One person may have trouble shifting her attention from one task to another, while another may have a tendency to pay attention to everything. For the latter, the way his shoes feel, the buzzing of fluorescent lights, the birds chirping outside, his teacher's voice and what he ate for breakfast may all present themselves as equally important. Another individual may not be able to maintain a consistent level of attention over a period of time, especially if the task at hand isn't particularly interesting. Many people with ADHD can hyper-focus and tune everything else out when doing something they love.

answerkeys

Teacher's Conference

No doubt there's a certain buzz in the air when over half the students in your classroom have ADHD. It is electric, exciting and definitely challenging. Strange things seem to happen a lot. The class butterflies may escape and be chased down the hall (by the entire class), or everyone may put more than double the correct amount of vinegar and baking soda into their model volcanoes—these are just two examples. Being immersed in a world of pre-adolescent hormones exacerbated by ADHD was never boring; to the contrary, it was usually exciting and beautiful. Brainstorming sessions were energetic and, at times, explosive. Class projects became masterpieces; lectures became adventures in storytelling. I was pushed to be a better teacher as I strove to not only keep my students' attention, but also to maintain and focus it. Classroom routines and responsibilities were the most essential lessons; academic curriculum was only relevant when everyone could do what they were supposed to do and be where they were supposed to be. What's the point of reading together from a novel if some students' books were in their backpacks, lockers or the backseat of the mini-van?

If your child has ADHD, then you are very familiar with this above-average level of chaos and disorder. Going from his bedroom to the kitchen, your child might be distracted by photographs on the wall, toys left in the hallway or the sound of the garbage truck. He might forget what he's doing, even in the middle of a task like taking a shower. His body may be constantly in motion, as if his internal motor were permanently on "high." Being the parent of a child with ADHD can be frustrating, exhausting, exhilarating and awe-inspiring. Your child is able to see things that no one else sees and understand the world from a unique and beautiful perspective because of, rather than in spite of, his attention difficulties.

There are three main symptoms of ADHD: hyperactivity, impulsivity and inattention. Hyperactivity and impulsivity tend to go hand-in-hand, and can be detected as early as preschool. Inattention often doesn't show up until later. There are three main types of ADHD: the hyperactive-impulsive type, the inattentive type and the combined type (hyperactive-impulsive and inattentive).

An individual with hyperactivity/impulsivity may…

- Have difficulty sitting still during a meal or in the classroom.
- Have difficulty waiting in line or taking turns.
- Blurt out answers before hearing the entire question.
- Talk non-stop.
- Fidget with hands or feet; seem squirmy or wiggly.
- Display emotions without restraint.
- Seem to lack a "filter" and say whatever comes to mind.
- Be more motivated by an instant reward, rather than delayed gratification even if the immediate payoff is much smaller.
- Need to stay busy all time.
- Try to do many things at once.

An individual with inattention may…

- Get bored with a task quickly.
- Miss details and make careless mistakes.
- Be easily distracted by extraneous sights and sounds (a dog barking in the distance, someone tapping his pencil, children playing outside).
- Skip from one unfinished task to another.
- Frequently lose things: keys, books, shoes, toys, etc.
- Have difficulty following directions carefully.
- Appear to be "spacey," lethargic or slow-moving.
- Have difficulty processing information quickly.

Most of us could recognize many of these behaviors in our children, our spouses, even ourselves. Trying to do too many things at once is an occupational hazard of parenthood, and all of us have lost our keys more than once. I certainly hope that my young children will be avid daydreamers. It is only when these behaviors are exhibited consistently over a period of at least six months that you should consider the possibility of ADHD. It is very important to remember that ADHD is a medical condition that can only be diagnosed by a trained professional. You cannot diagnose your child—neither can his teacher, soccer coach or the mom down the street whose son has ADHD. If you are concerned that your child might have ADHD, start by talking to his teacher and pediatrician. Some pediatricians specialize in ADHD, and are comfortable doing a thorough evaluation and making a diagnosis. Many will refer you to a trusted specialist. Be wary of any doctor who quickly dispenses a diagnosis of ADHD and a prescription to go along with it. While medication can be a very valuable tool for managing ADHD, it isn't a decision to take lightly. A thorough evaluation is needed to correctly diagnose ADHD and rule out any other conditions that might produce ADHD-like symptoms. Below is a list of things to insist on when having your child evaluated:

According to the National Resource Center on AD/HD, the cornerstones of an ADHD evaluation are:

- Parent and child interviews.
- Parent and teacher-completed child behavior-rating scales.
- Parent self-report measures.
- Clinic-based psychological tests.
- Review of prior school and medical records.
- Individually administered intelligence testing, educational achievement testing or screening for learning disabilities (only necessary if not completed within past year).
- A standard pediatric examination or neurodevelopmental screening should be considered in order to rule out any unusual medical conditions that might produce ADHD-like symptoms.

151

answerkeys

Homework

Assignment #1

Make a list of your child's strengths. Challenge yourself to uncover the strengths that may be a direct result of her ADHD. For example: boundless energy, sensitivity to the world around her, athletic prowess and creativity. Share this list with your child, and thank her for the way she makes your life better, fuller and more beautiful.

Assignment #2

Think through a typical day with your child and make a list of the times and/or activities that seem to be pitfalls. These could include: getting dressed in the morning, brushing teeth, homework or bedtime. Don't feel bad if it seems like you are writing down every moment of the day. The goal is to break the day down into manageable moments, and then come up with strategies to make the worst moments better for everyone. More often than not, increased planning, structure and a little creativity can make a big difference. The mother of one of my students, for instance, put a giant X made out of fluorescent masking tape on her kitchen counter to remind her son where to put his backpack. He always knew where to find it when racing out the door in the morning. Having well-rehearsed, consistent routines is important for every child; it is critical for children with ADHD. (See lesson on *The Importance of Routines*, page 167.)

Assignment #3

Again, think through a typical day with your child, but this time make a list of the times that are magical. You may not get these moments everyday, but when you do, they can be transformative. Looking at the good times and understanding what made them good can help you create more of these opportunities for you and your child. Does she love to listen to you read at night? Does she love to play basketball with you or ride her bike? Is he fascinated by baseball cards or dinosaurs? Is bath time a celebration? Try to isolate what it is that makes these times rewarding for your child, and strive to integrate more of that special ingredient into your everyday lives.

Academics

Assignment #4

Make an intentional effort to catch your child doing something well. When you do, offer lots of genuine and enthusiastic praise to support this positive behavior. Try to make sure that the compliments you give your child outnumber the corrections. Many kids with ADHD can get beaten down by hearing, "Don't touch that!" or "Sit still!" over and over again. Look for and celebrate good choices—even if they are something basic like: "She kept her hands to herself on the playground, or she remembered to put away her backpack. If these are accomplishes for your child, then celebrate them.

Words of Wisdom

- Spending time outdoors is important for all of us, but it is crucial for individuals with ADHD. Studies have shown that time spent in nature can significantly reduce the symptoms of this condition.

- There are many treatment options for ADHD. Medication is often one very effective component of an overall treatment plan; behavioral therapy has also been shown to be effective. Many people believe that changes in diet can lessen the symptoms of ADHD. Perhaps you are passionately opposed to any type of medication, or maybe you think all the talk about milk allergies and sensitivity to food dyes is nonsense. My advice is to be reasonable and open-minded. Be willing to investigate options on both ends of the spectrum. Make these decisions carefully and with the guidance of a professional, rather than alone at your laptop while frantically searching the Internet. There are no quick fixes. ADHD is a lifelong, chronic condition that requires professional medical attention.

- Have reasonable expectations for your child. Experts estimate that the social and behavioral maturity level of a child with ADHD is about two-thirds of their actual age. For example, if your child is six, she might have the maturity level of a four-year-old in some areas. Uphold your family's standards of behavior, but view your child with loving and understanding eyes.

answerkeys

Questions for the Teacher

My child has ADHD. How do I help him make friends and foster strong peer relationships?

Every child has strengths, and children with ADHD are no exception. Plan your child's play dates, birthday parties and other time with friends around his strengths. Playing soccer at the park may be a better choice than a trip to the art museum. Discreetly observe your child playing with his friends, and watch for pitfalls and problems. Children with ADHD may act impulsively and be unaware of the impact their words and actions have on their friends. It can be helpful to role play situations at home in advance to avoid embarrassment and hurt feelings. If your child seems to be oblivious to facial expressions and other non-verbal cues, try watching a sitcom (reruns from older shows like "The Cosby Show" and "The Brady Bunch" work well) with the sound muted and see if your child can pick up on the actors' feelings simply by watching their body language.

My child has a friend with ADHD. Sometimes he gets a little wild when playing at our house. What are some strategies I can use to make our play dates a positive experience for both children?

Safety and structure are two important things to remember to help any play date go smoothly, but they may be especially helpful when hosting a child with ADHD. Choose an activity that suits both children. Your child may be able to spend hours building intricate contraptions out of Legos®, but another child may lose interest and move on to something else. Playing at the park or in your backyard with you close at hand are usually good options. It's also helpful to have a definite end-time set for the play date. Limiting play time can increase the chances that things will go smoothly.

Sources

"CHADD : Children and Adults with Attention Deficit/Hyperactivity Disorder. http://www.chadd.org (accessed July 17, 2010).

Hallowell, Edward M. and John J. Ratey. *Driven To Distraction: Recognizing and Coping with Attention Deficit Disorder from Childhood Through Adulthood.* New York: Touchstone, 1995.

Academics

Today's Lesson:
Dyslexia

I was, on the whole, considerably discouraged by my school days.
It was not pleasant to feel oneself so completely
outclassed and left behind at the beginning of the race.

– WINSTON CHURCHILL

Chalk Talk

Dyslexia is a language-based learning disability. Dys- means "difficult" and lexia means "words," so together, it literally means having difficulty with words. Many people associate dyslexia with reversals and "seeing things backwards." While many dyslexics do substitute b for d and vice versa, it is incorrect and misleading to say that they actually see things backwards. There is an identifiable, biological basis for this frustrating and often debilitating disorder. Studies using neuro-imaging have shown that people with dyslexia use a different part of their brains than most of the general population to read words. Using the part of the brain that typically processes images rather than language, it is believed that many dyslexics read an individual word almost as if they are viewing a picture or object. This is not a wrong way to read, simply a less efficient and often less accurate way. Words and images do not behave in the same way, therefore looking at a word with the "picture" part of your brain can be misleading and frustrating. An apple is an apple, no matter which way you turn it, but if you look at the letter "d" it could easily be the letter b,d,p,or q depending on your perspective.

Teacher's Conference

As a native English speaker with no knowledge of Chinese, discriminating between the following two characters 软 新 and reproducing them accurately would be very difficult. Imagine how frustrating it would be to have the same trouble with your native language. Working with students with learning differences, I see the enormous effort and struggle that can go into the seemingly simple task of reading a word. Reading, unlike speaking, is not a natural process. All over the world, with limited exceptions, everyone speaks. But not everyone reads.

Reading can be divided into two main parts: decoding (reading individual words) and comprehension (understanding the meaning of what one reads). Written language, and most basically the alphabet, is a code made up of symbols. In order to read, one must be able to understand and break the code. Individuals with dyslexia have a glitch at this most basic level of reading. Their ability to reason and comprehend is intact, or even advanced.

Homework

Assignment #1

If you suspect your child is dyslexic:

- **Gather information.** Start by talking to your child's teacher. She may be able to give you a better picture of how your child's abilities and struggles compare to other children his age. If your preschooler writes his name backwards, it doesn't necessarily mean he is dyslexic. Reversals and backwards writing are developmentally appropriate at this age. Ask your child's teacher or pediatrician for an age-appropriate checklist to give you an indication of the likelihood that your child may be dyslexic. Remember that dyslexia is a medical diagnosis that can only be made by a trained professional. Checklists simply provide a starting place to help you clarify your concerns and give you language to help you describe your child's behavior and learning style. See Question for the Teacher below.

- **Don't overreact.** Familiarize yourself with typical, developmentally appropriate milestones for your child's age. (See lesson on *Developmental Readiness: Is Your Child Ready for School?*, page109.) If you know what is typical, then you will be better able to determine if your child's behavior and abilities warrant a closer look. When my daughter was three, she started trying to write her name. About this time, an art project came home from school with her name written backwards. I would not have been concerned about any other three-year-old who did this, but of course since she was my baby, I could feel my heart beating just a bit faster. When I casually asked her about it she told me she just wanted to write it that way because she had drawn "a bowl of scabitti" on the other side and didn't have room. Give your child plenty of freedom to grow and learn, but trust your gut. If you are concerned, ask for help.

- **Take action.** Be very wary of waiting for your child to "grow out of" his or her difficulties. For some children, more time is what is needed; for others, waiting simply widens the gap between them and their peers. Studies have shown that almost all children with learning disabilities can eventually reach grade level if they receive intervention before Kindergarten. Trust your instincts, and be a persistent and loving advocate for your child. Get her tested. A parent or teacher cannot diagnose dyslexia, so seek out a trained professional in your school district or in the private sector to assess your child's language learning abilities. There are several types of formal testing, all of which have names that sound much scarier than they actually are. A "psycho-educational" evaluation focuses primarily on educational issues and should include IQ testing. A "neuro-psychological" evaluation will address educational issues and IQ, as well as a broader range of cognitive or "brain" tasks. Some diagnosticians will provide "language-learning evaluations," which provide a comprehensive assessment of a child's academic strengths and weaknesses but may or may not include an IQ score. Any of these three types of testing can help determine if your child has dyslexia or other learning disabilities. Early identification and intervention are essential to ensure your child's success in school.

Assignment #2

If your child is diagnosed with dyslexia:

- **Don't panic.** A diagnosis of dyslexia can be overwhelming, but doesn't have to be debilitating. Going to college and having a successful, fulfilling career are goals well within your child's reach. Dyslexia intensifies and amplifies the importance of one of the main jobs of every parent: to help provide opportunities for their child to learn, flourish and thrive.

- **Educate yourself.** As your child's most powerful advocate, the more you know the better off you will be. Dyslexia does tend to run in families. It is very common for a parent to hear about a child's diagnosis and have flashbacks of miserable school days, filled with anxiety and humiliation. If this is the case, you already have an intimate understanding of how it feels to be dyslexic. However, if you always did well in school and easily learned to read, your child's struggles may be baffling. If this is the case, I would highly recommend attending a learning disability simulation, which can give parents and teachers a first-hand look at what it's like to have a learning disability like dyslexia. Some school districts and hospitals provide workshops for parents.

- **Put together a support team.** This could include your child's teachers, a dyslexia or reading specialist (either at your child's school or in the private sector), a speech and language pathologist, the school counselor or psychologist, the school principal, a specialty teacher (music, art, drama, etc.) or coach to help cultivate and encourage your child's strengths and interests. Be wary of tutoring centers. I have talked to many heartbroken and frustrated parents who have spent a great deal of time and money at places that advertise "guaranteed" or "instant" results. A dyslexic student will have difficulty in a chain tutoring center in the same way that he or she struggles in a traditional classroom setting. Look for a specialist who is trained in a structured, sequential, multisensory approach to remediate dyslexia.

And don't forget to have some support for you, too—your spouse, a friend, local and national organizations, parent support groups and online resources can help provide much needed encouragement and information.

- **Make a plan (or two or three…).** With members of your support team, determine what services, interventions and/or modifications are available and appropriate at school and at home. Consider the latest technology. For example, audio books (including textbooks) can be a very important tool for an older dyslexic student with lots of assigned reading. There are also new types of voice recognition software that can adapt to a user's voice and convert the spoken word directly into text. Be flexible. "The plan" will change over time. No plan, school or teacher is perfect. Be persistent. There is no quick fix or cure for dyslexia, but this doesn't mean you have to settle for an inadequate plan. Be a strong advocate for your child. And above all, be hopeful.

- **Allow yourself to grieve.** Although this may sound strange after my encouragement to be hopeful, I think it's important. As parents, it's excruciatingly painful to watch your children suffer and struggle. Grieve the change in your expectations and the loss of time and money and energy spent on helping your child. Grieve the losses she will bear as well. They are real. Allow yourself to grieve so that with open arms and a free heart you can embrace your child exactly as she is.

Cheat Sheet

Neuro-imaging: a non-invasive way to produce images of a person's brain.

Multisensory teaching: an approach to teaching that involves using techniques for engaging a student's eyes, ears, voice and hands in a structured way to learn and reinforce new skills.

Sources

Shaywitz, Sally. *Overcoming Dyslexia: A New and Complete Science-Based Program for Reading Problems at Any Level.* 1st ed. New York: Alfred A. Knopf, 2003.

Neuhaus Education Center. http://www.neuhaus.org (accessed July 17, 2010).

The International Dyslexia Association. http://interdys.org (accessed July 17, 2010).

Academics

Questions for the Teacher

Is my child dyslexic?

Although there is no simple answer to that question, there are some "red flags" to look for if you think your child may have dyslexia or another language learning difference. Keep in mind that all of us exhibit some of the following behaviors from time to time. Look to see if your child consistently exhibits several of these behaviors. If your child is struggling to learn to read, or if you or your child's teacher has noticed that some of the following behaviors are interfering with her learning, then she may need to be evaluated.

Oral Language

- Late in learning to talk
- Difficulty pronouncing words (speech is difficult to understand, persistent mispronunciations)
- Difficulty with singing songs, playing rhyming games, or nursery rhymes
- Difficulty following directions
- Does not use age-appropriate grammar or sentence structure when speaking
- Difficulty learning the alphabet
- Limited oral vocabulary
- Difficulty with word retrieval or naming
- Difficulty with directional concepts such as left and right, up and down
- Difficulty with concepts of time such as before and after, yesterday, today and tomorrow

Reading

- Difficulty learning letter sounds
- Difficulty learning to read
- Slow, hesitant, or laborious oral reading
- Misreads or omits frequently used, small words
- Poor comprehension while reading silently or aloud (Comprehension may be significantly higher when listening to a passage.)

Written Language

- Difficulty spelling
- Difficulty getting ideas on to paper
- Difficulty proofreading

Today's Lesson:
Autism Spectrum Disorders

Hope begins in the dark, the stubborn hope that if you just
show up and try to do the right thing, the dawn will come.
You wait and watch and work: You don't give up.

– ANNE LAMOTT

Chalk Talk

What is autism, exactly? It's a question that even the foremost experts grapple with today. It is a complex, yet not uncommon disorder affecting thousands of families. Today one in approximately 100 children are diagnosed with autism, making it more common than pediatric cancer, diabetes, and AIDS combined (www.autismspeaks.org). Autism is thought to be a "neurobiological" disorder, meaning that it manifests itself in the brain and nervous system. Although there is currently no genetic, chemical or neurological test for autism, experts believe that the brain of a person with autism is essentially wired and organized differently. Many behaviors associated with autism are thought to be coping mechanisms —an autistic brain's attempt to process a world that it's just not wired for.

Autism is one of several disorders, which together are known as Autism Spectrum Disorders. The root of the word autism comes from the Greek prefix auto- or aut- meaning "self, spontaneous, directed from within." Autism impairs a person's ability to connect with, communicate with and relate to other people—which can cut a parent's heart deeply. To be a parent is to be attached, connected, committed and heart-breakingly in love with your child. Anything that threatens that relationship, as autism often does from the inside out, can be devastating. Even so, there is great hope for those who struggle with autism.

Teacher's Conference

While in the classroom, I worked with and came to love a handful of students "on the spectrum." Some diagnosed, some on the brink of diagnosis. Some who would stand out in a crowd, some who would rather stand alone. One particular student stands out in my mind, not for how much he learned or the friends he made (he was remarkably well-loved), but for how much he and his parents taught me.

At the beginning of the year, his cheerful parents met with me to talk about "their son's Asperger's". They said it like they were talking about his dimples or his imaginary friend—something cute and remarkable. I really did not know what to say. I kept thinking to myself, "Do they not know how serious this is?" I am embarrassed to admit that I spent the better part of the school year trying to explain to them that Asperger's Syndrome, which is on the autism spectrum, really is a big deal and that in the real world, outside of our sweet, quirky class where eleven-year-old boys still love playing dinosaurs at recess (with high-pitched shrieking to rival a dog whistle and occasional, full-body T-rex attacks)…outside of this safe haven, their son would have trouble making and maintaining real friendships. What in the world was I thinking? Does anyone make real friendships in middle school? Is that even possible? And how much more real does it get than being able to fully and completely be oneself all the time. His parents saw Asperger's Syndrome as a gift, and it became one. How completely life-changing.

Talk about autism is everywhere these days: magazines, the evening news, books, talk shows and the internet. Much of this talk is about finding a cause and a cure. So far, neither of these things has happened. Now what? What if those of us who love and care for someone with autism choose to see it as a gift? Not just the individual as a gift, but autism as an actual gift: the awkwardness, the fear, the loss, the frustration, the bewilderment and unpredictability, all of it. What if we stage quiet, powerful revolutions in our homes and classrooms by seeing all these things as a gift? What if we focus on making the future better, rather than focusing on making our children better?

A monumental lesson for all parents to learn, especially parents with exceptional children, is that we cannot make our children do anything. What we can do is choose our own behavior and create an environment in which our children are most likely to thrive, succeed, grow and learn. I find that most of my blood-boiling moments as a parent occur when I am trying to control my children's behavior—especially the kind of behavior that I really can't control (i.e. bodily functions—eating, sleeping, pooping and the like.) As any sleep-deprived new mother will tell you, you cannot make a baby sleep. But you can make it *much* more likely that she will sleep well by providing a soothing environment and a predictable routine, and by making sure her basic needs are met.

When your child has autism, there are more behaviors that fall into this "you can't make me" category. Often children with autism may be overwhelmed by too much external stimuli, and sensory overload can lead to tantrums or withdrawal. As a parent, you know that there is very little you can do to control your child's response in the heat of the moment. However, you can anticipate what situations may be especially challenging for your child, and plan accordingly. You can also teach him coping strategies for dealing with stressful situations. Because of what I have seen in the lives of children with autism and their families, I believe that the moment when parents come to the humbling and petrifying realization that they cannot change or control their child is the moment when true healing and growth begin.

Taking the pressure off your child to progress or to "be healed" can dramatically change the entire family dynamic. This doesn't mean that you give up hope. Instead, it means giving hope some room to breathe, opening up more space for hope in your lives. Shifting your focus from making your child better to making the future better for your child can have a positive effect on how you approach each day, each challenge, each setback and success. Making the future better can mean so many different things like increasing awareness in your community; taking time for yourself, so that when your child's next meltdown or outburst comes you'll be better equipped to handle it; strengthening your support team; spending sweet time with your child doing whatever he wants (my friend's son loved everything about washing machines, so they would go to Sears and wander the appliance section); or spending time with your spouse and your other children, who may feel left out at times.

Widening your focus can illuminate more opportunities for success. Instead of success being measured in single words, a lack of seizures or a decrease in tantrums (all of which are really big deals), it can also be measured in moments of strength and grace in the face of the unthinkable, minutes spent doing something for yourself, and bursts of laughter. Making the future better can and must mean working with and teaching your child, and finding the best plan of treatment. But having her actions, choices and abilities—all of which are beyond your control—as your primary focus is exhausting and self-defeating. Imagine what it would be like if your entire family's happiness depended on your "getting better" or becoming "more like other moms." The pressure would be unbearable. Although it probably is never articulated or even intended, this kind of pressure is a very common reality for kids with autism and other disabilities. They can feel the stress and weight of unmet expectations in the air. Who can heal or grow in this kind of environment?

If your child has autism, and even if he doesn't, it is critical that you find a way to honestly say to him: "I accept you exactly as you are. If you never, ever change, I am okay with that. I love you here and now, all of you, just as you are." After all, isn't that what all of us want to hear, that we are loved just as we are? Autism is a crucible of sorts that leads parents to be either accepting or combative—or a little of both. Ultimately, however, wholehearted acceptance of your child just as she is, is your most powerful weapon.

Homework

Assignment #1

If you suspect your child is autistic:

- **Gather information.** Experts now say that signs of autism can be seen as early as age one. Start by talking to your child's pediatrician. The following website (http://depts.washington.edu/dataproj/chat.html) has a checklist sometimes used by pediatricians at a child's eighteen-month check-up. Even if your child is older, checking this list to see if he did or still does exhibit any atypical behavior can provide helpful information for your family doctor.

- **Take action.** Be very wary of waiting for your child to "grow out of" his or her difficulties. For some children, more time is what is needed; for others, waiting simply widens the gap between them and their peers. Trust your instincts, and be a persistent and loving advocate for your child. If you still have concerns after speaking with your pediatrician or family doctor, a developmental pediatrician is the next person you need to see.

Assignment #2

If your child is diagnosed with autism or an autism spectrum disorder:

- **Don't panic.** This diagnosis may seem like the end of the world, but it's not. It is life-altering, but not life-ending. Give yourself some time and space to grieve. Surround yourself with people—a spouse, family member, friend, pastor, someone who understands your need to just vent—who won't judge or offer unsolicited advice.

- **Educate yourself.** As your child's most powerful advocate, the more you know the better off you are. This is especially challenging with autism spectrum disorders. There is an overwhelming amount of information out there regarding treatment and causes of autism, but a good developmental pediatrician can guide you in making treatment decisions. The following website (www.autismspeaks.org) provides good description and comparison of most of the current, mainstream interventions used to treat autism spectrum disorders.

- **Put together a support team.** This will probably include your doctor, a therapist, a psychologist and teachers. Don't forget to include support for yourself. Many parents who are the primary caregivers of children with autism find that their child's needs are so involved and that their treatment plan is such that they have trouble trusting anyone else to take care of their child. Include your spouse, a relative or close friend when learning about and being trained in any procedures or specific methods that you will use with your child. Be confident that there is at least one other person who knows what your child needs and is able to care for her when you are sick, unavailable or taking a well-deserved break.

- **Formulate a plan.** With the help of your support team, determine what services, interventions and/or modifications are available and appropriate at school and at home. Be flexible. "The plan" will change over time. Autism is considered to be a lifelong condition, and your child's needs will change.

- **Plan for the future.** Just thinking about estate planning is difficult for any parent. And while it's critical for parents to be responsible and think ahead, it's especially important for parents of children with special needs. An individual with autism may not be able to live completely independently. Consider the very real possibility that your child may need to be provided for far into the future. It may be helpful to speak with a financial planner about what resources that are available for families with special needs children.

- **Choose to be grateful.** This is a terribly powerful choice. Heartbreaking, life-changing and almost impossibly difficult. Be satisfied with your child just as she is. Love her fiercely just as she is. Be thankfully present in the moment and hopeful for the future.

Cheat Sheet

A diagnosis of autism is given when all of the three following areas of development are significantly affected: social interaction, communication and repetitious behaviors/restricted interests. (www.autsimtreatmentcenter.org). The two following conditions are also considered to be "on the autism spectrum":

Asperger' Syndrome: An individual with Asperger's will typically exhibit behaviors similar to those of "classic" autism. These may include difficulty "reading" people's faces, body language and other important social cues; speaking with little or no emotion or having unusual speech patterns; and having an intense interest in one specific subject. The main difference between Asperger's syndrome and typical autism is that there are no signs of significant cognitive difficulties in those with Asperger's; the individual's IQ will fall in the normal to superior range.

Pervasive Developmental Disorder, not otherwise specified (PDD-NOS): This diagnosis is given when an individual exhibits some symptoms of autism, but does not match the criteria closely enough to warrant this diagnosis. But it's not necessarily a "milder" form of autism. One symptom or set of behaviors may be minor, while another may be more severe.

 HIGH FIVE to **Jeff Rice**, Head of the Tuttle School at the Briarwood School in Houston, TX.

Sources

Autism Awareness Centre, Inc. http://www.autismawarenesscentre.org (accessed July 17, 2010).

Autism Speaks. http://www.autismspeaks.org (accessed July 17, 2010).

Autism Treatment Center of America: The Son-Rise Program. http://www.autismtreatmentcenter.org (accessed July 17, 2010).

building a bridge
between home & school

If you bungle raising your children,
I don't think whatever else you do matters much.

– JACQUELINE KENNEDY ONASSIS

Heather

After teaching for over a decade without children of my own, I have been surprised by how I feel now that I'm on the other side of the fence. I have been plagued with feelings of anxiety and anticipation at different times—when I dropped Maya off for her first day of preschool, or when I attended my first parent/teacher conference as a mom. Fortunately, I can say that school has been a great experience for my daughter and me. She is safe, loved, and encouraged at school, while I am both well informed and encouraged as a parent. Even in preschool it's important to build positive relationships and get involved. Let your child see the powerful partnership you have with her teacher.

It seems we're always looking for ways to better our children and ourselves, ways to get organized, build healthy relationships, and instill a good work ethic. So many of these valuable skills can be learned from a well-run classroom. I love the creativity that school can inspire, whether it's thinking outside the box to keep twenty backpacks off the floor, watching new friendships blossom over a play dough sculpture, or motivating children to eagerly learn something that could seem boring and dull. Bring this vibe of excitement into your home, and make learning, cleaning and everyday living manageable and fun.

Melissa

As new parents, my husband and I attended birthing classes. We bought the safest crib and car seat; we read all the baby books twice, and triple checked that there was never a choking hazard in sight. Now, our children are growing older, and their needs have changed from that of simple safety to that of wanting independence, yet still needing guidance and instruction. Some of the most useful tools we can give them will stem from our efforts to build a solid bridge from home to school. Our kids will spend many years in a classroom. What better way to prepare them for the challenges of life than by ensuring they are prepared to meet the demands of school, no matter their age or grade level?

Jennifer

I love school. I was one of those book-loving, hand-raising, gold-star kids. I played school for fun. I still linger in the school supply aisle when I shop. Helping students find peace and success at school has become my passion as an adult. Why is it, then, that the thought of sending my oldest child to Kindergarten sends a tangible shiver of anxiety through my body? Katie is a capable, confident, spunky little girl. I'm not worried about her—I'm worried about me. It's so difficult to place my child in someone else's hands. Her teachers won't know her as I do, but that's the point. They will draw out a side of her that is new and just coming into being. My job will be to support, reinforce and supplement what she's learning and who she's becoming both as a student and a person. Good teachers reach out to parents and include us in our children's school lives. But we, in turn, need to reach out to our children's teachers and help to build a strong bridge between home and school. I challenge you (and myself) to find the balance between letting go and reaching out, and to tell our children through our posture and our presence that we believe they have what it takes to make it out in the "real world," and that they're in good hands.

Patina

As parents we have many jobs. Most of these relate to preparing our children to become independent and productive in a way that fulfills them. From the time our children enter school until the time they don a cap and gown, they will have spent most of their time in these two worlds: home and school. So it's critical that both worlds work together for the betterment of the whole child. Parents and teachers alike have unique perspectives and insights that when combined, offer a more complete understanding of children and their strengths, gifts and challenges. It's an invaluable and powerful partnership.

Today's Lesson:
The Importance of Routines

Success depends on previous preparation,
and without such preparation there is sure to be failure.

– CONFUCIUS

Chalk Talk

Getting out of the house sounds easy enough, right? If you always have extra time because you and your children are early birds, skip this lesson. But if you're like the rest of us—your mornings resemble a circus juggling act and getting out of the house is not a pleasant experience for anyone— then it's time to establish a home routine. Following a routine and providing a structured environment will not only make your life easier, it will teach your children personal responsibility and independence.

When preparing for the next day, I put most everything I'll need by the door, including the notes I write reminding me not to forget the things by the door. On Maya's school days, I have her bag packed, blanket tucked in her nap mat and her lunch already prepared or ready for heating. Since the age of nineteen months, Maya has been responsible for her lunch bag; she carries it to the car and to her classroom. She has loved this job so much actually that we have trouble prying it from her fingers when it's time to put it away. When I pick her up in the afternoon, she points to her lunch bag, ready to carry it back to the car. Giving Maya a job teaches her responsibility, makes her feel like a big girl and gives me one less thing to worry about.

Teacher's Conference

How is it that one teacher can round up twenty kids, get them where they need to be, with what they need, on time, *and* keep a smile on her face? Practice, training, organization and following a routine. Teachers set the tone for the day as students arrive each morning. They greet students with a smile at the door as they welcome them to a day full of learning and fun. This allows teachers to see the face of each child, check moods and attitudes, and be ready to listen or allow students a little time to decompress. When I was teaching, if I saw a child with a sad face walk into my classroom, I could help with the problem right then to get the student's day on the right track.

Teachers also monitor the morning routine, making sure it runs smoothly. Students know where to put belongings, what they need to do next and even what kind of voice they should use in the classroom. Labeling items with students' names or labeling areas also keeps things organized. Teachers post charts (word charts or picture charts) to show each step in the morning routine as well as the schedule of the day so students know what to expect. Believe it or not, kids like structure. One of my favorite ways to set a calm and inviting environment was with music. It would always put a smile on my face to hear a student hum along with Enya.

As a parent, however, I have to confess that it's easy to drag my feet on occasion. But I've learned that a little procrastination becomes a big headache! You are in charge of setting the tone for your day and your child's day, so avoid frustration and problems by planning ahead. It puts your child in a bad position when he arrives late for school and without his things. You may be thinking, "But my child is making us late," and "I told him to get his homework!" Of course your child must take ownership for his belongings, but this can and will only happen after he has developed a sense of personal responsibility. And he can only develop this if you set an example, teach the appropriate behavior and then model how to follow through with that behavior. Following a routine at home is essential to being prepared and getting out the door on time.

Teacher Toolbox Tip

In September 2009, *Parenting Magazine* reported on a study by Ohio State University and Teachers College, Columbia University. They found that kids who grow up in an organized, calm home are more likely to have good early reading skills at ages five and six. Set mealtimes and bedtime, clear chore assignments, a family calendar, and keeping the TV off during dinner can all promote early reading skills. And this is just one of the benefits of establishing a functional and consistent home routine!

Homework

Assignment #1

Prepare and Organize the Night Before

Clothing

- Set out complete outfits.
- Put all accessories (socks, belt, hair accessories, jewelry) in a clear bag and drape it around the clothes hanger, or place items together in a designated spot.
- If you have evening activities that don't allow for nightly decisions, put together weekday wardrobes over the weekend. Depending on your child's age, she can do this independently with your approval or you can do it together. To avoid last-minute problems, once outfits are put together, keep them together unless there are sudden weather changes, rips or stains in the clothing.

Bath time

- Shower or bathe the night before.
- Brush or braid long hair to eliminate many tangles. You can always wet wild hair to tame it in the morning.

Breakfast

- Set out bowls, spoons, cereal boxes, cups or whatever you use. If you make a hot breakfast, put the skillet on the stovetop and have other items you need beside it. Set the table with plates, forks, spoons and napkins.

Lunch

- Pack lunch the night before. Make sure it is ready to just grab and go.
- If your child needs money, put it in a designated spot in her backpack.

Assignment #2

Teach Your Child to Follow a Routine

Plan and prepare for your morning, afternoon and evening routine. Just as following a school routine keeps a classroom running smoothly, teaching your child to follow a daily home routine will help keep your household running smoothly, too.

Morning

- If your child has trouble getting out of bed in the morning, open the blinds to let the sun shine in. You may also want to adjust his bedtime accordingly. What child wants to go to bed earlier? Move bedtime up fifteen minutes for every morning you struggle to get your child out of bed. You should see a turn-around within days.
- Use a picture or word chart to remind your child of each step in his morning routine. Example: wake up, make your bed, wash your face, get dressed, eat breakfast, tidy breakfast area, brush your teeth, gather belongings and a star at the end to represent a special treat (e.g. phone call to a grandparent, walk the dog, dance to favorite tunes, read a favorite story together) if time allows. You can also recognize your child's efforts with a special treat when he earns a predetermined number of stickers for following the chart.
- Talk about time and exactly when your child should be ready to walk out the door. In addition, talk about how long the different parts of his morning routine should take. Put a clock in your child's bedroom or bathroom. If your child is too young to tell time, you can draw a picture of where the long and short hands will be, or tell him that when the long hand gets to a certain number it will be time to go.
- Set a good example. Modeling a productive, organized morning does not mean putting your shoes on in the car and brushing your hair at the red light. Wake up early enough for a calm morning and reserve time to talk to your family about the day ahead. Ask your child what she is looking forward to that day and let her know what you plan to do that day. Reward her with a special morning treat, such as a story, if you are all on time.

Afternoon

- Unloading the car after a long day at school or work can create a mountain of clutter. Depending on the space you have, designate a specific spot for backpacks and coats. Use hooks, bins, benches, baskets or cubbies and try to find a spot by the door.

- Check your child's folder for homework or notes. After she finishes her homework, make sure it goes right back in the backpack for school the next day. Also, be sure that any special items your child may need go into her backpack the night before. (for more tips, see lesson on *Time Management, Organization & Study Skills for Children*, page 93.)

- Set a good example. Model a structured routine for your child. Hang your keys, purse or briefcase in the same spot so you'll be ready to go the next day. If possible, charge your cell phone next to your purse. Keep a checklist and calendar by the door to ensure that you and your child have everything you need when you leave.

Evening

- Following your after-school activities and dinner, try to stick to a regular routine. Spending time together as a family and discussing your day is a great way to unwind.

- Prepare for bedtime—pajamas, brushing teeth and making time to read together every night.

- Be consistent with bedtime. Your child must be well rested in order to be energized the next day.

- Read at bedtime as part of your routine and to calm children before going to sleep. Have a predetermined number of books. Before Maya could count, I would always end with the same story so she would know we were finished reading for the night.

Continuing Education

Anything worth doing takes time and energy. Practice. Be patient with your child and yourself. As children get older, the schedule of activities, the amount of homework and gear, and the number of responsibilities will all increase—but it will seem like you have less time in which to get it all done. Starting regular routines now will help with time management and organizational challenges down the road. You won't always be there to pack his lunch and put his cleats in his sports bag. Remember, you are preparing your child for independence.

Mom Tip

Just as you work on managing your time wisely, do the same for your child. Kids can learn how to use their time efficiently by following the structure of a daily routine. Focus on the progress your child makes in following a schedule, and reward improvements. He will enjoy the predictability of his day and also learn flexibility as things crop up to change the schedule.

Today's Lesson:
Words as a Teaching Tools

Kind words can be short and easy to speak,
but their echoes are truly endless.

– MOTHER TERESA

Chalk Talk

Words have power—the power to heal, to encourage, to wound and to teach. This power lies dormant in words gone unsaid and runs amok in words unleashed. When I was a student teacher, our professor led my class of prospective teachers in a powerful, reflective exercise. She asked us to think back and recall words that had significantly impacted us, both positively and negatively. We had to list three positive and three negative things that someone in our lives had spoken aloud to each of us. Without exception, all of our lists included words spoken by our parents and our teachers. I have strong memories of words spoken by my father and mother, my high school English teacher, even my first-grade teacher. In every circumstance, these powerful words came from an obvious overflow of emotion, rather than a carefully delivered speech or intentional lecture. Your voice as a parent has immeasurable power to shape your child's heart and self-concept. The words you speak to your child will live beyond you and continue to wield their power long after your child has grown up.

Teacher's Conference

I truly learned the power of my words as a teacher when I tried to teach with laryngitis. Luckily, it was not at the beginning of the school year; I had my students well-trained by this point. Nevertheless, I was amazed by how well my students did when all I could do was point, gesture and whisper. I had spoken the words necessary to the functioning of my classroom so many times, that my students could say them for me. I heard my students reminding each other to do things like "use a classroom voice" and "get in your LLP" (listening, learning position). Your children can probably recite many of your often-used parenting phrases. I sometimes catch myself using the same words my mother used when I was a child. Words have staying power.

We often find ourselves using words to correct and direct our children, and this is an unavoidable and necessary part of parenting. But there are so many more ways to shape our kids' lives with our words. As a teacher, I considered every space my classroom: the hallways, the cafeteria, the playground and the carpool line. As a mother, every moment is a teachable moment. Find opportunities to share your wisdom, love, and guidance through your words.

Homework

Assignment #1

Reflect on your past. Take some time to recall words that have impacted your life. Recall both positive and painful memories. Write down the words and who said them to you. Keeping these memories close to the forefront of your heart and mind will help you make wise choices about what you say to your family—and how you say it.

Assignment #2

Record memories of your child. Take some time on a regular basis to write down stories about your children. They could be quick notes, journal entries, captions beneath photographs or descriptions in a baby book. Find a medium that works for you and use it. I am horrible at keeping up with my children's baby books and I can't stand scrapbooking. But we keep a small journal next to our bed, and whenever either of our children says something funny or profound, one of us (my husband or I) writes it in the book. We have a precious collection of quotes from our children, beginning with their first few words. Here's another example. I have a friend who loves to draw. So she fills each square of her calendar with a small sketch of something important that happened that day. Another mom I know uses a diary to write notes to her daughter. They take turns writing notes, questions and letters to each other and passing it back and forth, leaving it on the other's pillow before bedtime. Not only do they have a private, personal way to communicate with each other, they also have a record of their relationship to look back on.

Assignment #3

Redesign dinnertime. Choose one meal a week (or more) when your family eats together. Turn off the TV and cell phones, and eliminate other distractions. Create space for storytelling as you eat together, rather than waiting for a special occasion. Here are some ways to start:

- Ask everyone "What was a good part of your day?" Not necessarily the best part. There have been days when I've said, "I had a terrible day, I pass." Encourage everyone to share, but don't force it.
- Let your kids ask you a question about your childhood. My kids like to hear me tell about rescuing kittens out of floodwaters in our neighborhood when I was young, and about the time my husband got a fishhook stuck in the back of his hand. You will probably have some old favorites that your kids will want to hear again and again.

Cafeteria Line

Here are some more opportunities and ideas for using the power of words to enrich your parenting and expand your sphere of influence in your child's life:

Ask thoughtful questions. Trips to the grocery store, park or doctor's office can be prime opportunities for language and vocabulary development. When my daughter was singing Christmas carols one year, she asked me about "figgy pudding." I had to confess that I couldn't describe a fig very well. All I could come up with was that it was a brownish, purplish sort of fruit. On our next trip to the grocery store, I made a point of finding figs so she could experience them and know exactly how they looked, smelled, felt and tasted. By asking the grocer where and how figs grew, I learned something, too. Seeing the grocery store as an avenue for answers, not just another mundane errand, transformed our experience.

Questions are some of the most powerful kinds of words. They invite your child to be an active participant in what you are doing. Asking your child thoughtful, open-ended questions tells her that you care about what she thinks and what she has to say. Some examples of questions that lead your child beyond 'yes' or 'no' answers:

- Where do you think this came from?
- What do you think would happen if…?
- What do you think will happen next?
- What do you see?
- What do you think this is?
- What do you think this is used for?
- How does this feel?
- What do you think made that sound?

answerkeys

Mom Tips

- Even very young children can benefit from being asked questions. You might be surprised by your child's answers, even if he has very few words. A baby who can only coo or gurgle in response still appreciates being included in the conversation.
- Ask your child questions with a genuine sense of wonder and interest in what she has to say. Questions are not meant to be a quiz, but rather an invitation to draw near and to discover.

Wonder with your child: At different points in my journey, I have found myself seeking consolation and guidance from wise counselors. I first learned the power of the words "I wonder …" from a therapist as I was sitting vulnerable and confused on her couch. The strength of these words allowed me to consider a new perspective without feeling like it was being forced on me. Wondering also helped me to engage the power of my mind and imagination to see beyond my present circumstances. Here two different ways to use these words with your children:

- Beginning with "I wonder" to reach out to a hurting, frustrated child provides a way for you to offer your wisdom with no strings attached. For example, say "I wonder what would happen if you tried to talk to your friend about how you feel?" Wondering communicates the truth that you don't know everything (which he will be quick to point out to you), but that you might know something that could help.

- Modeling a sense of wonder for your child helps her to see the majesty and mystery in the world around her. For example, while on a walk with your child, say things like: "I wonder who lives inside that hole in the tree?" or "Look at those dark clouds, I wonder if it will rain at our house?"

The key to wondering is authenticity. If you say you are "wondering" but are actually seeking a specific answer or response from your child, it will backfire. Strive to regain a childlike inquisitiveness and a genuine eagerness for discovery before attempting to lead your child to wonder with you.

Read more than the words on the page: Books provide a great starting place for talking to your children. If thinking of meaningful things to say to your child seems daunting, this is a good place to start. I have friends with four young children, all under the age of six, and they are masters at this. My friend Jason can hold his three wiggly boys and baby girl on his lap and read them all a story, giving each of his sons a turn to notice special things in the pictures, count objects, and predict what will happen next. If he can do it, then so can you. Here are some ways to interact with your child while reading a picture book together:

Ask your child:
- How many _____ (balls, balloons, cars, bananas…) do you see?
- Which one do you like best?
- What do you think will happen next?
- What is hidden behind the _____ ?
- What sound does a _____ (cow, truck, trumpet) make?
- What do you think the word _____ means?
- Has this ever happened to you?
- How would you feel if…?

Have fun with words by:
- Leaving out the last word in a sentence for your child to complete
- Using funny voices for the different characters in a story
- Singing the words of a story
- Having your child act out a favorite story

Pick and choose a few of these activities rather than trying to incorporate all of them into each story time. I have had several of my overzealous attempts to liven up a story interrupted by my daughter's pleads to "just read the story for real, Mom."

Storytelling: Each of us is a born storyteller. It is written in our genes and given to us as a birthright. Whether you tweet, text, journal or joke, each of us has a story to tell and a desire to tell it. Stories are some of the most meaningful and potent kinds of words; they draw us together in community and pass on a legacy of love and experience.

A few years ago, before my husband's grandfather passed away, my husband and his brother sat with him after our Thanksgiving feast and asked him about his life. They pulled out a video camera and said "Tell us about Africa." What resulted was a priceless retelling of his journey with his wife to South Africa and their work fighting apartheid. We learned how they met Nelson Mandela. Pop Pop told stories only he could tell—what it was like to be newlyweds and start a family in a strange country, what it was like to fight for what they believed in and to live to see the fruit of their efforts. You probably have similar treasures in your own family if you take the time to ask and to listen. Here are some ways to make storytelling a part of your family:

- Provide opportunities for your children to spend time with their grandparents, great-grandparents and other family members. Ask specific questions and make time to listen. Document or record the life-changing, funny and historically significant stories your family is sure to have. I still remember my grandmother telling the story of how her father abandoned their family car on the side of the road one day after it repeatedly broke down. After that, they walked everywhere they went.

- Tell your own stories. My daughter loves to hear the story of when she was born over and over again. I am the only one who can tell her what it was like when she hiccupped inside me, making my whole belly twitch. You are the only one who can tell your stories, so make sure that you do. Write them down for your children to read and re-read. Tell your children how you met your spouse, what you remember about school, learning to ride a bike, or losing a pet.

- The best stories are often funny ones. Share little memories, even if they do not seem particularly profound or significant. I still laugh when my dad tells the story of how he played a trick on one of his younger brothers by rushing to the freezer ahead of him when he heard him planning to get ice cream. My dad put the family cat in the freezer seconds before his brother got there and hid around the corner to watch the bewildered cat leap out and onto his brother's head.

- Making up stories can be a wonderful way to connect with your children. I have fond memories of the "Ollie Ostrich" stories my dad would tell us at bedtime. One of my parents' best tricks was "green bean stories." A bite of a green bean—or any other vegetable—was the ticket to the next part of the suspenseful dinnertime story. We also loved "beep stories." One person would start a story and say "BEEP" in the middle, and the next person would pick up and take the story in a new direction.

Give your children meaningful praise: Thinking back on the most powerful words that have been spoken to me, I have to say that specific, meaningful praise has had the greatest impact on my heart and self-concept. Words from my parents, a teacher, a counselor and my husband come back to me when I am flooded with self-doubt and fear. Authentic, specific words of praise can act like an anchor for your children when the world and their own hearts tell them that who they are is not enough. Here are some important things to remember when praising and encouraging your children:

- Be authentic and honest. Don't lie to your child. He will know you are just using words to try and make him feel better.

- There is always something positive you can say to your child about even the most dismal of experiences. Look for the good and point it out to her. Be specific. Say "It took a lot of courage to try to climb to the top of the rope." Or "I am proud of the way you shook hands with the other team after the game."

- Comparing your child to someone else is not praise. Compliment your child directly, rather than in comparison to someone else. Say "You are a truly talented pianist," rather than, "You played so much better than everyone else."

- Be sensitive to the feelings and needs of all your children. Find opportunities to celebrate their gifts, and spend time with each child to tell them how you feel.

- Take your child's temperament into account when praising her. One child may love it when you make a big deal in public about her spelling bee victory, while another would prefer a private note.

- Don't wait for a special occasion or achievement to honor your child with your words. Celebrate and praise your child just for being himself.

- Victory, success and achievement are not the only opportunities for praise and recognition. Look for and recognize times when your child is compassionate, forgiving, polite, cooperative, gentle, thoughtful, patient, persistent or creative.

If you find yourself constantly nagging or correcting your child, make it a personal goal to thank, encourage and compliment your child more often than you reprimand him. Making discreet tally marks can help you be aware of the overall tone and nature of your words.

Today's Lesson:
Preparing for Parent-Teacher Conferences

In this complex world, it takes more than a good school to educate children.
And it takes more than a good home.
It takes these two major educational institutions working together.

– DOROTHY RICH

Chalk Talk

As a school principal, I remember telling parents, "You are your child's primary educator, and the school is here to support your efforts." I meant every word of it. But I'm not sure I truly understood or appreciated the words, "primary educator," until I had my own children. Even as a teacher, I have concerns about my children's performance in school. I have tons of questions regarding how to best set them up for success in a society that's academically oriented.

Research supports the notion that when parents and teachers work together, everyone benefits; students tend to earn higher grades, perform better on tests, attend school more regularly, have better behavior, and show more positive attitudes toward themselves and school. School programs that include strong parent involvement are also more effective.

In order to successfully build a bridge between home and school, parents need to foster a positive relationship with their child's teacher and other adults in the school environment. A vital part of these relationships is communication. And while communication between home and school may begin on the first day of class, its importance is perhaps most poignant during parent-teacher conferences.

Teacher's Conference

Teachers have your child's best interest at heart and are invested in her educational and long- term success. Strong teachers take pleasure in watching students accomplish goals and meet challenges. I still enjoy hearing about my past students and their accomplishments. Many of my former students have now graduated from college and are moving into the work force or entering graduate school. I feel inspired and proud that I played a small role in their success.

First of all, teachers get nervous about conferences too! They spend between one and three days in back-to-back meetings with concerned and sometimes frustrated parents. The purpose of a parent-teacher conference is not to solve every problem or address every issue. A conference is a jumping-off point for parents and teachers to form a partnership and work together to ensure the student's success.

Teachers want parents to feel empowered and be active participants in both the conference and their child's overall school performance. Research indicates that parental involvement allows teachers to focus more on the task of teaching and spend less time on behavioral issues. Additionally, by forming a relationship, teachers are able to learn more about a student's needs and then better address them in the classroom.

Homework

Before the conference
- Prepare for your child's conference like you would for any important meeting.
  - ◎ Assemble work samples (graded assignments, tests, quizzes, artwork, etc.) and any pertinent information.
  - ◎ Review standardized test scores and work samples, watching for positive and negative consistencies (always doing poorly on math quizzes, consistently performing high on the Social Studies portion of a standardized exam).
  - ◎ Talk with your child (see **www.theanswerkeys.com** for a list of questions you can ask your child).
  - ◎ Prepare a list of questions for the teacher (see **www.theanswerkeys.com** for sample questions).

During the conference
- Arrive on time and be yourself. Teachers want to learn more about students and their families, and conferences are a wonderful opportunity to do just that.
- Listen. Children behave differently at school than at home. Be open to what the teacher has to say. She is there to help, not hinder, your child's academic and social progress.
- Treat the teacher with respect, even if you disagree with an assessment or comment she has made. Wait

until you've heard everything she has to say. Becoming defensive right off the bat will inhibit your relationship with the teacher and prevent you from using your conference time in a constructive manner.

- ◉ If you become frustrated or angry, ask for another conference. Ask the teacher to put something concrete together for you so that you can effectively evaluate what she has said.
- Take notes.
- Make the most of your time with the teacher. Stay on topic. Use this time to discuss your child, not your issues with the school, questions about school policy or general questions you could have answered through email or by phone.
- Review your child's performance and behavior in auxiliary classes as well, and schedule separate conference if necessary (music, PE, computer, etc.). These may be areas where he shines or where you can note consistencies or inconsistencies in behavior.
- Create an action plan. Along with the teacher, make a short list of objectives for your child in each area of development: social/emotional, academic and physical. This will give you focus after the conference is over. Some examples include;
  - ◉ **Social/emotional:** work on shyness, confidence or developing peer relationships
  - ◉ **Academic:** learn to study independently for a quiz or short exam
  - ◉ **Physical:** be able to hop, skip or jump
- Create a plan of action for any follow-up items. This may include a follow-up conference where your child is present. If you are setting goals for performance and/or behavior, it is important that your child be part of the process.

Teacher Toolbox Tip

Making a list of objectives will allow you to provide your child with more focused assistance and enlist the teacher's help where it's needed most. She will also be able to keep you up to date on what is developmentally appropriate for your child at different ages and stages.

After the conference

- Keep your conference notes in a safe, accessible place so that you can refer to them if necessary.

- Involve your child in the process. Share conference notes where appropriate and talk with your child about any objectives you may have laid out with the teacher.

  - Discuss if the objectives are feasible and what your child thinks he needs to do to achieve them.
  - Discuss what you can do to support your child's efforts; tutoring, evaluating activity load, support materials (software, extra books, etc.).

- Implement any action plan.

- Schedule and attend follow-up conferences. Bring your child when appropriate.

  - Enlist the teacher's help with specific issues. For example, if your child is struggling with self-control, have the teacher create a behavior contract to track your child's progress.

- If a teacher has mentioned your child may have vision or hearing problems, make the necessary appointments and report back to the teacher with the results.

  - A teacher can better assist your child if she knows to seat her near the front of the room or can help handle the embarrassment she may feel by a new pair of glasses.

- If the teacher mentioned that she feels your child may have a learning disability, make an appointment to have her evaluated. See lessons on *Attention Deficit Hyperactivity Disorder*, page 149; *Dyslexia*, page 155; and *Autism Spectrum Disorders*, page 160 for additional information.

Early Childhood Programs: The Gateway to School

Early childhood education programs usually have very specific assessment materials with milestones for different points during the year. Preschool and pre-kindergarten programs are geared toward the development of your child's social skills, in addition to exposing them to beginning academic skills. If the school does not provide its list of objectives at the beginning of the school year, ask the teacher for one close to conference time. This will allow you to better prepare your questions. Keep in mind that parents must have realistic goals and expectations for their child's performance. Preschool programs are a child's gateway to school, and his first experience should be a positive one.

answerkeys

Questions for the Teacher

My child's teacher believes my child might have a learning disability. What are my next steps?

- **Don't panic.**
  Having a learning disability is life-altering, not life-ending. Learning differences simply intensify and amplify the importance of one of the most critical jobs of every parent: to help provide opportunities for their child to learn, flourish and thrive.

- **Educate yourself.**
  As your child's most powerful advocate, the more you know the better off you will be. Don't be afraid to ask questions, for example: "Can you give me a specific example of Jeff's 'off-task behavior'?" Making a list of questions for your child's teacher, doctor or other professional can be calming and empowering.

- **Treat yourself as an expert on your child.**
  Make a list of observations about your child that may be relevant. For example, how long it takes your child to complete his homework. Have there been any major changes at home, or any changes in your child's behavior, such as difficulty sleeping or changes in appetite or energy level?

- **Make a plan and take action.**
  Decide with your child's teacher what your next steps should be. This may include whom to speak with, where to go and what materials to bring. In order for your child to receive services and accommodations from the public school system, she will need an Individualized Education Plan (IEP).

I was completely blindsided by the teacher's comments? What should I do?

As a school principal, I always told the teachers that no parent should be surprised at conference time. It was their responsibility to communicate effectively with parents ahead of time and make sure they were prepared for the conference as well. Unfortunately, there are times when the lines of communication break down. Here are some management strategies for when the partnership between home and school does not materialize.

- Schedule a follow-up conference and ask her for concrete examples of what performance and/or behavior she is referring to. Ask follow-up questions to gather as much information as possible. Remember, this is about forming a partnership in order to help your child succeed.

CONTINUED ON NEXT PAGE

Questions for the Teacher

- Bring your spouse or your child's tutor to a follow-up conference. You will have another set of ears that can help you accurately assess your child's performance and implement an action plan for improvement.

- If you cannot find common ground, it might be prudent to make an appointment with the principal. She may be able to mediate the situation and provide clarity regarding academic and behavior standards, as well as school policy and practice.

- All children are bound to encounter at least one teacher they do not care for during their school career. If, however, you find that a situation has become unhealthy for your child, you may want to consider asking the principal for a classroom change. This option should only be considered for the most extreme cases.

Continuing Education

Parents' attendance at conferences drops dramatically as children move from the early grades into middle school and high school. However, studies show that parental participation plays an important role in a child's success throughout school. Don't back away just because your child is getting older and becoming more independent. There are many times when our middle and high school students need parental support more than our little ones. They are facing tougher decisions with tougher consequences, and they need your support more than ever to help them stay on track.

Conference tips for high-school students

- Make an appointment to meet with your child's guidance counselor. Because your child may see up to seven teachers per day, a guidance counselor is likely to have a handle on your child's overall performance. She can also direct you to teachers you may want to meet with individually.

- Use time with a guidance counselor to discuss your child's strengths and weaknesses, and also to discuss potential college or work plans. Knowing where your child stands academically will allow you to help him make better-informed choices about college and beyond.

- When appropriate, bring your child to conferences with teachers or the guidance counselor. Involving him in the process can lead him to develop a stronger sense of personal responsibility.

answerkeys

- With guidance, allow your child to set academic and behavioral goals.
- Find out what support he needs to achieve these goals.

- Make sure you have contact information for all of your child's teachers. You may not use it often, but if you run into an issue or a crisis arises, you will be prepared to deal with it effectively.

- If you see sudden changes in your child's demeanor, grades and/or attitude, consider speaking with coaches or any faculty advisors your child interacts with at school. They may be able to provide you with helpful information if your child is struggling at school.

Cheat Sheet

Behavior Contract: a written agreement about how a child will behave at school. It is usually created by the teacher and agreed to by the student and her parents. Behavior contracts include both consequences for negative behavior and acknowledgment or rewards for positive behavior.

 HIGH FIVE to **Sue Arnold**, third-grade teacher at Holy Family School in South Pasadena, CA. and mother of three.

Sources

http://www.colorincolorado.org/article/19843
http://www.education-world.com
http://www.education.com
http://www.myshortpencil.com
http://www.teachersandfamilies.com
http://www.parenting-child-development.com

Today's Lesson:
Learning Centers

Play gives children a chance to practice what they are learning...
They have to play with what they know to be true in order to find out more,
and then they can use what they learn in new forms of play.

– MR. ROGERS

Chalk Talk

Learning centers are designated areas where children can independently explore specific learning activities. Ask a child about his favorite part of the school day and besides recess, "center time" will probably be the answer. Learning centers or stations are used to reinforce or extend skills that a child has already learned. This allows a child to reference what he has already learned, build upon that knowledge and learn even more. Centers give children a chance to independently practice and explore skills and information through what feels like playtime. Since children learn by "doing," centers should be hands-on, fun, engaging and stimulating as they meet the needs of diverse learners. Open-ended centers encourage investigation and problem-solving while allowing children to use various parts of their brain. They also allow children to connect knowledge to the real world and apply knowledge in new situations.

In your home, you can use centers to foster curiosity in your child. Yes, you want to keep him asking "why" and welcome every question. The hands-on nature of the centers will provide an opportunity for your child to discover some of the answers to his many questions. Putting the time into making exciting and fun home learning centers will help your child move toward independence and create lasting childhood memories.

answerkeys

Teacher's Conference

Look inside an elementary school classroom during center time, and you may see what looks like organized chaos. The children are busy constructively moving about while the teacher may be working with small groups or individual students. In order for learning centers to be productive and successful, teachers must implement routines and reinforce rules for several weeks before students can work independently. Pictures and labels can be posted to show completed activities within each center; these are also helpful to show how each center should look when organized and clean. To eliminate interruptions, the teacher may assign a captain for each center or enforce specific learning center rules and signals, such as the "Ask three before me" rule (ask three others before going to the teacher), or use color coded cups (blue cup on top means center is running smoothly, red cup on top means that center needs teacher assistance). After a few weeks of training, center time runs like a well-oiled machine. The students have built independence—they know where to go and what is expected of them—and they are actively engaged in meaningful learning.

Centers look different from classroom to classroom. They can focus on one subject, various subjects or a theme. When I began teaching kindergarten, an example of a week of non-themed centers included: home living; computer; puppets; sand table; listening, reading and comprehension; math art activity; and a small reading group with me. The students would rotate through these centers and the next week, some of the centers would stay the same, others would change and the story, art and small group skill centers would be new. Many of these centers allowed students to develop social skills and explore, using a vivid imagination. An example of a non-theme-based center may be may be "My Name." The students would:

- Listen to the book, *Chrysanthemum* by Kevin Henkes, and draw favorite part of story
- Make a name necklace with beads
- Cut out pictures in a magazine to represent each letter in their name
- Shape the letters in their name with Play-Doh™
- Go on a letter hunt to find the letters in their name
- Make a name puzzle
- Work with me in small group

Centers have changed over the years. Later in my teaching career, we moved to literacy centers. During that ninety-minute block, all centers were literacy-based. Students would rotate through them and work in small groups, or individually with me. I have also found that kids also enjoy math centers, and they're a great way to differentiate learning. Giving students time for "free choice" learning centers later in the day was always a good way to remind them to stay on task so we wouldn't run out of time.

Homework

When creating learning centers at home:

Get creative! You don't have to spend money or have extra space to create fun, engaging centers for your child.

- Think about the space in your home and how you can utilize different spaces for various learning centers. You can create centers in your child's room, turn your bathroom or kitchen into a science laboratory, go outdoors for some messy exploring, etc.

- Use what you have. Examples of household items that can be used for learning fun: laundry detergent scoop, cookie cutters, coffee can lids for tracing, any size boxes, muffin pans, ice trays or egg cartons for sorting, measuring cups and spoons, cut holes in the lids of plastic containers for paint. Don't have a water table? Use your bathtub. Sand table? Use a shallow sweater tub meant for under the bed. You can put the lid on it and keep it outside when not in use. Need a magnetic board? Use a baking pan or coffee can. White board? Get a small piece of shower board cut at a home-improvement store.

- Make portable centers for on-the-go learning. Keep them in a space that your child can easily access. Store them in a cereal box or shoebox, paper sack or coffee can. Label the centers using simple text or pictures.

Focus on your child's interests.

- Evaluate your child's interests and start there. If your child loves science, begin with a science center. If cars are the latest and greatest, give your child things to build a ramp or racetrack and a variety of wheels. You can still focus on skills he is learning in school. For example, write letters on a piece of paper with lines between each letter. Give your child directions such as, "Park your car in the space that says b."

- Think of how your child learns best—kinesthetic (movement), tactile (create), auditory (speaking and listening), visual (looking)—and try to create centers to explore with all five senses

- After your centers are established and children have engaged in these activities several times, ask them about their centers. Examples: Which is your favorite? What do you like best about your at home center time? Is there a center at school that you might like to try at home?

Create a variety of centers.

- Think about skills and concepts your child has been learning. Each center can be made to target the concept on which you want to focus, but be sure to let your child freely explore and make new discoveries on his own. This will encourage your child to build his imagination skills which will help prepare him for school and life situations.

- Make an appointment with your child's teacher for tips on setting up centers. Ask specific questions such as: "How long should I expect my child to be engaged in the center before he loses interest?"

answerkeys

Cafeteria Line

Art

- **Puppets.** Get crafty and make your own or buy pre-made puppets. Put on a puppet show. Make a stage with cardboard box or perform behind the mattress. If your child loves dinosaurs, make a dinosaur puppet and let him put on a show. Have him write a story about the puppet.

- **Creative crafts.** There are endless possibilities. Have a wide variety of supplies, such as scissors (various kinds), glue, crayons, markers, glitter, paper sacks, pipe cleaners, pompoms, foam pieces, string or yarn, hole punch, stapler, variety of paper (wrapping, newspaper, colored, textured, etc.), beads, magazines, old greeting cards, paint and chalk.

- **Edible art.** Some of my fondest childhood memories are from making things with food. Edible art can be fun to use with a favorite book, seasonal or special interest. If your child is into spooky tales, make a ghost by dipping a cookie in melted white chocolate and use chocolate chips for eyes. If you have just read a Curious George book, make a sandwich look like a monkey using round cookie cutters.

Tool time

- Let your child practice hand-eye coordination with a hammer and nails. Stay close and supervise.

Play-Doh®

- Learn colors, shapes, size, make numbers or letters, stamp sight words, or just manipulate and use your imagination.

- Make your own play clay together. You can make different colors or scents. There are plenty of recipes online.

Puzzles

- Board puzzles to floor puzzles or even crossword puzzles, independently or as a family, puzzles are a great way to use your brain.

- Make your own. You or your child can write and decorate her name or draw a picture and cut it apart to make a puzzle.

Dramatic play

- Use costumes, uniforms, hats, masks, daddy's closet, etc, and pretend! Your child will enjoy looking at herself in a full-length mirror.

Home living

- In the kitchen, have a basket of cooking utensils, measuring cups, spoons and bowls that come out when you make dinner for your child to pretend while you cook.

Building a Bridge

- Give your child a mini broom, dust pan, feather duster, play telephone, etc. You may think, "Do I really do that?" after watching your little one imitate you.

Writing center

- Create a writing center at a desk or table.

- Have various writing utensils and paper, a white board, envelopes, an alphabet chart, a dictionary, and some folders.

- Send letters to family or a pen pal; email friends or family.

- Other fun ideas for a writing center: typewriter, sidewalk chalk, a clipboard for walking and writing, letter stamps. Practice letter writing on a large platter in chocolate pudding or shaving cream on a table.

- Stickers or picture stamps can be fun for writing stories. If your child needs encouragement, look for pictures in magazines or coloring books. Tell a story about the picture. Model this in the beginning so your child can see how you use your imagination to make up stories.

Reading center

- Create a reading center that is comfortable and inviting for your child by setting out pillows or bean-bags, filling shelves with a variety of interesting books, using a lamp, or having stuffed animals your child can read to. If you don't have space for a bookshelf, fill baskets or crates with books.

- Let your child read to a recorder and play it back for him; read with fun pointers like a wand, a whimsical fly-swatter, a microphone or a magnifying glass. Listen to audio books.

- Label things in your home for your child to read. They will love reading familiar words as they begin reading.

Building

- Use a variety of materials and let your child build away with Legos®, wood blocks, bristle blocks, shoe boxes, cardboard boxes or popsicle sticks.

Magnets

- Use a variety of magnets: alphabet magnets, number magnets, picture magnets.

- Take a favorite magnet around the house to find out what is magnetic.

- Make a magnetic fishing pole by tying a string around a magnet that had a hole in the middle. Tie the string to a pole (I used the stick that turns the window blinds.). I made games, such as cutting out fish shapes, writing letters on each one and attaching a paperclip. My students would "go fishing," and match capital and lower case letters or put letters in order as they caught the fish. You could make it work for so many things! Examples: Have questions written on the fish to check for comprehension or just for fun, solve math problems and fish for the correct answer, match colors or shapes.

Bath time fun

- There are many bath time products that make for great, clean fun, such as paint, crayons, magnets and shaving cream.
- Make your own floating flashcards by using Styrofoam plates. Write letters or numbers on them, and put them in order; practice sight words.

Computer

- There are many great sites and games available for children of all ages
- Make sure to preview sites before letting your children explore (see lesson on *Using Computers & the Internet Responsibly*, page 200.)
- Help your child type a letter to a friend or family member.

Share. Give your child the opportunity to talk about her findings and discoveries. Resist the urge to give your child an answer or correct his answer. Being "right" is not always the goal. Part of the fun is the imaginative aspect of the activity. Let him show off a new masterpiece, or give a review of his favorite book.

Continuing Education

Your child will not grow out of learning centers, but into new ones that will explore new interests. Help her dive deeper into interests and hobbies as you transform centers with activities and materials that will challenge her and foster curiosity. These will continue to change as your child develops new passions. Follow her lead, and provide centers that will be important and meaningful to her. We want our children to develop a life-long love of learning.

Mom Tip

Don't stress about the mess! Think ahead, and use easy-to-clean materials like washable paint and markers. Also, be sure to remind your child that she is responsible for cleaning up the center, or it may go away. At times, jump in and have fun playing with your child!

Teacher Toolbox Tip

Many local museums and other attractions have activities on their websites that can be made into fun learning centers. Start by checking in with your local children's museum for ideas and connections. You might be able to visit the museum, learn something new and then extend your knowledge at home.

HIGH FIVE to **Shannon Black,** Reading Specialist in Nashville, TN and mother of two.

Today's Lesson:
How to Build a Home Library

The man who doesn't read good books has no advantage
over the man that can't read them.

– MARK TWAIN

Chalk Talk

Everyone knows that reading is essential to your child's success. But how can you expect your child to read everyday when there is nothing to read? If your DVD collection occupies more space than the books on your child's shelf, then you should consider re-stocking and replenishing your home library. Thinking of books that you loved as a child is a wonderful way to start picking out books for your own kids. I have a worn copy of *The Lonely Doll* by Dare Wright that belonged to my grandmother. I recently pulled it out of a box and flipped through it, amazed by the strength of the memories that the black and white photographs brought back. The very best moment was finding "Betty" (my grandmother's name) written in little girl print and "Jennifer" (my name) in giant letters underneath. I instantly remembered sitting on my grandmother's big brass bed the day she gave me the book and the felt-tipped pens she always used. I immediately dug out my own felt-tipped pen and had my daughter write her name, "Katie," underneath mine. Then I read her the story that had once been read to me by her namesake. There is such beauty and power in shared storytelling. Books are more than objects and educational tools; they are purveyors of wisdom and keepers of memories.

Teacher's conference

When I was a classroom teacher, we regularly had DEAR (drop everything and read) time. Everyone had to stop what he or she was doing and read for a given amount of time. During silent reading time, it was tempting to check my email or grade papers, but I always kept a book at my desk to read along with my students—to show them what it looked like to read silently for a sustained amount of time—and enjoy it. I wanted my love of books to be evident and contagious. Working with students who struggled with reading, it became critical to teach them to love books rather than fear them. If your child is a reluctant reader, you may be facing similar battles at home. Reading aloud to your child is an essential part of this process. It allows him to enjoy books that he may not be able to read on his own yet and to share the story with you. My husband recalls listening to his dad read *The Hobbit* aloud to him while he washed the dishes every night, washing each dish very slowly so that he could hear more of the story. Reading aloud to your children can become a wonderful, memorable time.

My husband and I both love to read, and we both love books—but this love of books looks different for each of us. I don't think I have really read a book until it has been bent, dog-eared, spilled on, and splashed by bathtub water. In my mind, to love a book is to devour it and wear it out. One of my favorite books is my battered copy of *Jane Eyre*, which I've had since eighth grade. The cover is literally falling off.

My husband's love of books is more reverential. He always uses a bookmark, and lays a book on its front cover after reading it to counteract any bending or curling that may have occurred while holding the book open. When giving books to your children, expect their love of books to fall somewhere in the middle of these two extremes. Of course you know that anything given to a child can become a weapon, impromptu potty seat or serving dish, so help your child learn that books are special—not chew toys for the dog. Be sure to choose board books for babies and toddlers. Their chunky size and cardboard pages are just the right size for little fingers, and they can withstand a bit of chewing as well.

It's never too early (or too late) to start building a home library with your family. One of the best baby showers I have attended was a book shower. Everyone brought one of their childhood favorites.

Homework

Assignment #1

Become a reader. Before you concern yourself with what your children are reading, choose a book or two for yourself and read. Don't make a big production out of it, especially if this is a new or infrequent undertaking for you—it won't seem authentic, and your kids, especially older ones, will feel put off and manipulated. Do read where your children can easily see you enjoying yourself.

Assignment #2

Create a book list. Make a quick list of books you loved as a child. Anything from *Corduroy* to *The Chronicles of Narnia*. Start to add some of your old favorites to your family library. Check your parents' shelves to see if they kept any of your old books.

answerkeys

Assignment #3

Visit your local library. Your library is a great, affordable way to check out new authors and discover new interests. Investigate the public library's website. You may be able to search for and request a specific book, and have it delivered to your local branch. No more frustrating, fruitless searches and trips across town. Some libraries will even allow you to download audiobooks from their website for free. Many libraries have story time during the day; your and child and you can listen together to a story being read aloud.

Assignment #4

Commit time to reading aloud. Put your feet up and read to your kids while they fold laundry or do dishes. Read aloud with your spouse before going to bed. Have an older child read to a younger sibling. Play audiobooks in the car.

Cafeteria Line

Set up multiple "libraries" throughout your home. Have special shelves for your personal books, and place them out of harm's way. Make your kids' books readily accessible.

Here are some examples of creative ways to make sure that a book is always within your child's reach:

- Low book shelves or baskets on the floor make great storage for books in your children's bedrooms.

- Stow lightweight books in your diaper bag or child's tote for reading on the go. Put a few books in the car to help long drives go by more quickly.

- Sew book pockets into your child's bed skirt for easy access at night. Placing small bookshelves on the wall beside your child's bed can also encourage quiet, independent reading before bedtime.

- Put children's cookbooks on a low shelf in or near your kitchen to encourage your child to choose a recipe or simply admire the pictures of delicious treats.

- My mother remembers tucking several books into my crib after I fell asleep at night. I would find them in the morning and "read" them, buying her a few extra minutes of sleep. When she heard the third book hit the floor, she knew it was time to roll out of bed.

- Rotate your selection. Organize your books by theme. Put some books away and pull them out at the appropriate season or time. This will help keep things interesting and fresh. Visit your local library to supplement your collection of books. Your child will look forward to special holiday books or books she just hasn't seen in a while. My daughter loves to read my old copy of *Betty Bear's Birthday* by Gyo Fujikawa on the night before her birthday, just as I did when I was her age.

- Ask for and give books as gifts. My goal for next Christmas is to give only books as gifts to my friends and extended family. Easy to order online, easy to wrap...I am practically giddy at the thought of how simple it could be. Encourage friends and relatives to give your children books as gifts for holidays

Important Types of Books to Read with Children*

Psychosocial: Books that address and resolve issues related to social and emotional development are particularly helpful for young children who may not have the maturity or vocabulary to express their fears and frustrations. Look for books that address relationships, emotions, identity, separation and fears. Some of my personal favorites include *Someday* by Alison McGhee and Peter H. Reynolds; *Bedtime for Frances* by Russell Hoban and Garth Williams; *You are My I Love You* by Maryann Cusimano; *Supersister* by Beth Cadena and Frank W. Dormer; and *The Giving Tree* by Shel Silverstein.

Multicultural and Historical Picture Books: Books that help children become knowledgeable about history and culture can be powerful teaching tools. Look for books that demonstrate the beauty and connectedness of all people; socially conscious books; books that celebrate diverse backgrounds; and books that highlight a new culture, country, language or historical time period. Among the books I particularly like are *Bee-Bim Bop!* by Linda Sue Park and Ho Baek Lee; *Yo! Yes?* by Chris Raschka; *Mama, Do You Love Me? and Papa, Do You Love me?* both by Barbara M. Joose and Barbara LaValle; *The Legend of the Bluebonnets* by Tomie dePaola; *Sadako and the Thousand Paper Cranes* by Eleanor Coerr and Ronald Himler; and *Twenty and Ten* by Claire Huchet Bishop.

Language: Books with beautiful language are a delight to read aloud. Even very young children will begin to pick up on the rhythms, rhymes and word patterns in books and begin to read along with you. My children often love to finish a sentence for me or predict what word will come next. Look for books that support oral fluency, vocabulary, patterns of language, grammar concepts, sounds, rhymes and rhythms, the alphabet and poetry. Some of my personal favorites are *Brown Bear, Brown Bear, What do You See?* by Eric Carle; *Allison's Zinnia* by Anita Lobel; *Many Luscious Lollipops: A Book About Adjectives* by Ruth Heller (she has written a book about each part of speech); *Read-Aloud Rhymes for the Very Young* compiled by Jack Prelutsky and illustrated by Marc Brown; *The Real Mother Goose* by Blanche Fisher Wright; and *Alphabet City* by Stephen T. Johnson.

(Continued on next page)

195

answerkeys

Mathematics: Reading books can be a fun and visual way to introduce and reinforce math concepts like symbols, patterns, shapes, numbers, size, counting, comparison, numeracy and measuring. Here are a few wonderful books to read with your child: *One Guinea Pig Is Not Enough* by Kate Duke; *Color Zoo* by Lois Ehlert; *How Much Is a Million?* by David M. Schwartz and Stephen Kellog; and *Over in the Ocean: In A Coral Reef* by Maryann Berkes.

Narrative Books: Storytelling is perhaps the most powerful and compelling part of reading aloud. Narrative books do just that—they tell a story. To build your child's comprehension and captivate her imagination, it is important to read her books that tell a story, conveying a written account of connected events. Fantasy books, folk and fairytale books, and chapter books fall into this category. Some of my favorites include *The Three Questions* (based on a story by Leo Tolstoy) written and illustrated by Jon J. Muth; *The Princess and the Pea* by Lauren Child; *The Paper Bag Princess* by Robert N. Munsch and Michael Martchenko; *Madeline* by Ludwig Bemelmans; *The Chronicles of Narnia* by C.S. Lewis; the *Harry Potter* series by J.K. Rowling; *The Hobbit and The Lord of the Rings Trilogy* by J.R.R. Tolkien, and the *Anne of Green Gables* series by L.M. Montgomery.

Human Differences: Books are a meaningful and effective way to help children learn to value all people, despite and even because of their differences in physical abilities, gender, age and background. Look for books that highlight how all people, no matter how seemingly different, share common concerns and experiences. These are some of my personal favorites: *Now One Foot, Now the Other* by Tomie dePaola; *Swimmy* by Leo Lionni; and *Free to Be You and Me* by Marlo Thomas and friends.

Scientific: Books are a great resource for helping your child begin to explore the natural world. Science books can help her notice, wonder, and ask questions about the world around her. My list of books to recommend includes *From Seed to Plant and The Honey Makers* both by Gail Gibbons; *Parts* by Tedd Arnold; *Mister Seahorse* by Eric Carle; and *D.K.'s Eyewitness Books* series (various authors).

Aesthetically Pleasing: Beauty can capture the heart as well as the eye, and books are no different. Books with beautiful illustrations can help your child learn about line, shape, space, color, texture, composition and perspective. Some of my favorite children's book illustrators include Susan Jeffers, Eric Carle and Ezra Jack Keats. Each year, the American Library Association awards the Caldecott Medal to the artist of the most distinguished American picture book for children. Ask your librarian or bookseller for help finding Caldecott winners to see some magnificent illustrations.

*adapted from "Eight Books that Will Change a Child's Life: A Summer Institute on Children's Literature" by Patsy Cooper and Julia Watkins and the staff of the Rice University School Literacy and Culture Project

Mom Tip

- Do a little research before handing a book to your child. Some books, especially those marketed to "young adults" may contain subject matter that you think is inappropriate for your child. Ask a librarian or your child's teacher for suggestions. Many local and chain book stores have knowledgeable staff members who can recommend books and also keep you informed of new books by certain favorite authors. Read the book yourself before giving it to your child. When in doubt, stick with the classics.

- When building your home library, choose books that you will also enjoy. Nothing is more miserable than suffering through a story that you can't stand.

- You can browse online at www.barnesandnoble.com, and instead of having a book shipped to you, ask them to hold it for you at the location of your choice. They will even send you an email when it's ready—just walk to the cashier and pay for it.

- Used book stores are excellent resources for finding great deals on books and making a little money on books you don't need or want. Garage sales can also be gold mines. I found a treasure trove of books in the garage of a retired school librarian, and bought them for $1.00 each. Also, many public libraries have an annual book sale to purge their shelves of unwanted books. Most are hardbacks in excellent condition and sell for a few dollars or less.

197

Tips from the Librarian: How to Choose Books for Your Children at every Age

Birth to age three:
- Buy sturdy board books and put them on a shelf your child can reach easily. Try not to worry about them getting ripped or broken.
- Read to your child every day. Take turns picking out books so you can introduce new books, and your child can also exert some control over the content.
- Look for fun books with bright pictures or rhyming words.
- Most children this age love to hear the same book over and over. They are comforted by and learn best from repetition.

CONTINUED ON NEXT PAGE

answerkeys

Ages four to six:
- By age four, kids have the stamina for longer storybooks (to be read aloud) and short early reading books that they can try to read when you are both ready.
- Early non-fiction books are also appropriate. Try to find books about topics they like, e.g. firemen, construction, zoo animals, princesses. Look for large clear illustrations and only a couple of sentences per page.

Ages seven to eleven:
- As kids learn to read, keep a good mix of read aloud and graduated early reader books. Second or third grade can be a time to transition to reading shorter chapter books to your child. Read a chapter a night to keep her engaged.
- Keep in mind that non-fiction reading skills tend to lag two years behind fiction skills until the end of high school. Without a plot to "drag" you through the book, it's harder to stay focused, and there are often unfamiliar vocabulary or reading words. Be sure that dinosaur book is in your child's comfort zone or they will be easily frustrated.
- The main goal is to continue to build reading stamina by finding things your child likes to read. "Series" books, a monthly kid's magazine subscription, or reading the sports page every day are good ways to get kids excited about reading.

Ages twelve to eighteen:
- One of the best sources of information is YALSA (Young Adult Library Services Association), a division of the American Library Association. The website includes updated and archived booklists for many topics and book awards, as well as information for parents and teachers. http://www.ala.org/yalsa/
- A "Young Adult" or YA literature designation does not mean the book is age-appropriate. Always check for reviews online or look through the book to be sure the content is appropriate, especially for middle-school students. Some YA fiction is very explicit.
- If you have concerns about the content, use it as a starting point for a discussion with your child. Talking about a book can be easier than discussing reality and may lead to healthy, meaningful family conversations. Use open-ended questions: "What did you think?" "What if you had a friend who behaved like that?" or "How would you feel in that situation?"
- Literature can be an escape for all ages, and more importantly, a way for kids to sort out what they are thinking and put their own values to the test in a hypothetical situation. Just because they are reading about a teen character making poor choices doesn't mean they plan to make bad choices, too.

CONTINUED ON NEXT PAGE

Building a Bridge

Tips from the Librarian: How to Choose Books for Your Children at every Age

- For struggling or disinterested readers, choice is the most important factor. If they have an interest, let them follow it. Help them find appropriate books about planes, fashion design, baseball, whatever hooks their interest. Struggling though a "classic" you chose will only discourage them.
- The goal at this age is to create proficient readers, capable of tackling any text that is put in front of them. Newspapers, magazines, comics, graphic novels, novels and non-fiction texts can all be part of a rich reading life.

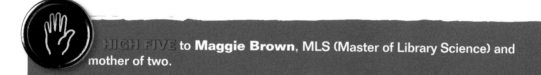

HIGH FIVE to **Maggie Brown**, MLS (Master of Library Science) and mother of two.

Sources

Center for Education. http://centerforeducation.rice.edu (accessed July 17, 2010).

Cooper, Patricia M. "Eight Books that Will Change a Child's Life." Lecture, A Summer Institute on the Uses of Children's Literature from School Literacy and Culture, Houston, TX, July 21, 2009.

Today's Lesson:
Using Computers and the Internet Responsibly

*Teach a man to fish, feed him for a day. Teach a man to use
the Internet, and he won't bother you for weeks.*

– UNKNOWN

Chalk Talk

I admit it. I'm a tech geek. I love the computer. I love the Internet. I love making photos albums on my Mac, downloading tunes onto my iPod and making slide shows with iMovie. Blogging? Love it! Facebook? I'm addicted! There are nights I've spent so much time on the computer that I go to bed with a crick in my neck and an ache in my shoulders. Call me a glutton for punishment because I wake up the next morning and do it all over again!

Part of what keeps me interested in the Internet is the vast amount of information available and the evolving world of technology. The World Wide Web offers access to things that were once unavailable to the general public. I will confess that I actually enjoy looking at satellite images of the homes my family has lived in over the years. I love to peruse real estate in exotic places while simultaneously learning how to caulk my bathroom sink.

If you were born in the 1970s or earlier, you probably remember eight-track tapes, record albums and cassettes. You may remember one of the first home computers, the Apple 2E. With its black and white graphics, it was the hottest item on the market. Fast-forward to the technology that is available to children today, however, and it will likely make your head spin. From handheld devices to MP3 players, children are being brought up in a technology-fueled environment. And chances are, regardless of whether or not you possess a love of technology, your child does or will when he gets older.

Computers are an integral part of our society and a significant part of many children's academic and social lives. There is no doubt about it, the Internet is a valuable tool and can greatly enhance a child's educational experience. Having access to so much information, however, also brings with it the task of navigating the

Building a Bridge

Internet responsibly in order to avoid potentially severe pitfalls. When children have access to the Internet, some of these risks include:

- Exposure to inappropriate material
- Harassment and bullying
- Viruses and hackers
- Legal and financial problems
- The risk that your child might agree to meet someone who isn't who he claims to be online

The federal Children's Online Privacy Protection Act (COPRA) was created to help protect kids online. It's designed to keep anyone from obtaining a child's personal information without a parent knowing about it and agreeing to it first. Even with federal protection, however, a child's first line of defense against online predators, bullies and con artists is her parents. As parents, we need to teach Internet responsibility because kids can access computers in a variety of places—friends' homes, the library, school, via laptops and on cell phones. And while security measures at home are a positive step, teaching sensible behavior in conjunction with those measures will give you greater peace of mind.

Teacher's Conference

One of a school's most important jobs is to keep students safe. One of the ways this is done is by monitoring student use of the Internet. Schools may use several different tools to ensure that students are safe when using the Internet on campus—Acceptable Use Policies (AUP), codes of conduct, firewalls and, most importantly, adult supervision.

Even with all these measures in place, it's still possible for a school to experience a breach. When I was a school principal, we had an incident in which a student came across pornographic material, even though we had a filtering system, code of conduct, acceptable use policy and adult supervision. Although the eighth-grade student accidentally accessed the inappropriate site while she was searching for a statistic about breast cancer, it brought to light the risks involved in allowing minors access to the web.

Fortunately, the technology teacher was able to use the incident as a segue into how to appropriately conduct an online search; we all learned a valuable lesson that day about the benefits and drawbacks of having Internet access on campus. This story underscores just how important it is for adults who care for children to always be vigilant when it comes to the Internet.

answerkeys ──────────────────

Homework

For households with children under the age of five (including kindergarten)

- Think about the future. Talk to your spouse about how much exposure you want your child to have to computers, TV, related games and the Internet.

- Create a usage plan that is age-appropriate. Research regarding when children should begin using computers is mixed. My ad vice is to err on the conservative side and follow the general guidelines for television usage; none under the age of two and no more than one hour per day for children ages two to first grade (both TV & Internet usage).

- If you plan to use a firewall or blocking service, look into what systems might work for you and your family. See our resource list for some age-appropriate options, or talk to friends about what they use in their homes.

- Talk to your child's teacher or day-care provider. If they offer computer class, make sure their computer use policy is in line with what you want for your child.

For households with children in elementary school (first to fifth grades)

- Educate yourself.
  - ◎ Take a ride on the Information Superhighway.
- Google yourself.
- Conduct some searches.
- Get familiar with the web.
  - ◎ Take an introductory course to strengthen your skills.
  - ◎ See **www.theanswerkeys.com** for some wonderful websites for parents, teachers and children.
- Set up a computer-savvy home.
  - ◎ Keep the computer in a common area, not in individual bedrooms. Insist that laptops be used in a common area as well.
  - ◎ Make sure you know your child's passwords and what sites he uses on a regular basis. Check out the sites and make sure they're appropriate.
  - ◎ Install a firewall and/or blocking software.
  - ◎ Set up a family email account so that you can monitor the emails your child sends and receives.
  - ◎ Set up "hours of operation" for the computer. Make sure they are during a time you are home and can monitor child usage.
- Check the Acceptable Use Policy and Code of Conduct for computer usage at your child's school, and make sure they are consistent with your values.
  - ◎ Review them with your child and make sure he understands both the school's expectations for his behavior and the consequences for misusing the Internet.

Building a Bridge

Kid-friendly sites should include the following:

- **Live moderation. This means the site monitors all live chats and online activity on the site.**

- **Chat filters that block inappropriate language and the ability to write numbers (this blocks a child from giving out her phone number).**

- **A requirement that a parent's email address be given for registration (this will help you track your child's online activity),**

- **Options for pre-canned chats for young users. This means that the conversations are pre-written and children click on them, as opposed to being able to write their own words**

- **Accreditation from BBB, CARU and Connect Safety (see website for more details)**

⊚ Use the school's policy as a starting point for your home Acceptable Use Policy. Many school and district policies have begun to include Internet usage both on and off of campus. This is a great way to address usage in a variety of areas (library, friends' homes, etc.).

⊚ Make an appointment with the principal, teacher or technology director to ask questions about the school's policy and their strategies for keeping students safe.

- Create a family Acceptable Use Policy (AUP)

⊚ Children need to know you are watching them and can access their accounts at anytime.

- They also need to know and understand the consequences if they…

⊚ Bully online.

⊚ Enter sites you have deemed off limits.

⊚ Open an email or social networking account without your permission.

⊚ Send or purposefully receive inappropriate pictures or information (this can include racist information or sexually explicit material, hate speech material or anything else you deem inappropriate).

For households with children in middle and high school

- Make sure you have followed the guidelines outlined in the elementary age homework section.

- Open the lines of communication with your teen.

- Follow through with tough consequences if your child violates your Acceptable Use Policy. Your child will live if he doesn't have access to the computer for a specified period of time. A good teacher will support this if you explain to her that your child was not using the Internet appropriately.

  - Have your child pay you to type an assignment or paper.
  - Drop him off at the library to do research. All of the information he needs is available offline, too.

- Periodically check your child's settings and history folder. Even Google your child from time to time. Teenagers are still children who often do not use the best judgment. And while I encourage parents to allow their children to feel the sting of consequences from making a poor choice, I also don't want a photograph or immature post to keep a child from getting a summer job or worse, keep him out of the college of his choice. Some high schools, colleges, volunteer organizations and employers will use Google and social networking sites to evaluate applicants. You will be better prepared to guide and assist your child if you do, too.

Words of Wisdom for Middle & High School Students

- **Think about what you post.** Once it's on the web, it's out there for everyone to see. A wise friend of mine once said, "Don't put anything on the Internet that you wouldn't want to see broadcast on the ten o'clock news." Additionally, if you wouldn't say it to the person's face, why would you put it online?

- **Don't talk about personal issues with anyone.** This is especially true if it's a new friend or someone you met through a chat room but have never met in person. Unfortunately, many people lie about who they really are on the Internet. Sharing personal information with someone you don't know can lead to trouble.

- **Don't give out personal information to anyone online.** This goes for your address, the name of your school or anything else that might allow someone to find you without your knowledge or consent.

- **Avoid in-person meetings.** Never agree to meet someone you've met online. Again, because you have never seen the person, you don't know if he is who he says he is.

- **Make sure you utilize the privacy settings on any social networking sites you use.**

Mom Tip

If you catch your child sending inappropriate messages or bullying another child online, send a clear message that it is wrong. My suggestion, and one that I used when I was a school principal, is to make the child who wrote the message read it aloud for you to hear...insults, foul language and all. From a developmental perspective, many children do not have the cognitive ability to truly understand how hurtful their words are to others. They may not even know the meaning of some of the words they use. Because they don't have to see or hear the person's reaction as they would in person or on the phone, many kids don't realize the impact their words can have. And it's only after they read those words aloud and hear what they really sound like to others that the point hits home. It is not just about the consequence, but also about the teachable moment.

Cafeteria Line

- Don't ever use a recognizable photo of your minor children on a public site. Never list geographical locations for family events where the general public can view them.

- Be mindful of what you choose to view and/or download from the Internet. Bookmarking adult sites or downloading adult photos can fall into the unsuspecting hands of your child. Even some retail/ fashion sites may have content or images that you wouldn't want your child to see.

- When posting photos on family web pages or social networking sites, never post a photo of someone else's child without her approval. No parent wants an unauthorized picture of her child on a site where she has no control over who sees it.

- Credit card information, etc. should not be stored online for automatic purchasing purposes. Many kids are smart enough to access a site and start ordering.

- Use an Internet browser that allows you to check its history folder (Mozilla Firefox, for example). If your child continually violates your Acceptable Use Policy, consider removing the computer until he demonstrates that he's mature enough to handle the privilege of having a computer in the house.

- Be mindful of applications that are available for phones, especially those with access to the Internet. Don't overlook the importance of monitoring your child's phone. Children can easily download inappropriate material.

◎ The following devices have Internet capability: Nintendo Wii, X-Box 360, Playstation 3 and the iPod Touch. (This is not an exhaustive list).

• Buy your child the simplest phone available. If you take away the temptation, he is less likely to make poor choices. Children don't always use the best judgment, so don't put your child in a situation he is not mature enough to handle. Save the camera and Internet accessible phones for college.

Teacher Toolbox Tip

Many kids know how to erase a computer's history folder. There are software programs that will keep a running log of all sites accessed on a certain computer within a given time frame (week, month, etc.). In addition to teaching your child the values of honesty, integrity and how to follow directions, installing one of these programs will allow you full access to what your child is viewing online.

Continuing Education

Parents are the first line of defense when it comes to their children and exposure to inappropriate material or negative choices online. Stay on top of your child and be vigilant in your efforts to protect him. Understand, however, that despite your best efforts, your child may still come into contact with some negative aspects of the Internet.

Warning signs of inappropriate online behavior
• Spending long hours on the Internet, especially at night.
• Phone calls from people you don't know. Hang-ups when you answer the phone.
• Your child receives gifts, letters or packages from people you don't know.
• Your child suddenly turns off the computer when you enter the room.
• Your child suddenly withdraws from family, friends, sports or other hobbies.
• You discover unusual or unauthorized charges on your credit card.

If you believe your child has developed an unhealthy attitude toward the computer, seek the professional advice of a licensed therapist. A strong therapist can help you get a handle on the extent of the problem and set up a plan to address the issue with your child.

Questions for the Teacher

What is the appropriate age for my child to begin visiting sites with chat rooms?

This is really more of a question for Mom and Dad, than just the teacher. All four of us agree that there's no hard and fast age at which children miraculously become mature enough to enter chat rooms and interact responsibly with other site users.

Look to sites for basic guidelines and enforce those rules. For example, Facebook has a minimum age usage of fourteen. Your child should not have a profile if she is younger than fourteen. Differentiate between sites where you have some control over who sees your information (ex: Facebook) and chat rooms that may be open to anyone and allow access to your personal information.

How do I handle bullying?

Please see the Cyberbullying section of lesson plan on *Approaching Bullying*, page 21.

What is "Sexting"? Do I even want to know?

"Sexting" usually refers to teens sharing sexually explicit photos via cell phone, but inappropriate photos are also being transmitted via the web. The practice can have serious legal and psychological consequences, so you do need to know what it is and some details about how it can affect your child.

- "Sexting" is illegal. Sending, receiving or forwarding sexually explicit material of minors is considered to be the distribution of child pornography. Children under eighteen have been prosecuted for this offense.

- If your child is caught sending or receiving "sext" messages, deal with it immediately through both conversation and consequences. If feasible, enlist assistance from the parents of other kids involved in the incident.

answerkeys

Words of Wisdom

Cars are fantastic! They give us freedom. They allow us to visit new and exciting places. In many ways, having access to the Internet is similar to having a car. Surfing the net gives us a certain amount of freedom, and provides us with opportunities to meet new people and see new places. And it allows children to visit online locations without parental supervision.

Unlike the Internet, however, children are not allowed to get a driver's license until they reach the legal age and demonstrate they are capable of handling such a large and potentially dangerous piece of machinery. Parents need to prepare their kids for responsible Internet usage as they would prepare them to drive a car. The Internet is full of potential hazards and requires that people have the appropriate knowledge, maturity and training to use it properly. Don't allow your child to "drive the Information Superhighway" until he is ready to take on the responsibility that comes along with that new-found freedom.

Cheat Sheet

History Folder: a file on one's desktop that contains all of the sites accessed on that computer for a specified period of time.

HIGH FIVE to **Carrie Pacini**, founder of www.thetastefullife.com, the Mom2Summit, and mother of two; and to **Ben Jones**, CA, CEO of www.sixdegreegames.com.

Sources

http://www.safekids.com
http://www.cnn.com
The Center for Missing and Exploited Children (http://www.missingkids.com)
http://www.kidshealth.org
http://www.thexlab.com
http://shine.yahoo.com (social networks)
The Federal Bureau of Investigation website (http://www.fbi.gov)

Today's Lesson:
Fostering Independence

If you raise children to believe they can accomplish any goal
or task they decide upon, you will have succeeded as a parent, and you will
have given your children the greatest of all blessings.

– BRIAN TRACY

Chalk Talk

My parents have probably given me a thousand gifts throughout my lifetime: birthday presents, Christmas gifts, graduation presents and "just because we love you" gifts. Zeroing in on the most precious one, then, might seem like a daunting task. But, truthfully, one thing pops right into my head without a moment's hesitation: the gift of independence.

I still remember my first major piano competition. I was so nervous, my hands were ice cold as I drew them out and my fingers hit the keys. I'd like to say that my anxiety melted away and that I performed Bach like a virtuoso. Unfortunately, that scenario couldn't be further from the truth. I bombed so hard you could hear a pin drop when I finished—and not in a good way. I was crushed.

As I walked back down the long center aisle of the auditorium, I looked at my parents, tears streaming down my face, and saw nothing but encouragement and acceptance in their eyes. That's when I knew I could pick myself up, dust myself off and begin again. I stayed with the piano, and while I never made it to Carnegie Hall, I still enjoy playing.

My point is that from a very young age, my parents encouraged me to be strong and independent. By offering me experiences that forced me to put myself out there and see what I was made of, they helped me build my self-confidence and develop an individual identity I would never have achieved on my own. They celebrated with me when I succeeded, and they comforted me when I didn't.

answerkeys

All parents should want their children to grow up to become mature, responsible and independent adults. Living at home at the age of thirty-five is no one's idea of success, is it? Unfortunately, much of today's parenting advice seems to undermine the goal of raising independent children. Parents are told they need to coddle their children, keep them from failing, and basically avoid any of life's harsh realities until absolutely necessary. But it's completely unrealistic to think we can shield our children from hurt, ugly words and pain.

Teacher's Conference

Teachers strive to foster independence in their students. From peer tutors to classroom jobs, they use a myriad tools to help students develop a strong sense of self. Nothing is more satisfying to a dedicated teacher than to hear the following year's teacher comment about how her new class is so independent and mature.

I used to employ the "ask three before me" strategy in both my first-grade and middle-school classrooms. I required that students attempt to solve a problem or answer a question three different ways before asking me for help. This allowed me to teach them several important life lessons.

- They learned to advocate for themselves and develop their own voices.
- They developed the ability to choose different strategies to solve problems, thus improving their critical and abstract thinking skills.
- They also learned that it was okay to turn to an adult for assistance, but only after they had exhausted their own resources.

Homework

There are many simple, well-planned strategies you can use at home to help your child become independent. Here are some ideas for different age groups:

Birth to crawling
Help your child learn to entertain and comfort himself.

- Swaddle your child and place him on his back in the middle of a play mat. As he gets a bit older, or if your child does not like to be swaddled, place him on his back in the middle of the play mat.
- Hang toys from the play mat bar, and turn on some soothing music.
- Make sure the area is safe and free of potential hazards.

- Allow your child independent play or rest time on the mat for five minutes.

- Feel free to stay close by if you're nervous, but you should be far enough away so that your child cannot see you or hear what you are doing.

- If your child begins to fuss before time is up, walk over, soothe him with words and touch, and then walk away again.

- Gradually increase your time away in five-minute (or less) increments until your child can stay unattended for about twenty minutes.

- When you return from your time away, show your child cuddly affection and praise her for doing well while she was on her own. Although children at this age have a limited understanding of spoken language, they do understand positive cues and reinforcement. Talking to your child about learning to entertain herself will help her reach the next milestone.

You may think this is crazy and won't work, but I used this strategy with both of my kids and they have developed into children who can amuse themselves with either independent or dual play, without my having to intervene or entertain them for extended periods of time.

The underlying idea is that your child learns, from a very young age, that he can be alone and comfort or amuse himself. The *On Becoming Baby Wise* series, written by Gary Ezzo and Robert Bucknam, provides even more information about this technique.

Mom Tip

Swings, vibrating chairs, ExerSaucers® and other contraptions that help entertain little ones are awesome, and I highly recommend them—in moderation! Using an outside source to constantly soothe your child will only lead to his dependence on that device for comfort. Do you have a friend who can only get her child to sleep if she straps him into his car seat and drives him around the neighborhood? Children need to learn to comfort themselves, and the bonus is that teaching your child to comfort himself will also promote healthy sleep habits.

Crawling to two years

- Take a look at the kinds of toys that inhabit your home. Do they simply provide instant gratification, or do they challenge your child to make choices and solve problems? If you notice a lack of simple puzzles, stacking toys or building blocks, start adding them to your repertoire. But don't accumulate too many toys, as this can cause overstimulation.

answerkeys

- Sit on the floor and teach your child how to use unfamiliar toys. Practice with him, and then give him an opportunity to do it on his own. Once he learns how to use a new toy, encourage him to use it independently. Model and practice using the toy as needed, but always have the goal of moving away for a period of time so that he can do it himself. Resist the temptation to jump in and offer assistance at the first sign of frustration. He can learn a great deal through a bit of trial and error.

- Ask your child questions or give directions that require him to think of an independent answer. "What color are the blocks?" or "Can you show mommy where the square is?" will make him think about his answer and apply the knowledge he has acquired through activities and reading.

- If your child is constantly looking to you for answers or to play with a toy, redirect his behavior, both physically (move him toward the toy or bring him back into the room with the toy) and verbally ("Why don't you stack the rings by size?"). Consistently and lovingly steer him toward independent play. Don't get frustrated. Practice makes perfect, and you can rest easy knowing that many children need lots of practice!

- Two is a wonderful age to begin having your child clean up his toys. Many kids at this age are eager to show off their independence and often want to do things by themselves. Sing a song or count to twenty-five while your child picks up toys. Encourage him to count with you or to pick everything up before your song is over. Keep your expectations reasonable, knowing that if he puts one to two toys away by himself about half of the time, you're off to a successful start.

- Use constructive feedback. Acknowledge your child's feelings, reward positive choices, and encourage him to make the right choice again the next time.

Children who can entertain themselves, solve their own problems, come to their own conclusions, overcome life's challenges and fight some of their own battles are in a better position to succeed in life because they possess the necessary skills to tackle adversity on their own.

Two years to Kindergarten
- Continue supplying your child with toys that challenge her, both physically and mentally.

- Provide your child with "alone" time everyday. Allow her some room to explore, breathe and use her imagination without you watching her every move. Encourage her to color at the table, work a puzzle, or build an amazing tower all on her own. Make sure to praise her efforts, no matter how small.

- Use a chart or some other system to track progress. If your child still has difficulty playing independently, set a timer. Reward him with some time together with you when he meets a new time milestone. Talk to him about how good it feels to accomplish something on his own.

- Schedule play dates. Learning to share, negotiate and solve age-appropriate problems is a great way to encourage your child to develop his own identity.

Remember to keep your expectations in check. You may do all of the above and still have a child who needs consistent handholding, encouragement or praise. That's okay. From birth to Kindergarten, it's all about teaching and not as much about results. If you keep things consistent, you'll see your child grow and mature in ways you never thought possible.

I bought a wooden puzzle of the United States when McKenna Kate was two-and-a-half years old. By that point, we had already moved from California to Florida to Minnesota, so I wanted her to begin to understand something about the places we had lived. I taught her how to use the puzzle. We practiced. I encouraged her to make little strides on her own. I taught her the states where we lived and where they went on the puzzle. We practiced some more. I was amazed to find her constructing the entire puzzle on her own about six months later. It took that period of time for her to develop the ability to independently work the puzzle. Now, she is a puzzle wizard and loves putting them together all by herself. She has even begun to teach her brother how to work puzzles, too.

Elementary school

- Create and maintain a routine to keep your child organized and aware of what happens next. Kids are more likely to do well if they feel in control. Although it may seem odd, providing your child with structure will actually encourage him to become more independent (see lesson on *The Importance of Routines*, page 167.)

- Help your child learn to advocate for herself. Use occasions, like when you're in the car together, to run through certain situations with your child. "How would you approach your teacher if she graded you wrong on an exam?" is an excellent question. Teaching your child to respectfully speak to authority figures is a wonderful way to encourage independence. Walk through different scenarios and the right or wrong ways to address them. Use both real life situations your child is currently facing ("How should you approach your coach about giving you more playing time?") as well as hypothetical situations your child might encounter ("How would you deal with a class bully?") so that he is prepared for whatever comes his way.

- Resist the urge to solve all his problems. This is a tough one, but we all know that we learn more from our mistakes than from our successes. When he forgets his homework, let him experience the consequences. Falling down at seven or eight carries a much smaller consequence than failing a college course because he never learned to turn in assignments on time.

- Even in elementary school, negative events and consequences can be teachable moments. If your child fails a quiz because he didn't budget his time effectively, work with him before the next test. I am an advocate for allowing children to experience life's bumps and bruises; but as parents, we are also responsible for equipping our children with the tools they need to succeed.

answerkeys

Middle school and beyond

Ah, the minefield otherwise known as the teen years. Many children are itching to gain their independence during this time, but have a hard time expressing themselves and figuring out how and where to fit in.

- Ask yourself, "Do I really know my child?" Talk to your spouse and discuss what you really know about your son or daughter.

- Watch your child for a week and try to remain silent—in other words, don't criticize. Within reason, allow your child to be himself for that week. Watch. Observe. Discreetly take notes if you need to. The idea is to better understand who your child is becoming and how you can continue to support his growth as an independent thinker and doer.

- Ask yourself how important it is to win every battle. Many problems with this age group occur because both the parents and the kids want control. Inventive hairstyles and trendy outfits are temporary and changeable. Support your child's attempts, within reason, to figure out who she is and who she wants to be. Very few, if any, adults have the same hairstyle or taste in clothing as they did in junior high or high school. Pick your battles and save your absolute "no's" for things with more permanent or life-changing consequences.

- Talk with your child. Many parents don't think their middle- and high-school aged children are listening. They are.

- Listen. Listen without judgment, without shaking your head, shuddering or peppering the conversation with your own thoughts. Slow down, keep your two cents to yourself, and really listen. Paraphrase back what you heard from her, and ask if you understood her correctly. Teenagers often feel that no one understands them. If your child feels you accept her and actively listen to her, she will make better independent decisions AND come to you when she really needs help.

- Understand that you probably won't agree with all of your child's choices. You may want her to take Spanish as an elective, but she might choose music. Delve deeper. Talk with her about her choice. Learn something new about her. Instead of placing your wants and expectations on her, step back and appreciate her desire to take a different path. A painful, yet necessary, part of successful parenting is allowing our children to make independent choices. You are there to be her guide.

Cafeteria Line

- If your child has trouble settling down or constantly tries to get your attention, set an egg timer for a predetermined time period and have your child engage in independent play that does not include media (TV, computer, hand-held games, etc.). Gradually increase the time as he becomes more comfortable entertaining himself.

- Consider enrolling your child in a mother's day out, preschool or pre-Kindergarten program, especially if she is having trouble being independent from you. A small amount of time away can do wonders for a child who is have trouble developing her sense of self. Experienced teachers will tell you that children often act differently at school than they do at home. This may provide your child with a wonderful opportunity to grow into her own little person.

- Provide your child with opportunities to become personally responsible for his belongings and actions. Place a checklist of items he needs to bring to school everyday (draw pictures if he is too young to read—backpack, lunch/snack, sweater, homework, etc.) in his room or near the front door. Teach your child how to follow the list. Practice together. Empower your child to do it himself, and resist the urge to re-mind him or go back and get things he's forgotten. Allowing him to take responsibility for his things and actions will help him become more independent. This concept can also be applied to sports gear and equipment.

- Encourage your child to engage in creative activities that allow her to identify who she is. Collages are a great way to bring out your child's personality. Make one with your child and then discuss what's on it. I bet you will learn a lot about who your child is and who she wants to become.

- Have your child plan a family event. Allow her to de-sign it the way she wants—food, decorations, music, etc. Give her an opportunity to take on some respon-sibility for something she is excited about. When children are actively engaged in an activity, they try harder.

- Take your child on a road trip. This is a wonderful way to reconnect and re-energize after a week of hectic schedules. Spending time together without the stress of outside commitments can help strengthen the bond you have with your child.

Teacher Toolbox Tips

Use tips from other lessons in the book. Here is a quick checklist of activities that will help your child become independent.

- **Create a home routine (see lesson on *The Importance of Routines*, page 167).**
- **Assign your child chores beginning as early as two years old (see lesson on *Chores*, page 75).**
- **Allow your child to begin making simple choices with minor consequences at a young age (see lesson on *Choices*, page 12).**
- **Encourage your child to engage in unstructured "alone" time each day.**
- **Set up a study station to encourage your child to learn to complete homework/ study on his own, only asking for help when necessary (see lesson on *Creating a Study Station*, page 135).**
- **Encourage your child to engage in volunteer activities that take the focus off of his needs and desires. Seeing himself as part of a larger world will help him grow into a more independent and empathetic adult (see lesson on *Promoting Service Projects & Volunteerism*, page 46).**
- **Use positive and negative experiences to teach your child how to deal with adversity.**
- **Accept your child for who she is, eccentricities and all!**

answerkeys

Words of Wisdom

There is a difference between fostering independence and forcing your thoughts and opinions onto your child. You can be an involved parent without cramping your child's personal style. Part of building her sense of independence is to support her efforts to become an individual with her own thoughts and opinions. Remember that independence and the confidence it gives your child is one of the greatest and most rewarding gifts you can give him.

HIGH FIVE to **Sue Arnold**, third-grade teacher at Holy Family School in South Pasadena, CA and mother of three.

Sources

Bucknam, Dr. Robert, and Gary Ezzo. *On Becoming Babywise*. Treasure Publishing, 2007.

Mogel, Wendy. *The Blessing Of A Skinned Knee: Using Jewish Teachings to Raise Self-Reliant Children*. 2006. Reprint, New York: Scribner, 2008.

Duckworth, Angela L. & Seligman, Martin E.P. "Self-Discipline Outdoes IQ in Predicting Academic Performance of Adolescents." *Psychological Science* 15, No. 12 (2005). https://camcom.ngu.edu/Science/PSYC/PSYC%202385/Dr.%20Dobson%27s%20Spring%20 2009%20Course/Article%20Review%20I/Biological,%20Cognitive%20and%20Social%20Development%20Articles/Self%20 discipline%20and%20academic%20success.pdf

Jaramillo, J. "Vygotsky's Sociocultural Theory and Contributions to the Development of Constructivist Curricula." *Education* 117(1996).

Today's Lesson:
Making & Keeping Friends

The better part of one's life consists of his friendships.

– ABRAHAM LINCOLN

Chalk Talk

That familiar expression "quality, not quantity" comes up over and over again in parenting—especially as it relates to the time we spend with our precious little ones. This rule also applies to the friendships our kids make along their journey to adulthood. Children who develop healthy, caring relationships with their peers are likely to do well in school and in life. Don't be concerned if your child only has one or two best buddies. Research has shown that it's the ability to form meaningful connections, not the number of connections that counts.

As a mentor mom to my church's preschool mothers, I have come across many worried and frustrated moms whose children are struggling socially. Some preschoolers are very shy, while others may be impulsive or aggressive. Social skills are not something that a parent should simply address as the need arises. Having an attitude of "kids will be kids" when your child comes home crying from school is the same thing as teaching your child to swim by throwing him in the deep end of the pool. It's painful and not very effective.

These days, parents invest hours and countless dollars on teaching their toddlers "ABCs" and "1, 2, 3s," plugging them into "brainy" videos and playing classical music. Teaching social skills is just as important as teaching academic skills. While some kids may be naturally outgoing and friendly, others may need some practice and direct teaching in order to make and keep lasting friendships. So how do we help our children form deep, healthy relationships when we cannot make and keep friends for them? We offer ways to prepare them for different social situations, teach respect and compassion, and what to do when there are bumps along the road.

answerkeys

Teacher's Conference

As a classroom teacher, I have seen many young children make small mistakes like leaving out a number when counting, or stumbling over a beginning sound while learning to read. Watching my students struggle with their studies never bothered me nearly as much as seeing a child left out of an activity or sitting alone at recess.

Strong teachers have known for years how important socialization is for the growth of the whole child. Children with strong social skills have the tools to form healthy friendships and maintain a high level of self-esteem. The reverse is also true. Students without basic social skills, such as following directions, sharing, taking turns, or showing respect for others and their property, will likely suffer from low self-esteem, have few friends and come to dread their eight-hour school day. If basic social skills aren't taught early, the "socially challenged" child may go on to suffer from isolation and depression.

In the classroom, I witnessed common social struggles such as:

- Invading another's personal space. Many kids don't know how much personal space is appropriate. Space is different when you are talking to a close friend or to someone you've just met. How close should you get while standing in line? Some kids need to be taught this.
- Difficulty sharing and taking turns.
- Speaking without thinking. Some kids don't have a good filter and will say whatever comes to mind.
- Too much competitiveness or aggression.
- Inability to read body language and facial expressions of others.

The key to helping your child is to figure out how he is struggling and where the breakdown is occurring. Then work on this skill at home with role play—talk through the steps, and model the best response.

Children's social education is as important as their academic education. As parents, there are many things we can do to help our children develop social skills. When our child does poorly on a spelling test, we have a good idea of how to help. For instance, have him write the words three times each and make flash cards. Having a plan of action makes us feel useful and generally brings results. Approach your child's social struggles in the same way. If you teach your child to treat others with kindness and respect at an early age, you set him up for success. When problems arise, and they will, respond quickly and consistently. Have a plan.

Homework

Assignment#1

- Set age-appropriate reasonable goals. It isn't reasonable to expect your child to be completely free of social struggles. You simply want to equip your child with the skills necessary to face the inevitable challenges.

Assignment #2

- Take action when problems arise. If your child is struggling to make and keep friends, identify your child's specific trouble spots. Try to pinpoint exactly how things are going wrong in a social setting. Observe your child interacting with his friends before you try to intervene.

Assignment #3

- Recruit your child's teacher. At conferences, ask the teacher what she observes at school. If she sees problems, try not to make excuses. Instead, ask for suggestions and the names of classmates who might be good playmates for your child. Teachers are happy to help and want to see your child succeed with his peers.

Long-term Projects

- Model the desired behavior. Remember, those little eyes are always watching you. Do your best to demonstrate the behavior you want to see in your child. Remember, have fun and be patient.

- Teach basic courtesy. During your child's first year say "Hi" and "Bye" for her, and wave her little hand until she can do it on her own. When your child is two and three, make sure she says "Hi" and "Bye" herself. For ages three and older, model and encourage eye contact and a smile. Others will give your child lots of praise for such a nice greeting. This positive feedback builds confidence in relating to others.

- Teach respect and thoughtfulness for others. "Please" and "Thank you" truly are magic words. They can turn a child's new acquaintance into an adoring fan. Manners are not like Sunday clothes—they need to be used both inside and outside the home. I always try to say "Please" and "Thank you" to my children, and they do the same for me and their siblings.

- Teach compassion. For example, if a friend is unable to attend your child's birthday party, drive to his house and let your child deliver a party favor. If your neighbors are going out of town for the weekend, let your child feed their dog. By doing so, he'll get positive feedback from the neighbor, which will encourage him and build his self-confidence. For preschoolers, praise is a great incentive. As children grow older, they will learn to be kind without expecting anything in return.

- Teach your child to wait his turn. When my son, John Henry, was big enough to hold a door, he would do so for people when we were at a restaurant, church or the grocery store. By doing so, he received

219

praise "for being a little gentleman." This reinforced the behavior I wanted to see in him as a man and made him feel like a big boy. Our house rule is to always put our guests first. When he had friends over he allowed them to take the first turn or pick the first cookie. Play dates run more smoothly and friends are eager to be invited back. Children who are always allowed to put themselves first have a difficult time making friends.

- Teach your child empathy and take the focus off her. Sometimes your child just walks into someone else's bad day. Teach her to always try to give people the benefit of the doubt. Talk through possible scenarios that could have happened occurred morning. For example, maybe Cassie missed the bus, or got in a fight with her brother before school. Taking the focus off your child will make her feel better and not add to the conflict.

- Teach your child to "walk away" with confidence. There will always be children who seem to delight in upsetting others. An effective strategy is to say "So?" and walk away. For example: Say your child's shirt has dinosaurs on it and another child tells him that dinosaurs are for dumb babies. What should your child do? Say "So?" and walk away. If he doesn't react, it's not much fun for the teaser. Teach him not to stand around and display his hurt feelings. Instead, teach him to leave without appearing bothered. Offer different scenarios, and let him practice saying "So?" and walking away.

- Teach problem solving. Listen and help him develop a plan. On your weekly trip to the park, for instance, your child finds all the swings occupied and gets upset. At his eye level tell him, "I understand you love to swing and I see that you are disappointed, but the swings at the park are for everyone. Let's think about what our choices are."

  - Tell him he could stand by the swings and wait so that he's next in line.

  - He could ask a friend to play on something else with him and hope that a swing frees up later.

  - Then ask him, "Which do you choose"? Assure your child that he will have another opportunity to swing next week. If your child makes a good choice, tell him how proud you are of him. Praise him for waiting his turn and for playing nicely with other friends. If he starts screaming and crying, warn him that you will both will leave the park if the inappropriate behavior continues. If he ignores your warning and keeps screaming, take him by the hand and go home. Try again next week.

Mom Tip

Research has found that the number of friends a child has is not nearly as important as the quality of those relationships.

Very few people are born with a natural ability to become the "class favorite." Therefore, as parents, we need to prepare our children at an early age by talking about how one's choices and behavior affect others. Create frequent and regularly scheduled play dates so that your child can interact with children his own age. Provide opportunities for your child to have fun while practicing appropriate social skills.

Cafeteria Line

Here are some fun games and helpful strategies that you can implement with your child.

- **Smile with your voice.** This is what we call the telephone manners game. My daughter, Whitley, was so excited when she was finally allowed to answer our home phone. This meant that she was well-practiced and ready to greet others with a smile in her voice. Good phone manners are important. My children all enjoyed playing the phone game, where I would call them on their toy phone several times a day pretending to be a plumber, teacher, school friend or even Grandma. They would think my different voices were so funny! Whitley enjoyed learning to use a "smiley voice" as she called it. "Sehorn residence" followed by "May I ask who's speaking?" Then she would ask the caller to please hold while she got her mother. As I picked up the phone, the caller usually commented on what a sweet little receptionist I had. Remember, safety always comes first. Teach your child about phone safety; good manners are just one part of this important skill.

- **Play the eye color game.** As your children get older they will start to want to order for themselves. This is an excellent opportunity to practice making eye contact when you are speaking to someone. When your family goes out to dinner, allow your children to politely order for themselves. As soon as the waitress leaves, ask your children who can guess the server's eye color. Whoever guesses correctly gets to choose the dessert for the table. Making eye contact when speaking shows respect for others. Keep in mind that for particularly shy children it may be just a glance while ordering. That's okay, it's a start.

- **Organize social events.** Host after-school activities, play dates and sleepovers so you can watch your child's social skills in action. Never embarrass your child if he makes a mistake. Instead, say, "Let's talk over here." Step out of the sight of others and then speak in a low voice at his eye level. Discuss what happened, make sure he understands, and then let him return to the group.

answerkeys

- **Be the chauffeur.** Whether carpooling to and from school, or driving to Tae Kwon Do lessons, this will provide you with another opportunity to bring your child together with other kids. Volunteering to drive on field trips also gives you valuable information about what's going on in your child's world.

Questions for the Teacher

What if my child is...?

Painfully shy

- Don't push your child. It will only make things worse.
- Try to create situations in which your child can be friendly without having to say much. For example, talk to your child's teacher about letting her bring doughnut holes for the class. At lunch, she can walk around and pass them out. Pack fun cartoon or party napkins in her lunch box so she can give them out to friends—enough for everyone. This can start easy conversations between children. Embrace baby steps.
- Organize a play date with a child whose temperament and interests are similar those of your child.
- Teach your child to smile when she meets others. Sometimes this is a good replacement for a hello.

Bossy

- Instead of having a play date at your house, have it on neutral ground like a neighborhood park. This prevents fights where "MINE" is the word of the day.
- Talk to your child in advance about how other people do not like being told what to do. Ask her if she likes being bossed around. How does it make her feel?
- Role-play with your child taking turns, sharing and listening to others. Read books about bullies and being bossy.
- Play a simple board game that involves structured turn-taking. Discuss and agree upon the rules of the game before starting.

Overly Aggressive

- Teach her to keep her hands and feet to herself at all times and to respect other people's personal space. Always follow through with the consequences, and use your judgment about whether the physical move was malicious or just impulsive. Malicious moves warrant immediate consequences.
- Have play dates with children of equal size and temperament. For example, if your little tough guy has two older brothers, you may not want to start by inviting over the shy boy from next door.
- Choose low-key activities like board games, art projects and activities that allow for plenty of personal space.
- Stay close by to help.

Continuing Education

I am lucky enough to be the mom of two teenagers: my son, John Henry, who is seventeen, and my sixteen-year-old daughter, Murphy. I truly enjoy both of them. They are well liked by their peers and are able to make meaningful friendships. That is not to say that they are perfect or don't suffer from the same pitfalls as other teens. Getting through middle school and high school isn't a breeze for anyone. My kids have endured changing schools, making new friends, peer pressure, braces, hormones and rejection.

And they have turned out to be awesome individuals. People often ask me what I did to raise such kind, well-adjusted teens. Over the years, my answer has remained the same. First, I worked to create a firm foundation of social skills—the same ones presented earlier in this lesson—and I started when they were very young. I demonstrated and taught the desired skills, and then practiced. Over and over. And I kept it fun and positive. Next, I found a loving church that supported my family's values. My children have enjoyed being a part of our youth group and participating in mission projects over the years.

Even if your teen's social skills are firmly in place, there's still more you can do to help:

- Reassure your teen that she already knows how to make friends because of the friendships she has made in the past.
- Give your teen as much control as you can over wardrobe and hairstyles.
- Help your teen manage his homework routine. He needs time for fun and friends.
- Be a good listener. Try not to jump in with advice too quickly.
- Encourage your teen's interests and activities. It's a great way to meet new friends.
- Get involved at their school and church. Support their activities with your presence.
- Make your home a place that your teen and his friends want to be. Be available to supervise discreetly. Have your child's friends over to dinner and find opportunities to get to know their parents.
- Lastly, the most important thing you can give your teen is unconditional love, affection and support. Let her know that you love her no matter what.

answerkeys

Words of Wisdom

Prepare your child for the path, not the path for your child. We can't control what the world will throw their way, but we can teach our children how to deal with what they are thrown. Deliberate and meaningful parenting starts by teaching your child early on the social skills she needs to navigate her world.

Be honest with your child. Forget about pretending to be perfect. Let her know that growing up isn't always easy. We all experience rejection and get our feelings hurt from time to time. Share stories of struggles you've had while making friends as a child. Encourage her to choose friends who are positive and who make good choices.

HIGH FIVE to **Mary Hollis,** Executive Director, Cornerstone United Methodist Preschool, Houston, TX and mother of three

Sources

"Adolescent Health and Wellness: Starting High School : Helping your Teenager Adjust." Dr. Paul.
http://www.drpaul.com/adolescent/highschool.html

Wise, Nicole. "Helping Kids Make Friends." Family Fun.
http://familyfun.go.com/playtime/helping-kids-make-friends-701344/

Bauler, Gabriella. "Help Your Child Make Friends."
http://familyfun.go.com/playtime/helping-kids-make-friends-701344/

Parker-Pope, Tara. "What Are Friends For? A Longer Life." *The New York Times.* (April 20, 2009),
http://www.nytimes.com/2009/04/21/health/21well.html

Poole, Carla, Susan A Miller, EdD, and Ellen Booth Church. "Ages & Stages: All About Me." Scholastic. (January, 2006),
http://www2.scholastic.com/browse/article.jsp?id=3429

Frost, Jo. *Supernanny: How to Get the Best from Your Child.* (New York: Hyperion, 2005) Reference pages 40-43.

Today's Lesson:
Attention-Seeking Behavior

The way for a parent to get attention is to sit down and look comfortable.

– LANE OLINGHOUSE

Chalk Talk

"Mommy, come see my Play-Doh® cookies!"
"They look delicious, Emma."
"I can't find my rolling pin."
"It's right here."
"I can't find the pink cookie cutter."
"Here it is."
"I don't want Play-Doh,® I want to paint."
"I'll get the paint set as soon as I feed Elizabeth."
"Will you paint a flower for me?
"Mommy, Mommy, MOMMY!"

Does this sound like your house? If it does, don't worry. This is normal. All children need attention and approval. However, attention-seeking behavior can sometimes be more than annoying; it can be a real problem. Children are smart, and we teach them what does and does not work by our response to their actions. As soon as a toddler realizes that negative behavior gets her what she wants, then you're sure to see a lot more of the same misbehavior. Young children may whine, scream, hit, bite or throw themselves on the floor to get what they want. If this behavior is not handled properly, children will use this negative behavior to control their parents' every move and eventually become a nuisance to everyone around them. To create a positive change, you have to be calm, patient and consistent.

answerkeys

Teacher's Conference

A teacher is responsible for the academic needs and welfare of an entire classroom of children. Nothing drains her energy faster then one or two students demanding her full attention. An experienced teacher knows that she must get negative behavior under control in order to get on with the business of teaching.

I distinctly remember a precious little boy named Jack in my pre-K class who would blurt out answers and talk over the other children. He would push and shove to get the red marker at the art table. Instead of one pump of hand soap, he would pump half the dispenser, creating a slippery, bubbly mess. But the hardest thing was that he couldn't make a single mark on his paper without calling me to come see what he'd done. I'm exhausted just remembering it! The good news is that he and I worked together to change his negative behavior. By December, he was able to work independently, and I was confident that by May he would master the necessary skills to handle the challenges of Kindergarten.

Strategies used in the classroom translate beautifully into your home. Use these steps as a starting point, taking into consideration your own child's needs.

- First, I recognized that Jack's negative behavior hadn't come about overnight; he'd had four years to master his demands for attention. Be patient. It will take time and consistency for your child to "un-learn" behavior that has gotten him results in the past.

- Every morning I would review the class rules and how to appropriately get a teacher's or classmate's attention. Teachers know that teaching a skill without reinforcing, role-play and practice is a waste of time. Practice, practice, practice. Show your child the polite way to get your attention.

- I set up a system to reward Jack's and the other students' positive behavior. When your child uses the skills you have taught her, respond quickly and with lots of enthusiasm. Show her that a polite request will get quick results. (See lesson on *Chores*, page 75, for ideas about reward charts.)

- This was a good start for Jack, but he also needed to be reminded and redirected several times during the day. As long as I was consistent, I knew I would see continuous improvements in his behavior. Be consistent. As tempting as it is to give in to your child's whining and interrupting, you will lose valuable ground by taking the easy way out. Only give him the attention he seeks when he behaves appropriately.

- I also gave Jack a job each week. One week he passed out the lunchboxes and the next he was the patient door holder. After lots of praise, I saw his confidence and independence grow. Give your child a special job to encourage independence. A sense of accomplishment will lead to your child to try doing things on his own. He shouldn't always need your help or supervision.

- Lastly, and most importantly, if Jack was patient and had a good day I would give him five minutes at the end of the day to sit at my desk and tell me all about his art work. (He loved art.) His desire for attention was normal. He just needed to know how to channel it appropriately. Find special time every day to give your child undivided attention. If he can expect to spend quality time with you every day, then he may be less needy when you are trying to prepare dinner.

Homework

These are great techniques to use when your child engages in attention seeking behavior:

- Make a list with your spouse of the top three behavior issues you plan to work on together. Start small, and keep it simple. For example, work on helping your child keep her hands and feet to herself, stop whining, and stop yelling for you inside the house.

- Don't drop everything and run every time your child calls. Teach him that there are other people and situations that need your attention as well.

- Don't give in to negative behavior, such as whining, begging, screaming or hitting.

- Catch him doing something good each day. When he is playing independently, get down on the floor to give him a little hug and tell him how much you like how he plays with his toys.

- Give your child special time each day. On busy days, it may only be a ten-minute cuddle and a story…. but that's okay. Quality over quantity.

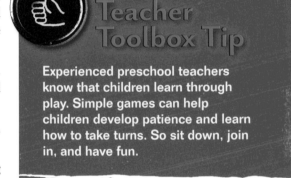

Teacher Toolbox Tip

Experienced preschool teachers know that children learn through play. Simple games can help children develop patience and learn how to take turns. So sit down, join in, and have fun.

Cafeteria Line

The most effective defense against negative attention-seeking behavior is giving your child your time and attention. Take pleasure in simple activities. Enjoy the simple times life offers you to spend with your child. Here are a few ideas:

- Sidewalk chalk
- Play in the sprinklers.
- Play board games. They're great tools for teaching kids about rules, taking turns and good sportsmanship. Read books on topics like patience, good manners, and kindness and sharing.

- At home spa treatments manicure/pedicure
- Backyard insect hunting
- Geology adventures, rock collecting
- Cooking
- Picnic at the parks

answerkeys

Questions for the Teacher

What can I do to help stop my child from biting?

- Many children between fourteen months and three years go through a biting phase that usually ends as soon as they are able to communicate their feelings and needs with words.

- Be patient as you work through this phase. Your frustration or anger can aggravate the problem. Take comfort in knowing that many children bite.

- Stay calm and give a firm, immediate response. If your child bites at daycare or school, enlist the help and support of his teachers. See if you can pinpoint when, where and who he is biting. If there is a pattern to his behavior, work to develop prevention strategies with the teacher.

- Take proactive steps to help your child deal with anger and frustration. Help him find safe and productive ways to express his feelings. (See lesson on *Anger Management*, page 36.)

- Give him extra love and attention if you notice the biting started after a major life change, such as a death, a move, birth of a sibling, divorce or starting at a new daycare.

What should I do when my child bites another child?

- Stay calm, and act quickly.

- First, give the child that has been bitten your full attention. Express your concern so your child sees you showing sympathy for the victim.

- Firmly tell your child that he is never allowed to bite anyone. EVER. Teeth are for chewing food not for biting people. It hurts.

- Explain to your child that the other child is crying because he hurt her when he bit her. Tell him he will now sit in Time Out, and when his thinking time is over you and he will talk.

- After several minutes in Time Out, get down on his level and talk about why he got frustrated and how he is never allowed to bite. Explain to him how we use our words to tell people when we are sad, angry or need help. (See lesson on *The Proper & Effective Use of Time Out*, page 41, for a complete guide to using it effectively.)

- End with a hug and reassure him that you still love him very much.

How do I handle it when my child kicks or hits?

If your child is hitting or kicking, handle the situation in the same way as above. You might say "Hands and arms are for hugging, or legs are for jumping and running not hitting and kicking." Tell him he must keep his hands and feet to himself because it hurts to be hit or kicked.

What do I do when my child has a tantrum and throws himself on the floor?

- First, make sure that he can't hurt himself or others. Move anything that may get damaged.

- If you are at a play date or store, calmly pick up his noodle body and wrangle him into the car seat and go straight home. (Leave your groceries if necessary) It may be a good night to order

CONTINUED ON NEXT PAGE

228

pizza. If he throws a kicking fit and you can't pick him up, stay calm. Just walk around the edge of the aisle in the store so you can see him, but he can't see you. When the tantrum subsides or ends, take him by the hand and go straight home. No words needed.

- If you are at home, try to stay calm and always walk away. Don't give him an audience. Remember, there should only be one hysterical person in a room. Make sure it's not YOU.

- Forget about trying to reason with him. He isn't listening, and you are wasting your breath. Wait until the tantrum passes to talk about what upset him and what a better solution might be.

If you respond consistently to your child's tantrums, you should see them disappear in time.

My child's whining is driving me crazy. How do I get her to stop?

- Children are results-driven. Teach him that you will not give in to whining.

- In the classroom, I would always tell my students that I couldn't understand their words when they whined. I gave the impression that whining was a foreign language to me. For example, you might say, "I would love to give you your sippy cup, but I cannot understand you when you whine".

- At home, I would repeat the whiny irritating voice back to my child, and she would burst into laughter and also become a bit embarrassed.

Here's the bottom line: Never honor a whiny request. But always respond to a polite patient request, even if the answer is no.

My son has started using bad language. What should I do?

- Do not allow bad language in your home. Even young children will pick up bad words if they see they get a big reaction.

- A nasty word spoken by an angelic toddler can be funny, but don't laugh. It will only encourage more bad language. For the very young, ignoring it can work wonders, too.

- Try to find out where he picked up those bad words. Listen to yourself more carefully, especially in traffic or when something goes wrong at home.

- Monitor the music he listens to and the TV shows he watches.

- The first time, give him the benefit of the doubt—he may not even know what some crude words mean. Talk about how important it is to know what words mean. Say something like, "That's an ugly thing to say, and we don't talk that way in our family. If I hear you use it again, you'll be sent to Time Out."

- Set firm limits with consequences when bad language occurs.

answerkeys

Continuing Education

Strategies for Older Children:

Younger children are not the only ones who engage in attention-seeking behavior. As a mother of two teenagers, I know they, too, can give you a run for your money! If your child chooses to engage in risky activities or displays behavior that is harmful to him or others, you should consult your pediatrician for a referral to a licensed therapist. If, however, your child is engaging in behavior that pushes the envelope or just your buttons, here are some strategies you can implement to help alleviate attention-seeking behavior;

- Establish a carefully thought-out plan with your spouse to address common teen pitfalls (smoking, experimenting with alcohol, poor grades, staying out past curfew).
    - When trouble arises, (and it will), implement consequences that involve your child's currency. You are more likely to get positive results if the consequences are swift, consistent and appropriate.
    - Older children and teens need accountability in order to become reasonable adults. Follow through with the threatened consequences. You are only as good as your word.

- Be your child's biggest cheerleader. Older children need praise just as much as our younger ones. Celebrate their accomplishments with enthusiasm, and support them with your physical presence. Even though your son may act as if he couldn't care less that you attend his basketball game, he does care. Be present!

- Involve other family members. Does your child respect his grandparents or have a favorite aunt or uncle or youth minister? If so, enlist their help to rein in your child's behavior. The more a child cares about someone's opinion of him, the more likely he is to behave in a manner that's going to please that person.

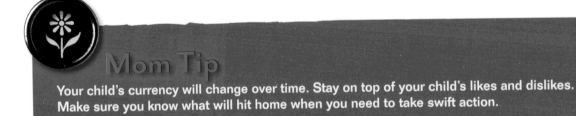

Mom Tip

Your child's currency will change over time. Stay on top of your child's likes and dislikes. Make sure you know what will hit home when you need to take swift action.

Words of Wisdom

All children thrive on attention from their parents. I know how hard it is to carve out chunks of undivided attention for your child. But understand that this time doesn't need to be super structured or fraught with expectations—your children just want to be with you. I don't think I have cooked a dinner or cracked an egg on my own since Whitley was two or three years old. Since I have to cook dinner anyway, I might as well make it a special time with my child. When you are washing a load of clothes, let her throw in everything that is blue or pour the soap in for you. I have found that a parent's positive attention is the cure for most children's negative behaviors.

HIGH FIVE to **Randi Raizner, Ph.D.**, child clinical neuropsychologist and mother of three.

Sources

"Child Behavior Challenge." Nickelodeon Parents Connect. (April 16, 2009), http://www.parentsconnect.com/questions/child-behavior

"How to Handle Attention-Seeking Kid?" Ygoy. (March 13, 2008), http://parenting.ygoy.com/2008/03/13/how-to-handle-attention-seeking-kids/

Frost, Jo. "*Supernanny: How to Get the Best from Your Child.*" (New York: Hyperion, 2005) Reference pages 34, 73-83.

"Handling an Attention-seeking Child." Family Education. http://life.familyeducation.com/behavioral-problems/punishment/42962.html

McCormick, Tim and Sal Severe Ph.D. *How to Behave So Your Children Will Too!.* (New York: Viking, 2000)

Today's Lesson:
Car Talk: A Classroom on Wheels

A mother's role is to deliver children obstetrically once,
and by car forever after.

– PETER DE VRIES

Chalk Talk

I love my car. I love that it safely holds my kids and all their gear. By the end of the week, the floorboards sometimes look a bit like my son's bedroom—covered in socks, balls, loose papers and whatever treasures have been found on the playground that week. I must admit that if we got stranded in a snow bank, an unlikely event in Texas, we could surely survive for three days on all the half empty juice boxes, water bottles and goldfish wedged between the seats.

But my wheels do more than deliver my precious cargo. What I love most about my car is that it is a rolling classroom where I share important information and ideas with a captive audience. Even better, the car gives my children a place to share what's on their minds. In the car, they have my full attention—no phones, computers or chores to interrupt the conversation.

Teacher's Conference

Even if you aren't a teacher by profession, you're a teacher by virtue of being a parent. You are your child's first and most influential teacher. Use the time you spend in the car to your advantage. There are endless ways to use these valuable hours in the car to promote academic skills, reinforce social skills, and set appropriate expectations for behavior. What's more, as your kids grow older, you will covet this precious time together as a chance to get to know them better.

Building a Bridge

Teachers love to impart meaningful information to their students. Most don't just leave teaching at the classroom door at three o'clock. My husband will certainly tell you that at times, when we were on a family vacation, it felt a little like a class field trip, with constant checks, drills and instructions before the fun started. I guess that explains why my car has been a natural extension of the classroom.

Car time is connection time. Looking back over the countless hours I've spent in the car, I have come to realize that many of my most meaningful conversations with my children have taken place while driving. My son is not a "Let's sit down and have a heart-to-heart talk" kind of guy. By nature, most boys like to be engaged in an activity while they are talking. As a teenager, our heart-to-heart connections have sometimes come while he was fiddling with the radio or glancing out the window. Now that he's off to college in a few months, I look back and cherish those times.

So even when I am fortunate enough to not be in the car, and I notice that one of my children seems bothered or particularly quiet, I'll say, "Hey, do you want to go get a drink or an Icee with me?" Over the years, this has become their cue that for the next twenty minutes or so, they will have my undivided attention. They usually confide in me about what's bothering them before we return.... although sometimes, I need to take the long way home.

Sometimes, just plugging the kids in can be tempting, especially since cars today come with DVD players, headphones and all kinds of electronic gadgets. Make hard and fast rules for watching videos and playing handheld games in the car. Do not allow your children to simply tune out. Use this valuable time to reconnect with them instead.

Homework

Volunteer to drive carpool. Being in the driver's seat with your children and their friends gives you a daily or weekly opportunity to know what's going on with teachers, upcoming assignments, friends, bullies or who has a crush on whom. Carpooling also allows you to see how your child interacts with her peers.

What's more, carpooling can be just plain entertaining. One time, when I was driving four kindergarteners home, I listened as the girls chattered on about Barbie and their new school shoes; the boys, on the other hand, stuck to two main topics: poop and fighting animals. "My dog pooped in the living room" was followed by "My baby brother peed in the tub last night" and then fits of laughter. Before I could redirect the conversation, one asked the other, "What would happen if a silverback gorilla fought an African elephant?" The good news is that as boys get older their conversations tend to be more about trucks, sports and classmates.

As your children enter middle and high school, carpooling continues to give you a peek into their lives. I learned that the quieter you are, the more freely they talk. Sometimes it's like they forget you're in the car. If you turn down the radio and tune in, you will hear a lot of what is going on in your child's life.

answerkeys

The Car Talk technique:

Below is an example of how I review appropriate behavior before we exit the car:

- Never unbuckle a seat belt or open a door until all of the expectations for their behavior have been discussed and you have checked for understanding. Do an oral fill-in-the-blank test. It's quick and the children think it's fun. (Sometimes I sing it. This gets their attention and makes them laugh.)

- "Whitley, while we are in this restaurant you are not allowed to get out of your __(chair)__ and run around. We also must use our inside __(voices)__ when speaking. Other people will be enjoying their dinner, and we would not want to disturb them. Your uncle invited us to dinner tonight and it is important that we use our __(good manners)__ and remember to __(thank)__ him for dinner before we leave."

- Check for understanding. "Now before we go in, can you tell me what you are not allowed to do and what kind of voice we need to use in the restaurant? Also, whom will we be thanking for dinner tonight? Awesome job, thank you for remembering."

- Praise and expect success. "Your dad and I are always so proud of you. You always have such nice manners. Thank you. After dinner we may have time to get ice cream if our evening goes as planned."

234

Assignment#1

Start today, take charge and set a positive tone in your car. Get off to a good start, not rushing or speeding in the morning. This de-stresses your child's morning and ensures a peaceful ride to school. Setting the tone for the day is as important as a good breakfast.

Examples of setting a peaceful tone:

- Hang your keys by the door.
- Charge your cell phone the night before.
- Have all backpacks, lunchboxes and homework ready by the door.

(For more tips, see lesson on *The Importance of Routines*, page 167.)

Assignment #2

Set age-appropriate expectations for any situation. An ounce of prevention ("car talk") is worth a pound of cure. Next time you are on your way to Grandma's house, church, a birthday party or anywhere else, discuss the appropriate behavior and your expectations for that particular situation.

On the occasions when appropriate expectations are not met and misbehavior occurs, then it's time to implement swift and well thought out consequences:

- Take your child by the hand, give a quick "good-bye" and drive straight home from the party.
- If you happen to be four hours away from home, at Grandma's house, find a quiet area and place your child in Time Out.

(For ways to approach this issue, see our lessons on *Discipline Versus Punishment*, page 29, and *The Proper & Effective Use of Time Out*, page 41.)

As far back as I can remember, my children and I have used this Car Talk technique. Wisely using the few minutes of drive time, along with the minute before we get out of the car, has greatly improved our behavior.

By "improved behavior" I mean, it greatly reduces the number of times I had to use excuse myself and my child from the table for a talk, or repeat the constant reminders of what I thought should have been clear by now.

Assigment#3

Start a meaningful conversation with your child on your next leisure drive when you expect to be in the car for a while. Take a chance. You may be surprised by what you learn and how great and wonderfully unique your child has become. Avoid questions that elicit 'yes' and 'no' answers. Ask more open-ended questions. This will encourage more discussion.

For example, "I also had to read, *To Kill a Mockingbird* in high school. What did you think about the ending?" or "Your fourteenth birthday is coming up next week. How would you like to celebrate?"

Mom Tips

- **Plan ahead to avoid the drive-thru junk food routine. Pack a cooler with sandwiches, fruit and veggies, or whatever healthy treats you have on hand. For those twenty minutes between soccer and ballet, stop at a park along the way for an impromptu picnic and some much needed down time. It saves money and teaches healthy eating habits.**

- **Bring your child a healthy snack or treat when you pick her up from school. She will appreciate this, and it will help her to relax and put her in the mood to share about her day.**

- **Be patient. Silence can sometimes be a good thing. Your child may be testing you to see if you are really willing to listen and keep her issues confidential.**

answerkeys

Cafeteria Line

In the car, make the most of these valuable minutes (or hours). When I found myself spending more than two hours a day shuttling children to and from three different schools, the teacher in me began finding ways to use this time to our advantage. Here are some ideas for using car time as teaching time:

Babies & toddlers

- Play music. Small children love fun and silly music.
- Sing songs about rhyming, colors, animals, sounds and other fun subjects.
- Talk to your child about what is outside the window: animals, different vehicles, trees, stores and schools.
- Roll down the window and give names to the different sounds you hear: birds, sirens, horns, rain, motorcycles or even squeaky brakes!
- When baby makes a sound, you say something in reply. This "game" lays a foundation for conversational turn-taking.

Preschoolers

Play I Spy with your child's color and letter of the week. Use what you're child is learning at school. Check with your child's teacher to learn the color and letter of the week, and look for them as your drive. If this week's color is yellow, count the number of yellow cars you see on your way to school. If the letter is "B," have her point out all the road signs, billboards and storefronts that have a "B" in them.

- Point out signs and letters, stop signs, gas stations and restaurants — anything with letters and shapes).
- Attach information to the seat backs for your child to look at while riding. Post your cell phone number so she can learn it. Jennifer's daughter Katie, learned Jennifer's cell phone number this way. You could also do shapes, letters or money (one dime = two nickels).
- Put age-appropriate books in the backseat pocket for your child to read.
- Talk about your neighborhood, who your neighbors are and who lives in each house you pass.
- Start discussing directional words, such as left and right, under, over and through.
- Discuss opposites: stop/go, in/out, fast/slow.
- Sing fun songs (ask your child's teacher what songs they sing at school).
- Expose your child to other languages and classical music by playing educational CDs

Building a Bridge

Elementary schoolers & older children

- Some school material, such as math facts, telling time or spelling words, can be reviewed orally—but make it fun, not more homework.

- If your dashboard has a digital clock, ask how many minutes until the next hour.

- Brainstorm different ways to stay organized with schoolwork.

- Make up some Mad Libs or short stories. Have your children take turns filling in the blanks with nouns, adjectives, colors or places.

- Have a Spelling Bee. See who can spell the most words correctly. Don't forget the grownups. Bring a small dictionary for word ideas.

- Twenty Questions. Think of an object; it can be anything. The first question the player will ask is: "Is it a person, place or thing." The player can ask any 'yes' or 'no' questions. Try to ask questions that help narrow down their ideas until they are able to guess the object. If the child can do it in less then twenty questions, they win!

- Keep the latest copy of *Guinness Book of World Records* and some joke books in your seat pocket. Children love these.

- If your car has a compass, talk about direction. North, south, east, west. Ask things like, "We drove west to get to school. What direction will we drive to get back home?"

HIGH FIVE to **Dr. Elwanda Murphy,** retired Natchitoches Parish Superintendent of Schools, Natchitoches, LA and mother of four children, including me.

Sources

Smith, Laurel. "Car Travel Games for Big Kids," (December 15, 2009), http://www.momsminivan.com/bigkids.html

Authors' Acknowledgments

Heather

Thank you to Lucy, Ellen and Kathleen for opening the door and giving us this amazing opportunity. I would like to thank my husband, Stephen, for believing in me and walking with humor and love in our ever-changing parenting journey. To Maya, for adding the perfect spice to our love story and for showing me how to be her mommy. Thank you to my parents, in-laws and grandparents for their encouragemnet and continuous support. Thank you to my teacher friends for sharing their insight and wisdom, and for their devotion, energy and passionate teaching that guides our future adults. Thank you to my students who not only rewarded me, but also taught me more than a classroom ever could. Finally, thank you to Melissa for the invitation, and to Jennifer and Patina for hopping on board. It has been a fun ride!

Melissa

So many people to thank, so little time. This feels a bit like an Oscar acceptance speech. And, since I won't be at that podium anytime soon, I'm going to make the most of this opportunity. First and foremost, thank you to Lucy, Ellen and Kathleen at Bright Sky Press for taking a chance on four moms with an idea. What a beautiful idea it turned out to be. To Carrie, who introduced us to BSP, to Nancy, my wordsmith, to Barbie & Nicole, my sanity keepers, to the women of MOPS, and to Amberly who told me to "just write a book"— you girls rock! Thank you to the fantastic educators I've had the pleasure of working with- your dedication and passion make me want to be a better teacher. Thank you to my students for giving me hundreds of smiling reasons to go to work each morning. Thank you to the parents of my students for opening your car doors everyday and allowing me to be a part of your children's lives. Thank you to Monsignor Connolly for being such a fabulous moral compass. Thank you to my godmother, Marie, who showed me the art of being a teacher. Craig/Steph, Rob/Alison & Shannon/Eddy—thanks for being such wonderful siblings, parents and uncles/aunts. To my parents, Art & Maryanne, and to my in-laws, Mac & Nancy—thank you for being truly amazing marriage partners, parents and grandparents. To my children, McKenna Kate and Mac III, you have introduced me to a level of unconditional love I never thought possible. To my husband, Mac, I would say something sweet and mushy, but that would only freak you out; I know you know how much I love you. Lastly, to my fellow authors—Heather, Jennifer and Patina—thank you for saying 'yes.' It was an honor to walk this journey with you.

Jennifer

Truly the best part of writing this book has been coming to the end and realizing how many people I have to thank. While I hope readers will find wisdom and insight in the words we have written, it cannot compare to what I have learned on this journey.

Many heartfelt thanks …

To Paul for loving me through this process and enduring an extra measure of insanity. Thank you for being steady, insightful, compassionate, patient and tender.

To Katie and Luke for being patient and understanding as I wrote and for being your wonderful selves. I like you just as much as I love you—which is as big as the ocean, as big as ten moons, bigger than big.

To my parents, there is no me without you. I could not ask for more loving, supportive and dedicated parents. You have taught me to celebrate triumphs with enthusiasm and artistry, and to weather crises with hope, resourcefulness and determination. You never once doubted that I could do this. Thank you for believing in me. I love you.

To Emily, my sister and my friend. You are always there for me. My life is better because of you. I am a better mom because of you. No one makes me laugh harder than you do.

To Billy and Chris. One of the greatest parts of being in our family is knowing without a doubt that we would all drop everything and come running if any one of us needed help. You are each a great part of my community of support. I am so grateful for you. Growing up with "the boys" made childhood much more of an adventure. I am so glad that you are my brothers.

To Debbie for being the world's best aunt/babysitter/Lego® builder/doll stylist/tea party hostess/baby whisperer. Thank you for caring for my kids and for me with such patience and love.

To Lucy, Ellen, Rue, and Kathleen and everyone at Bright Sky for understanding our dream—even as it was just beginning to unfold—and for helping it to take shape and become a reality.

To Carrie for being the networking diva that you are, a treasured friend and an inspiring mom.

To Peggy, Margaret, Paige, Jane and everyone at Beehive for making my children's first experiences of school irresistible and loving. Being a part of this community has been my favorite part of being a mom.

To Carole and everyone at The Briarwood School for believing in me and allowing me to learn more than I ever taught. I still think of Briarwood as home, and it is an honor to do so.

To Susan and everyone at Speech and Language Remediation Center. Thank you for giving me my dream job, even when I didn't think I was ready to take it and for making "working mom" a title I hold with joy and gratitude. I am proud to be a part of such a strong, caring, and exceptional group of women.

To Anne for seeing me as a swan when all I could see was a terrified mess. You were my first solid step on this incredible journey of motherhood. I will always be grateful for your friendship and wisdom. Everyone should have a friend like you.

To my church community of Ecclesia, for being a people of remarkable beauty, generosity, honesty and compassion.

Lastly, to M, H and P for your commitment to this project and your friendship. It has been a life-changing adventure, and I am grateful for each of you.

Patina

First, I would like to thank my co-authors, Heather, Melissa and Jennifer, who are excellent mothers and a tough act to follow—and I don't just mean alphabetically. To Lucy, Ellen and Kathleen, a group of Super Heroes disguised as everyday women. To all the ladies of the West University Mothers Of Preschoolers, who welcomed me as a mentor and first gave me an audience to share my love of parenting. To Randi, Rita and Mary, my high-five women, who gladly gave their time and expertise. To my dear friends Kimberly, Erika and Angel…. thanks for being there. To Nancy Mendez, a talented writer and friend, whose encouragement on and off the page meant the world to me. To my brother, Blaine, for always pretending that I'm a cool, smart older sister. To Murphy and John Henry, my pride and joy, for reading over my lessons for accuracy and gladly giving your teenage two cents. To Whitley, my caboose, for renewing my joy in mothering while keeping my skills sharp and my spirit light. To my mom for always acting like she was awake when I called her at midnight and never being too tired to help. Lastly, to my sweet husband, Tim, who became a highly overeducated typist at times and slept many nights beside the blue glow of my laptop.

For **EXTRA CREDIT**, see our website **www.theanswerkeys.com** for further reading on the contents of each chapter